Through the Darkness

My Tumultuous Journey
from Roman Catholic Nun to Psychic Medium

by

Janet Nohavec

with

Suzanne Giesemann

Aventine Press

Published by Aventine Press
750 State Street #319
San Diego CA, 92010

www.aventinepress.com

Library of Congress Control Number: 2011922716
Library of Congress Cataloging-in-Publication Data
Through the Darkness

ISBN: 1-59330-706-3
Printed in the United States of America

Contents

To a God who loves all of us, a hundred thousand angels and
to St. Therese of Lisieux, the Little Flower.
Thank you.

To my parents, who never got to dance in this lifetime.
To my family, whose support shines through our collective trials:
Thank you.
To my nieces: Live bravely. Sing your song.
To my friends: Life wouldn't be as rich without you.
To the girls: We had incredible times.
To my church: Peace and love.
To our benefactor — our angel: My heartfelt gratitude for believing in me.
To my students: If you serve humanity and the spirit world,
I have taught you well.
To Suzanne — my author: Your poetry, integrity, and gift shine brightly.
To God, the angels, saints, and departed loved ones:
I have loved painting you back to life.
To my fellow mediums of integrity: Thank you for standing.
Mediumship is a gift from God - treat it as such
For all the hands that held me up when walking wasn't easy: Thank you.
Hum though life. Sing your song.
Bring light to all darkness.
Never, never, never give up, nor give an inch.
Like a lighthouse, shine for all to see God's light in you.

Foreword

I still have trouble seeing myself as the co-author of a book about a woman who talks to spirits. I have a pretty straight-laced background, having spent 20 years in the Navy with tours as a commanding officer and aide to the Chairman of the Joint Chiefs of Staff. You won't find any incense burning in my home or catch me wearing wrap-around tie-died skirts, but as I've come to find out, that image doesn't fit most medium these days, either.

Back when I was still in the Navy, I lived a pretty blissful life, free of the kind of tragedies you see on the news each night. When life is going smoothly, we don't always stop to ponder such deep questions as "Why are we here?" or "Is this all there is?" Then something comes along that thoroughly shakes your foundation and causes you to look at reality completely differently.

For me, my spiritual wake-up call was the death of my 27-year-old step-daughter, Susan—a vibrant, loving, sergeant in the Marine Corps. She was crossing the flight line at Marine Corps Air Station Cherry Point when she and her unborn son were struck by lightning—a literal bolt out of the blue. I'd always had an interest in the afterlife, but when Susan was so suddenly taken, I developed an insatiable need to know that her spirit was still with us.

I convinced my husband, Ty, to go with me for our first-ever reading with a medium. A by-the-book former destroyer captain, Ty was more skeptical than most, but after our experience that evening, even he became a believer. When this medium—who knew nothing about us other than our first names—suddenly felt "the headache of Zeus" (the god of lightning bolts) then brought forth a woman in her twenties who died rather suddenly, we both sat up and paid attention. When she told us that the young woman was accompanied by a baby boy who the female spirit wanted to introduce to us, the medium did more than just amaze us: she gave us back our Susan.

Subsequent readings with other mediums convinced me beyond a doubt that there's far more to this world than what we perceive with our five senses. As the author of several books, I knew that writing was *my* medium for sharing the message of mediumship with the world: that our spirit survives the transition we call "death," and that it's possible to communicate with those who have crossed over to the other side.

I met Janet Nohavec at the Spiritualist community in Lily Dale, New York, while there to conduct interviews for my first metaphysical biography, *The Priest and the Medium*. I couldn't help but be intrigued when I found out that Janet had once been a Catholic nun. Because of her rebellious nature, Janet wasn't your run-of-the-mill sister, and she isn't your run-of-the-mill medium either, touted by one expert as "second to none in America."

Her background, I learned, brought a steady stream of Catholics to her door—people who otherwise would never be caught dead with a medium. But it was Janet's reputation for bringing forth highly detailed evidence that turned my desire for a reading with her into a year-long wait.

When I finally sat with Janet, she didn't disappoint. She brought through our Susan, describing her personality perfectly and giving me details about her that she had no way of knowing. Then she brought through my father, who we'd lost only two months earlier. "There's a gentleman here who was pretty sick," said Janet, who knew nothing about my father or his recent death. "He had some kind of manual job around coal." Even if she had met my dad, it was unlikely that Janet would have known that decades earlier, when he first started working on the Pennsylvania railroad, decked out in striped coveralls and cap, he'd shoveled coal on the sooty black engines.

She correctly identified my father by name and asked why he was talking about a poem that someone had written at the end. I wiped at my happy tears as I told her about the ode to my father that my brother Brent wrote the week Dad died. My mother copied the poem and framed it for all of us to hang on our walls.

Janet cocked her head and squinted as she listened, then said, "He wants you to know that poem meant a lot to him."

Through Janet, Dad went on to talk about his piles of National Geographics, the silver dollars lying in a drawer at home, and his big black dog that I didn't know he had until my mother later confirmed that Dad once had a Doberman that he absolutely adored. My father told Janet that my mother was wearing his wedding ring (she was), that she was talking to his picture (every day), and that she somehow blamed herself for his passing (she did, although we all told her not to). Janet passed along a very clear message from my father to my mom: "She has to stop beating herself up about that. There was nothing she could have done. When it's your time, it's your time."

Thanks to Janet, I know that our loved ones on the other side see us kissing their pictures. They read our poems. They hear us when we talk to them. So talk to them. And don't cry at the weddings and the graduations and all the special events that you wish your loved ones had been there to see, because they're right there with you. They tell us so themselves, through gifted intermediaries like Janet.

Through the Darkness is as much about Janet's amazing evidential mediumship as it is about her incredible life. The fact that she was once a nun is only part of her compelling story. In these pages you'll read about a woman who was no stranger to abuse and dysfunction in her early years. She squarely faced her personal demons, then found the strength to stand up for her beliefs when faced with religious intolerance rarely heard of in America these days. Janet's journey led her to become an ordained minister and pastor of her church, *The Journey Within*. For a woman who grew up without love, she is now a loving example of selfless service to others.

As a writer, I'm blessed to help tell a fascinating story with such real-life drama and emotion. As a spiritual teacher and now as a medium myself, I'm awed to be associated with a medium who has a wide-open window to the other side. But equally important, having gotten to know Janet Nohavec personally over the course of this project, I'm humbled and honored to call her my friend.

Suzanne Giesemann

Preface

I remember when that movie came out a few years back ... *The Sixth Sense*. Bruce Willis played a child psychologist working with this kid who talked to spirits. There was one line where the boy says, "I see dead people." It became this big joke, kind of like, *Where's the beef?* Suddenly everybody's walking around saying, "I see dead people" and laughing. It didn't do a whole lot to help me in my present line of work. Mediums have a tough enough time getting respect as it is.

The movie might have been fiction, but I started seeing dead people when I was as young as that kid. I heard them, too, just like they were talking out loud. After a couple dozen visits, I finally got them to go away. I was kind of relieved at the time; I had enough to worry about without having people standing there looking at me when I was trying to sleep.

I'm not sure about the boy in the movie, but I know my sixth sense was honed at home. It's simple: When you live with lunatics, you learn to pay attention to the little things that other people never notice. When my father walked through the door, it wasn't the alcohol on his breath that gave him away, because vodka doesn't smell. I could read his energy. I knew when he was gonna beat the crap out of my mother without even seeing his eyes.

All I've ever wanted was a little peace. So I was pretty happy when the spirit people decided to leave me alone. They stayed away for a long time, and with nobody looking over my shoulder, I admit I ran a little wild. But you can only be self-destructive for so long before life catches up with you. Somehow I survived those years, but not without some scars. My past is written on my face. Literally.

I'm the last person my family expected to become a nun. It surprised the heck out of me, too, but it seemed like a good idea at the time. So there I was getting ready to take my vows, and the spirits started showing up again. Go figure.

I guess they thought by then that things had calmed down enough that I could handle them.

Not exactly.

I found it a little disconcerting to see dead people walking around the convent. My sixth sense told me loud and clear not to tell the novice directress that I saw deceased nuns hanging out in the cemetery. She had enough baggage of her own to deal with. Luckily, I found some books that helped. I read everything I could get my hands on about Catholic mystics like John of the Cross and St. Therese. It was comforting to learn that Joan of Arc heard spirits, too, but we all know what happened to her.

In time I realized that rebels don't do well as nuns, and I left that life behind. I might not have been burned at the stake, but for a while there I was sure I'd burn in Hell. I finally saw a counselor who didn't look anything like Bruce Willis, but after a few years of therapy, at least I learned I wasn't crazy.

Once I accepted my abilities as the gift that they are, the spirit people started working with me. With the help of some real-life angels, I went from Sister Janet to Reverend Nohavec, Spiritualist minister and pastor of my own church. There was a while there when I wasn't sure I was on the right path—that I'd ever find my peace. Just when things would start to go well, someone or something would block my way.

I used to wonder, *why me?* as I got knocked down over and over and over. Then I realized that we're all here to learn certain lessons. It's like we're in school, and life is one big test. God's gonna keep throwing the same stuff in your face until you get it right.

I never did like school much.

Chapter 1

Demon Child

At five years old I didn't know my numbers too well, but I didn't need to count to know that something was missing from the family photo album. Someone, that is, and that someone was me.

I sat cross-legged on the floor of the living room and frowned at the oversized book. I closed it, then opened it again from the beginning. There was Dad in a rare photo with my mom. He usually stood behind the camera. Wiry but muscular from long days of building houses, if you put my father next to Frank Sinatra you'd swear they were twins. My mother, with her dark hair piled atop her head, could have passed for any one of the starlets that used to pose with Ol' Blue Eyes.

I turned a thick black page and studied the pictures of my older brother and sister back when they were young enough to both fit in my mother's arms. Michael came over on the ship with my parents, but Mary was born right there on Ellis Island. Speaking of twins, Mary was one, but her brother died at birth— something I knew better than to talk to my mother about.

I flipped past all the pages of smiling Michael and Mary. Those photos were a good seven or eight years old; no reason for me to be there. I slowed when I came to Nancy and Irene.

Born three years after me, yet only a year apart, my two younger sisters bonded with each other. Photos don't lie, and these told the truth as I knew it: Michael and Mary formed one pair, Nancy and Irene another. I, Janet, was the odd child out. I bit my lip and turned the pages backward, then forward. With a ten year gap between the two pairs, I should have been right there in the middle, born in 1957, but none of the little faces had my blue eyes or light brown hair turned dark by the black and white film.

I closed the pages and pushed myself to my feet. Holding the album close to my chest, I shuffled toward the kitchen. I stopped just before the doorway and peeked at my mother from the hall. She didn't see me as she shook some Comet onto the counter and scrubbed at an invisible stain. The purple blotch under her right eye had changed to a swirly yellow and green, but everything else about her face told me it was safe to proceed.

I crossed the linoleum and looked up at her. I averted my eyes from the mark on her cheek. She avoided my gaze altogether.

"Mom?"

She stopped scrubbing and looked down at me. "What do you want, Janet?"

I hesitated, then gathered my courage and held out the album with both hands. "Why aren't there any pictures of me?"

She glanced at the book. Her lips twitched and her eyes narrowed. "Can't you see I'm cleaning?"

I took a step backwards. I could see that very clearly. It was a wonder there weren't any photos in the album of my mother mopping the floors or washing the windows. The real-life picture of my mother—the one I saw every day—was of a woman cleaning to the point of obsession. Long, long after the floors shined and the windows sparkled, my mother scrubbed and scrubbed, polished and polished, then scrubbed some more. Was it any surprise that her weapon of choice when I did something wrong was a mop handle?

I hung my head and said nothing.

"Go outside and play. I don't have time to answer silly questions."

I returned to the living room. I laid the photo album in its place of honor, then did as my mother said. I went out the front door, pausing to check left and right. The coast was clear—no kids in sight. I hurried through the grass to the back yard. The playhouse sat empty. On some days its emptiness reminded me of my solitude. Other days, as now, it served as my refuge.

I ducked through the little door and sank onto a kid-sized chair. I hummed a few notes of a tuneless song, then glanced at the doorway and smiled.

"Hello, Sarah. Come in."

I held onto the chair beneath my bottom and shifted a few inches to the left to make room for my visitor.

"How are you today?" I asked, facing the empty seat across from mine.

I nodded my head and smiled in response as my guest described the details of her wonderful morning.

"Your hair looks very pretty," I commented.

I imagined Sarah running a hand through thick blonde ringlets that made Shirley Temple jealous. She told me that she liked the color of my blouse, and I thanked her. As always, Sarah was far too polite to mention the ugly patch on my right eye. She understood why I'd cheated on the eye test a while back, peeking at the chart when no one was looking. I thought if I could pass the test, I wouldn't have to wear the awful patch, but I couldn't win either way. If I didn't wear it, all the other kids would tease me about my lazy eye. All the kids but Sarah.

"I asked my mother about the photo album," I told my friend.

Sarah listened with great interest.

"She wouldn't tell me why there aren't any pictures of me, but I know why."

Sarah tilted her head to the side and waited.

"I'm adopted."

My friend nodded wisely. I knew she'd understand.

Had my mother told me the real reason for my absence in the album, I might have understood, too, but she shared little with me. If I'd known that my parents had barely enough money for food when I was born, I would have realized that buying film and developing photos was too much of a luxury.

I learned years later that those days in Nutley, New Jersey, were far more bleak than I was aware of at such a young age. Things only started looking up when we moved to Franklin Lakes. By the time Irene and Nancy came along, my father had found more work building houses. Once again they could afford to take photos of their babies, but I guess my eye patch would have ruined the pictures.

I had nothing to complain about, really. The hard times in Nutley couldn't hold a candle to my parents' lives back in Poland. Back then, according to my mother, "Heaven was a piece of bread covered with lard."

My father, Miro, was born in Pilsen, Poland. My mother, Helen, came from Lvov, Czechoslovakia. They pronounce the town "love," but there wasn't much of that for either of them growing up. After dad's father killed himself, dad's mother abandoned him. The orphanage where he ended up ran out of boys' clothes, so my father had to wear girls' things. Try and picture a tough little kid all alone, forced to wear a skirt, and you'll get an idea of why he might have had a few problems.

Unlike Dad, my mother had a big family, with two parents and five brothers. She didn't fare too well during the war, either, ending up in a work camp starving and alone. Conditions there were pretty awful, but at least the Catholics like my mother weren't exterminated. Still and all, she never saw her family again and never bothered to look for them.

When she met my father, he seemed like a good catch. Some gypsies in the camp told her that life would never be easy if she married Miro Nohavec. She took all their other superstitions to heart, but ignored that helpful bit of advice. I got a lot of my parents' history second-hand, but my mother told me to my face that she should have listened to those gypsies.

A slight motion over the playhouse door caught my eye. I looked up and flinched as a tiny black spider scurried across the wood frame, then swung gracefully across to a corner beam. My mother's words echoed in my ears as I stared at its acrobatics: "See a spider before noon, have good luck; see a spider after noon, have bad luck." I did a quick mental check: we had already eaten lunch, but if I was lucky it might not yet be twelve o'clock.

Not willing to take any chances, I apologized to Sarah for leaving so abruptly and abandoned the playhouse. I stood in the yard. If it was after noon, I didn't want to run into any of the neighborhood kids; their teasing was brutal enough under ordinary conditions. At least I hadn't killed the spider. According to my mom and the gypsies, that would have sealed my fate.

I ducked into the garage where I'd be safely out of sight. Looking back now, it must have been after noon, for there, in the corner, stood a stranger staring back at me—an adult male, same as my father … the scariest of the scary.

I bolted into the house, shrieking all the way, "Mom! Mom! There's a man in the garage!"

She followed me back to the spot where I'd stood moments earlier and where I now pointed at nothing but air.

"He was right there!" I insisted.

My mother stuck her head out the door and checked the yard, then came back to stand beside me.

"There's no one here now, Janet," she said, her voice tinged with impatience. "Are you sure you weren't imagining things?"

I trembled as I shook my head. I knew that I made up most of my friends. Sarah was the perfect playmate, but I never fooled myself into thinking she was real. The man who'd appeared before me, however, was not in my imagination. I'd seen him in three dimensions—in full, living color.

"What did he look like?" my mother demanded.

"He was about as tall as Pop, but real skinny. The bones in his cheeks kind of stood out." I stared, panting, at the corner where I'd seen him. "He was dressed all in black—in a black suit and a tall black hat. He even had a little black beard on his chin."

The color drained from the bruise on my mother's cheek. She took a step backward and crossed herself. "Get in the house now," she said, pointing at the door. As I stepped past her, she looked over her shoulder and shuddered.

She didn't mention the incident at dinner, and I didn't bring it up. My father had come home from work in a good mood, and the rest of us treaded lightly all evening.

That night I crawled under the blanket on the couch. There weren't enough rooms to go around, so I often traded beds with Michael. For once I was glad to be in the living room. I could hear my parents talking even through their closed door.

"Janet says she saw a man in the garage today," came my mother's muffled voice.

"What?" my father said. "Why didn't you tell me before?"

"Because I think she made it up."

"Then why bring it up now?"

"It's the way she described him …"

I tilted my head to hear more clearly. My mother detailed the stranger exactly as I'd seen him, down to the beard, the black hat, the suit, and his build.

"So?" my father said.

"It sounds just like your father from those pictures you had back in Poland, but Janet's never seen those photos."

"What are you saying, Helen? That Janet saw my dead father in our garage?"

My eyes widened. It was my grandfather? The man who killed himself? But the man I'd seen wasn't dead.

"This can't be good," my mother said. "It can't be good at all."

My father said something in Polish that I didn't understand, followed by my mother's equally foreign response.

Then she said something I understood all too clearly. It was something she'd repeated countless times before … "God doesn't like the Nohavecs."

I rolled over and closed my eyes. I was beginning to believe her, myself.

* * *

My father's good humor didn't last. It never did. He came home from work a little later than normal one evening not long after the incident in the garage. I shrank back into the corner of the living room where I was playing with my dolls and focused on his feet. The line he walked was straight except for a slight hitch to the right before he caught himself and continued on to the kitchen.

I took that as my cue to go outside for a while. I walked to the edge of our yard and sat on the curb. The parking lot of the Lutheran church across the street was half filled with cars. They had activities on weeknights, and whatever was going on over there must have just been finishing up. I pushed at some pebbles with the toes of my shoes and watched the families file out a side door.

Two boys I recognized from school chased each other in circles around their parents, slapping at each other and laughing as the adults walked on, oblivious. I also knew several of the girls who walked hand-in-hand with friendly looking fathers. I often envied the children on Sundays when I'd see them going to the services. Their clothes were so pretty and they all looked so happy. My mother had told me that I was baptized in a Catholic church, but our family didn't go to Mass. From where I sat, being a Lutheran looked pretty nice.

I heard our front door open and turned around. My father filled the frame; smoke from his cigarette swirled around his head like a dark gray aura. Our eyes met and I tensed.

"Pupa!" he called out, and my insides shriveled.

Perhaps if I'd reacted more quickly I might have stopped him from calling out the awful nickname a second time, but instead I sat stuck to the curb, too horrified to move.

"Pupa! Come and get ready for bed."

He turned around and went inside, leaving me at the mercy of my schoolmates' stares. They did nothing to disguise their amusement.

"Did he just call her *Poopy*?" one of the boys said gleefully to the other.

"No ... he called her *Pooper*!" said the other before his mother shushed him with a wave of her hand.

The boys laughed raucously, and even the girls looked delighted. I knew they'd waste no time sharing with everyone at school this delicious bit of news about the kid with the eye patch. I stood and slinked back into the house, invisible if I couldn't see them.

Once inside, I headed for the kitchen, but stopped, frozen, at the sound of breaking glass.

I heard my father growl, then yell, "You stupid woman! You think we have money to buy new things?"

My mother's answer came out an octave higher than usual. "It was an accident."

"Don't just stand there; clean it up, you lazy pig."

The thud of my father's shoe sinking into soft flesh made me clutch at my stomach with both arms. I leaned into the living room wall and ducked my head as more shattered glass exploded from the kitchen.

"There—clean that up, too, while you're down there!"

Another crash. "And that!"

"Get out of here, you lousy drunk!" my mother yelled back, crying now.

"Who're you calling a drunk, you good for nothing *kurwa*."

Another crash, a smack, a thump, and I took the stairs to the second floor two at a time.

Grateful that Michael had the couch that night, I shut the bedroom door behind me and stripped off my clothes. I pulled on a cotton nightgown and crawled into the small bed. Clutching the covers to my throat, I turned to face the far wall and looked up—straight into the eyes of my grandfather.

My father's tirades terrified me, but the sudden presence of this bony, black-clothed man in my bedroom raised my fear to a new level. I pulled the covers completely over my head.

"Please don't come in here," I said aloud. "Please, please just go away."

I peeked out to find that not only had the man not gone away, he was now joined by an old woman dressed in equally drab clothes. The three of us silently stared at each other for an endless moment and I willed them to disappear.

Go away go away go away go away.

When they refused to vanish, I slipped back into the darkness under the blanket and repeated my pleas until the darkness filled my mind.

* * *

I had my hand on the latch at the back door when my mother shook my shoulder.

"Janet! Stop! Where are you going?"

I opened my eyes and looked around. Nothing made sense.

"You're walking in your sleep again," my mother said in a hushed voice, then pointed outside. "You see? Look at the moon. You're always more active when the moon is full."

"I'm sorry, Mom. I don't know how I got here."

She crossed herself. "I don't need this in my life, Janet. First you see your grandparents in your bedroom, and now you're walking in the moonlight."

I could have kicked myself for telling my mother about the apparitions at my bedside. What she didn't know is that the old couple continued to appear; their visits now numbering over a dozen. Looking back on it, I realize they usually showed up on the nights when my father really let loose. I suppose they could have been trying to comfort me, but as a little kid, their presence only added to my nightmares.

My mother glanced at the moon. "You know what you are, Janet?" She looked back at me and scowled. "You're a demon child."

I returned her gaze as the new label sank in. If my mother said it, it had to be true.

She dug her fingers into my arm and dragged me back to the couch.

"Is it your legs again?" she asked as I stretched out on the cushions. "Is that why you keep getting up?"

I'd recently started experiencing severe pains in both legs. I would cry in agony at night, bringing my mother rushing to my side. I think she was mostly concerned that I might wake up my father. The spasms became excruciating, but rather than take me to a doctor, she'd sit beside me and rub moisturizer into my legs, all the while saying, "Be quiet, Janet, be quiet."

"My legs don't hurt tonight," I said, not mentioning the new ache in my chest.

My mother ran a hand through her hair and shook her head as she looked down at me. Then she glanced toward her bedroom. "I should have stopped after the first two," she muttered. "After them, everything else was a rape."

I remembered those words until I was old enough to know what they meant. It's hard not to take a comment like that personally, you know? But at the time—luckily—it went over my head. Her other words, however, still stung, and I played them over and over in my mind, long after she'd gone back to her own bed.

You're a demon child … a demon child … demon child …

I rolled over and pressed my face into the pillow so my crying wouldn't wake up my father. In between the jagged sobs I talked to the other mean and scary man in my life.

"Why don't you like me, God?" I cried.

My words came out muffled against the cotton and I burrowed in deeper. "What did I do that was so bad?"

Chapter 2

Chaos

Polish people eat a lot of potatoes. There are all kinds of things you can do with a potato: potato pancakes, potato soup, potato this, potato that. If you can get potatoes, you can live for a long time on them. When my father's business was going well, we ate meat and potatoes. If he couldn't sell any of the houses he built, we ate the potatoes by themselves.

In my ninth year, we started eating more meat. Dad's work was going so well that he bought a huge plot of land around a nearby lake. He planned to build one or two homes at a time, then he'd use the money from each sale to build another.

The first house he finished sat four miles down Pulis Avenue from the one where I saw my grandparents' spirits. The new house was bigger and fancier, with more bedrooms, so the seven of us moved in: Mom, Pop, Michael, Mary, me, Nancy, and Irene. My dead grandparents decided not to come along.

I guess all that hiding under the covers did the trick. Even when I started wandering around the old cemetery a couple of blocks from our new place, I didn't see any more spirits. I was real careful not to step on any graves, though, still terrified the ghosts would come and get me.

Our new house wasn't on the lake. My father planned to build the waterfront homes later. In the meantime, I was free to play on all that land to my heart's content. My mother never cared where I went or how long I stayed out, so I'd spend hours walking beside the lake and humming to myself. I liked playing with the turtles, and my artistic abilities came out when I'd paint their shells with nail polish. In the winter I'd twirl around the ice, convinced I'd be the next Olympic gold medalist. I had Dorothy Hamill shaking in her skates.

One thing that didn't change after we made the move was the trips to Polonia, the Polish bakery over in Passaic. Every time he'd get a little money, my father would take us for some of his childhood favorites like sweet *babka*, fresh from the oven. Sometimes it'd just be the two of us, and I'd let myself believe that my father loved me. Giving us food was the only way my parents knew how to show their kids affection. Forget touching. Rather than hugs and kisses, we got rye bread and kielbasa.

So you can imagine how I felt the November day my dad brought home the big frozen turkey. At school I'd been looking all month at posters of Pilgrims, baskets full of gourds, and these colorful cut-out turkeys with frilly little paper things on the end of the drumsticks. For days leading up to that Thanksgiving I pictured our turkey sitting in the middle of the table, roasted golden brown just like the cardboard ones at school.

Things were looking up from the previous Christmas Eve when my mother told us there wouldn't be any presents the next morning. I thought she was kidding. I woke up at sunrise, only to learn that Santa Claus had passed right by the Nohavecs' house. So when Thanksgiving day rolled around, I camped out early in the kitchen. I wanted to see how my mother was gonna cook a turkey that big.

Around nine o'clock my father stomped across the linoleum and pulled open the door on our big white Frigidaire. As my mother and I watched, he reached inside and pulled out the holiday's star attraction. I gaped in wonder, amazed that my father was going to help prepare the turkey. My wonder turned to worry when he turned on his heel and left the kitchen, bird-in-hand.

My mother hurried after my father, following him through the living room and out the front door. She returned moments later, her face as red as a Christmas light.

"Is Pop going somewhere else to cook our turkey?" I asked. The thing was so big, I thought it might not fit in our oven.

My mother spoke through pinched lips. "Your father is going to give it to someone else's family so he can be the big man today."

The wind rushed out of my lungs as if I'd been punched. "But that's our turkey," I said without air.

My mother picked her purse off the counter and dug around inside. She turned to me and held out a few coins, her face grim.

"Go to the grocery," she ordered, "and bring back some potatoes."

* * *

"Mom! You shoulda been there," I said, flopping down on her bed. "They cooked hot dogs and hamburgers … outside!"

My mother listened to my chatter while she brushed out her long hair in slow, even strokes. She talked to my reflection in her mirror without turning around.

"Did you behave yourself?"

"Of course, I did. They called it a barbecue, and I drank this soda pop called *Sprite* that was clear, like water, but really sweet!"

The slam of the front door cut short my mother's reply. We both turned toward the hallway, where the sound of heavy shoes on the stairs made both of us tense. Seconds later my father entered the bedroom. I took one look at his flushed face and jumped to my feet, putting my parent's bed between him and me.

"That son of a bitch raised the dam to get more water on his land, and now my best property is flooded!"

He sucked in a chest full of air, let it out in a roar, and kicked the dresser with the full force of his work boot.

My mother and I jumped at the loud crack. I stared, transfixed, at the yellow split in the smooth, dark mahogany.

"I'm gonna sue the bastard, then he'll see—"

The abrupt pause in his tirade caused me to look up from the damaged drawer. What I saw in his face scared me far more than a piece of split wood. He was staring at my mother with a look I'd seen countless times before. Alarm bells rang in my ears.

"What the hell are you doing?" he asked her.

"Stay away from me, Miro."

"You ugly bitch! Who are you fixing yourself up for?" My father lurched toward my mother and snatched the brush from her hand.

She shrieked as she fell backwards into her dressing table.

I choked back a sob, and my father turned toward me. He raised the brush above his head as if brandishing it at an intruder. "Get the hell out of my bedroom, Janet, before I give you a piece of this!"

I hugged the far wall and slipped out the door. My sisters and brothers peered into the hallway, but ducked back into their bedrooms as if embarrassed to be seen. With unspoken agreement, none of us ever talked about what went on in our house.

Huddled on my mattress, I hugged my knees to my chest and tried to disappear. It was impossible not to hear the terrifying sounds of slaughter—each slap, kick, and punch a distinctive note on the rising scale of violence.

I raised my head when my mother's screams grew too loud to ignore. *This time he's gonna kill her,* I thought, certain I wouldn't have a mother in the morning.

I pinched my eyelids together as tight as they could go and prayed so loudly that I finally blocked out all the noise.

The staff at Bergen Pines Hospital surely recognized the signs of domestic abuse, but this was the mid-'60s. What happened in the home was a private matter. Still, my mother looked so bad that this time they questioned my dad. I learned all this as she shared the details with one of our sympathetic neighbors over a cup of coffee a couple of days later.

"He told them I was trying to hurt the children, and that he had to stop me."

"My God! And they believed him?"

"They sent us home, didn't they?"

"It's not right, Helen. What are you going to do now?"

"What can I do? They might take my children from me."

"Surely Miro knows he almost killed you." The neighbor looked at my mother's battered face and shook her head. "Maybe this will make him change his ways."

The woman's prediction proved prophetic. My father did change his ways: From that day on he made sure his blows didn't leave any marks where you could see them.

As usual, my parents didn't speak to each other for days after that fight. My father glued the broken dresser back together and replaced the shattered mirror. But there was nothing he could do to fix the shattered pieces of my mother's soul. I sensed a new weariness inside her, but had no idea how overwhelmed she'd become just trying to survive each hour.

About a month after the big blow-up, I had a particularly good time at school. They'd held a field day—the first of its kind that I'd experienced, with fun games and activities that got us out of a full afternoon of classes. I rushed home afterwards to share my excitement and found my parents facing off in the living room. The house felt like a volcano about to erupt.

"You good for nothing bastard!" my mother shouted as she gripped her left side.

My father swayed like a dazed boxer as his eyes went in and out of focus. I tried to reconcile the rage I saw on his face with the man I'd caught crying the night before at the end of a sad movie on TV. The screen of our new television set now lay in jagged pieces on the floor.

Bits of glass ground into the carpet as I instinctively rushed to my mother's side. I guess I figured I could somehow get things back under control before my mother ended up in the hospital again. But I'd stupidly forgotten the one constant in my life: Just like my mother, I *had* no control.

My father was unstoppable that night. Fueled by alcohol, he'd gone well beyond reason. Behind me now, I felt the strength drain out of my mother. Mt. Saint Helen had no more fire left in her. As my father lurched forward, fists ready to swing, she did the only thing she could to save herself: She pushed me toward him to take the blows.

* * *

I waited with the neighborhood kids for the school bus to come down Pulis Avenue. We passed the time as we did most mornings talking about our classes and our teachers. I complained right along with everyone else, relieved to no longer stand out. My eye patch was ancient history. In the eighth grade now, fitting in was all-important. I dressed and acted just like a normal thirteen-year-old.

I glanced back at our house, glad that no one could see in the windows. Just like me, the exterior betrayed what went on inside.

127 Pulis Avenue was the third house we'd lived in on the same street—right next door to the one we lived in last. If somebody came along and wanted to buy our current home, we'd pack up and move into one of the others my father built. Sometimes I felt we lived a lot like the gypsies my mother grew up with.

I secretly hoped my father would find a buyer. I didn't really want to move again, but at least then my parents could pay the bills. It was bad enough sitting in the dark without my favorite TV shows, but with no electricity, even our stove didn't work. If my friends had peeked through the curtains the night before, they would have seen the Nohavecs in their big, fancy house cooking hotdogs in the fireplace.

The yellow bus came lumbering around the corner, lights flashing, and creaked to a stop. I trudged aboard and flopped onto a padded green seat with a practiced lack of enthusiasm. I didn't like school any more than the others kids, but secretly, I loved the bus. It carried me away from my hell hole of a home.

If I'd known the way my day would turn out, I might have skipped the bus ride and skipped town, instead.

First period math and second period social studies were bearable, but English class was another story. English had never been my best subject, thanks to my parents speaking Polish half the time. I was struggling just to stay awake, but my teacher, Mrs. Wilson, lost me altogether when she started diagramming sentences. I couldn't see how knowing the difference between a subject and a predicate was gonna help me get through the next day. When the door opened and Mrs. Wilson put down her chalk, I didn't mind the interruption.

I recognized the visitor, Miss Cartwright, right away. I'd spent my fair share of time over the last couple of years in the guidance counselor's office. Somehow the school had figured out that things weren't exactly perfect at home. I liked that Miss Cartwright actually listened to me, unlike my parents, who weren't the type to sit you down and talk things over.

My classmates and I shared curious glances as Miss Cartwright and Mrs. Wilson talked in muted voices at the front of the room. I started to get a little antsy, and when both women turned and looked at me, I fought an instant urge to cry. I'd learned from my mother to avoid attention of any kind, and now twenty-four pairs of eyes looked back at me.

"Janet," Mrs. Wilson said, "Please get your things and go with Miss Cartwright."

A murmur passed through the room, and I scrambled to think of what I'd done wrong. Then I noticed that Mrs. Wilson and Miss Cartwright looked more concerned than angry. My ears thundered and my brain shut down as I got to my feet. Somehow I made it from the back of the room to the hallway. The long, empty corridor felt cold and forbidding as I joined Miss Cartwright and walked toward her office.

"What's going on? Am I in trouble?"

"You're fine, Janet, but we had a call from your mother."

My nerves, already frayed, went on full alert. "What happened?" I asked as I put on the brakes. Is she all right?"

Miss Cartwright held out both hands. "Take it easy, now. Everything's going to be okay."

"What do you mean? What's going on? Where is she? What—"

The counselor patted my shoulder. "Let's go to my office and have a little chat."

She started walking again and I had no choice but to follow.

"What did my mother say?" I asked. I was breathing heavily now as if I'd just finished gym class, but Miss Cartwright was still playing dodge ball.

"Let's just step in here," she said.

I stopped again. "I'm not going in there until you tell me what's going on."

She stared at me for a moment, then took a deep breath. "Your mother said you shouldn't go home today."

I stood there, rigid, as I tried to make sense of her words: *I shouldn't go home today. Today I shouldn't go home.*

No matter which way I diagrammed the sentence, it only spelled trouble.

"Is it my father?"

"We don't know that, Janet. I'm sure— "

But I wasn't listening. The thoughts swirling around my mind picked up speed as my heart pumped out pure adrenaline. Frantic now, I began hopping from one foot to the other as if standing in a sizzling pan.

"I have to go. I have to see what's wrong." I bolted for the big double doors.

"Janet, stop!" Miss Cartwright ran after me and grabbed my arm.

I shook it off. "No! I think my—" I stopped just short of voicing my deepest fear—that my father had finally gone off the deep end. I clung to Miss Cartwright's words that my mother had made the call. If she was able to use the phone, there was the smallest hope that she was okay.

The counselor stared at me for a moment and our eyes locked. She loosened her grip and nodded. "All right. We'll go together."

I sat on the front seat of her blue Nova, fussing with my fingers as I directed Miss Cartwright along the familiar bus route. When we pulled up in front of my house, I was out of the car before she set the brake. Everything looked exactly as I'd left it a few hours earlier.

"Janet, wait!" Miss Cartwright called after me as I ran up the walk and turned the front knob.

When the door wouldn't open, I ran through the grass to the side yard. I peered in a window, and seeing nothing, slid it up. I hoisted myself over the sill and was inside before Miss Cartwright could stop me.

I looked left and right, then made a bee-line for the kitchen. The scene that greeted me there brought forth a sob and the tears I'd been holding inside. The normally immaculate counters and walls were spattered with dark, red blood. Crimson drops stained the sink, the stove, and even the ceiling.

I held a hand to my mouth and stumbled to the back door. Miss Cartwright stood on the other side peering through the small panes with one hand above her eyes. Her face mirrored my shock. When I opened the door, she stepped in. We stood side by side, gaping in horror at the grisly scene.

"We shouldn't be in here," Miss Cartwright said, yet she walked beside me as we followed the trail of blood into the hall. I could scarcely breathe, dreading with each step that I'd discover a bloody body to go with the stains ... whose—I didn't dare to imagine.

Room by room we searched the house, then retraced our path until I was convinced the house was empty.

"I'm taking you back to the school," Miss Cartwright said. I stole one last look at the chaos, then followed her to her car like a zombie.

The rest of the day passed in a blur. I spent most of it in Miss Cartwright's office, until suddenly, like a vision, my mother and sisters showed up. There was a lot of hushed talk with the counselor, then somebody explained to me that my father had cut himself pretty badly and went a little crazy. I stared at the wall and saw the gruesome scene that had greeted me earlier—an indelible image that my mother's scrubbing would never be able to erase. I had no trouble picturing my father stumbling around the kitchen, blind drunk, painting the walls with his blood.

There was no strong man to shore up the shaken Nohavec women that evening. Michael was off fighting the Viet Cong and my father had disappeared to fight his own demons. Mary got behind the wheel of our car and drove us all to a diner. She was the only one with a driver's license. Mom had never gotten hers. She tried twice, but her nerves got the best of her both times. Everybody's nerves were pretty well shot that night. I doubt anyone remembers what we ate. Later, we got a room at a hotel and stayed there a couple of days—long enough for dad and the man next door to cover up all that blood with a fresh coat of paint.

Ten days later, I sat with my friends in what would one day be the dining room of my dad's latest house. The four walls were framed in, but not yet dry-walled. The glow from Mark Simmons' cigarette provided just enough light to see his hand slide up Laura Harrison's leg. I ignored the love-birds and reached for the bottle Terry Jamison passed me.

I provided the house; my friends provided the booze. The arrangement had worked quite well since the previous year when I'd turned twelve.

I took a healthy sip, but I was long past the initial warm glow of that first swallow—blissfully beyond my pain. I stared at the label: Gilbey's gin, courtesy of some unsuspecting parent's liquor cabinet.

"I heard Mrs. Wilson is getting a divorce," Terry said.

Laura moved Mark's hand and sat up. "No way!"

I ignored my friends' gossip and stared at the moonlight streaming in where the hall window would go. I thought back to the surreal scene in our own dining room shortly after my dad cut himself. There we all were: my mother, my father, Miss Cartwright, and me, all sitting around the table having a discussion like normal people.

I never should have opened up to Miss Cartwright, but she'd forced me to talk. I guess after seeing the mess at my house, the school could no longer deny that something was seriously wrong at the Nohavecs'. Miss Cartwright had gotten me to admit how hopeless I felt, then asked me point blank if I was thinking of killing myself. After that, she set up the meeting at my house.

My parents listened and gave appropriate responses, but I could feel their discomfort like a scratchy wool coat in July. I'd brought unwanted attention on our family, and that could never be good. My father acted all concerned, as if he really cared. When Miss Cartwright got up to leave, they shook hands and everybody smiled. I'm sure she thought she made a difference.

I knew better.

Mark Simmons staggered to his feet. "Shit, you guys—it's after midnight. My parents are gonna kill me!"

My other three friends joined Mark in cursing and hurriedly stamped out their cigarettes.

I leaned back against a two-by-four and took another swallow of gin. I could stay out 'til three A.M. and no one would notice. A whopping two days had passed since Miss Cartwright's visit, and my life was back to normal.

Chapter 3

Cursed

The mechanic didn't look much older than me—probably eighteen. I couldn't help but notice how good-looking he was: tall and muscular with dark, brooding eyes. The white name tag embroidered on his blue shirt read "Eddie." At first I thought that having my car overheat and being towed to a garage was the worst possible luck. Now, with Eddie taking care of me, I wondered if the breakdown was a blessing in disguise.

Eddie leaned against the left front fender of my car, stared down at the engine, and shook his head.

"It's gonna cost ya 'bout 200 bucks to get this thing back on the road. You need a whole new radiator and a water pump.

My shoulders sagged. "But that's all I paid for the whole car!"

"Sorry," he said, but he didn't look like he meant it.

I stared at the battered blue sedan, the first car I'd owned and my only way of getting around.

"So?" Eddie glanced at the clock. "What do you want me to do?"

I looked back at him and said with disgust, "You can keep it."

He didn't say a word as I climbed across the front seat and opened the glove box. I emptied the contents into my purse, then backed up and plucked my last pack of Marlboros from the driver's door pocket. I glanced in the back. A couple of empty beer bottles peeked out from under the passenger's seat. He could keep them, too.

Ignoring Eddie's stare, I backed all the way out of the car and left him standing there. Outside the garage, I stood along the busy road and looked around to get my bearings. I'd been to this part of West New York plenty of times, but usually not in the daylight. A pay phone on the corner caught my eye and I headed for it, fishing a dime from my purse as I walked. Once inside the booth I put the coin in the slot and dialed my best friend's number.

"Hello, Debbie? It's Janet."

"Hey, what's up? You don't sound too good."

"My car broke down and I need a ride. Can you drive over to West New York and pick me up?"

"No problem. Where are you?"

"Right by the entrance to the Lincoln Tunnel. I'll be waiting on the corner by the Esso station."

"I'm on my way," she said, then paused. "You sure you're okay?"

"Yeah, sure," I said, then hung up.

The traffic noise climbed a few notches outside the booth. A dump truck belched black smoke in my face. I frowned, knowing it would take Debbie longer than I wanted to stand there on the corner. I looked back across the street at the garage. Several plastic chairs called to me through the big plate glass window. I could have spread myself across the whole row and slept for a week, but I had no desire to go back inside. When the tow truck that brought me there rolled up to the bay to remove my car, I turned my back and headed in the opposite direction.

I kept my head down as I walked. Losing my car was just one more blow in a string of painful losses that started stacking up right after our neighbor in Franklin Lakes raised the dam. When my father's property flooded, Pop made good on his threat and sued. The case dragged on for years, and while it did, he stopped building houses to fight his battle. He grew so intent on winning, that when the lawyers offered him a settlement, he refused to take the money.

So, instead of doing the right thing for his family, he lost everything. And I do mean everything. Without any income, the houses he hadn't sold yet went into default. They were all mortgaged by the bank, so the bank took them back, along with our car. That was bad enough, but it was nothing compared to the day when I came home from school to an empty house.

There stood my mother, crying and babbling on about the sheriff driving up with a moving van. She tried to block them, but they got past her. They took all our things, put them in storage, and put our family on the street.

I had to go and live with the Warrens, the family of a man my father knew, while I finished my last year of high school. My older sister, Mary, landed with another family, and my mom took my two younger sisters to a hotel. My father stayed there a couple of times, but his whole life had pretty much fallen apart by then—and ours along with it. When Mom got a small apartment in Oakland, New Jersey, not too much later, he didn't go with her.

You might think that staying with another family might have brought a little normalcy for once, but as far as the Warrens were concerned, I was nothing more than a boarder. I ate a meal with them now and then, but mostly I picked up a pizza or grabbed a burger somewhere.

I'd been working as a cashier at the Stop 'n Shop until we got evicted, then I started cleaning houses like my mom. To get to the jobs, I needed wheels. To pay for the gas and my food, I needed to clean more houses. I figured I needed money more than a diploma, so I quit school three months before graduation.

The sound of a siren shook me back to the sidewalk, and I winced as an ambulance squealed past. I caught a glimpse inside the small back windows where an EMT bent over someone on a stretcher. I wondered if the poor guy had been in an accident. Surely it couldn't be as bad as the wreck my life had become.

With no money and my family spread across New Jersey, I felt utterly alone. Cleaning houses wasn't the way I wanted to spend the rest of my life, but my parents had left me totally unequipped for the future, with no direction or life skills.

I stopped walking when I reached the high point in the road. I'd wandered onto an overpass with four lanes of traffic zipping by directly beneath me. I leaned on the railing, drained of all desire to go any further. I knew at that moment exactly how my mother felt every day of her life: completely overwhelmed.

I could jump from here and end this in an instant, I thought.

Then I pictured myself in the back of an ambulance like the one that had just sped past. It would be my luck to survive the fall, yet mess myself up completely. I stepped away from the edge and started back down the ramp. There was no sense in rushing the natural course of events. I knew that with the kinds of choices I'd been making lately, I'd be dead by 30 anyway.

* * *

Debbie showed up an hour later, all apologetic.

"Sorry it took me so long. I had to fix myself up."

"For what? To pick me up at a garage?"

She gave me a look. "I thought since we'd be right by the Lincoln Tunnel, we could zip into the city. I heard about a club in the village that won't card us."

"Sounds good," I said and leaned back against the seat. "I could definitely use a drink."

We parked on a side street off Greenwich Avenue and found the club. It was still early, so we wandered around soaking up the sights, hoping to see someone famous.

I don't remember who saw the *Psychic* sign first—me or Debbie—but it hooked me and pulled me in like a fish on a line. If there was any chance my luck would start to pick up soon, I wanted to know about it.

Next thing I knew I was sitting in front of a little babushka straight out of the movies. I'd never seen any of the gypsies my mother talked about, but this lady could have been raised by them. Short and round with dark hair and even darker features, she had me sit across from her at a round table with a scarf on it. A crystal ball and a deck of tarot cards completed the picture.

"Your aura is very dark," she said, picking right up on the fact that my life wasn't going so well. She might have actually had some real psychic abilities, but I think even the guy selling papers at the corner newsstand could have read the negative energy rolling off me that day.

Nevertheless, I soaked up her words—and believed them—as if she held the key to my happiness. When she got to the part about my love life, I leaned in even closer.

"I see a large eye hovering above you," she said, shaking her head. "An evil eye."

I pulled back, well aware from my mother's stories that evil eyes were real.

She squinted, made a tsk-tsk sound, and said, "You're never gonna have a boyfriend unless I remove your curse."

My chin dropped to my chest. My mother would certainly agree that I was cursed, and I couldn't deny it either as I reviewed the sorry facts of my life: I didn't have a home, I didn't have any money, and I no longer had a car. I longed for a boyfriend, but according to the psychic, that was one more "never gonna have" to add to my list unless I let her help me.

Well aware that I'd be heading to a club later with my girlfriend instead of with a date, I didn't hesitate too long before handing over the $25 dollar de-cursing fee. What I got in return was a tiny pouch to put under my pillow. I never opened the cloth to see what made it crackle like a bean bag, trusting only in its magic.

That night I placed the pouch on my bed sheet. I stared at it for a full min-ute, willing it to take away the awful curse, then covered it with my pillow. Just like the princess in *The Princess and the Pea*, I went to sleep that night sure that I could feel that little packet through the padding.

Three times I went back to Greenwich Village to get the pouch's powers renewed, but one month and one hundred dollars later, no prince came by to sweep me off my feet. With money tighter than ever, I finally had to give up and face the facts: The psychic was running a con. The only sweeping came from me and my broom ... working overtime to pay her fee.

Chapter 4

Wild Thing

My new car was a step up from the old one, if only in price. For $800 bucks I got a gold Chevy Impala with a torn Landau top and a driver's side door that wouldn't open. The rust spots along the underbody made the car look like it had survived a shootout with Bonnie and Clyde. That having been said, it had one thing going for it that my other car didn't: it ran.

I could afford the car thanks to my new job at The Owl and I restaurant, which was also a step up from cleaning houses. I started out waitressing, but I did a little cooking as well. My learning curve in the kitchen was kind of steep, considering I'd only ever helped my mother with things like goulash and pierogies. It didn't help that in our house we never ate vegetables. And I mean *never*.

With time, other things started going better in my life as well. Since I'd dropped out of school, it didn't make sense to continue boarding at the Warrens'. I happily packed my stuff and moved into my mother's apartment with her and my younger sisters. The place might have been small, but at least I had some semblance of a family again. None of us had gotten over the permanent state of shell shock from a lifetime of living with my father, but with him out of the picture, we no longer dreaded the near-daily explosions.

The eviction and breakup of our family took a toll on me, but deep inside I still had my dignity. I signed up for the first GED course I could get into and earned my diploma only a few months after the rest of my graduating class. I don't know that I needed a degree to work as a waitress, but at a time when I was feeling pretty powerless, that piece of paper meant a lot.

Waiting tables at The Owl and I wasn't the most high-class job, but I worked with some good people. Technically, The Owl and I was a restaurant, but they were better known for their bar. That's where they made their real money, and after work I'd join my co-workers for a drink or two. I was eighteen now—the legal age in Jersey in the mid '70s—and it seemed like a good way to unwind.

There was a group of us who liked to listen to the bands that played in the bars over in West New York. In case you don't know it, that's actually in New Jersey. It got its name because it overlooks the city skyline, but sitting across the Hudson River from Manhattan, it's about as far from glamorous as Harlem is from Hollywood.

One night after a particularly busy shift I felt like letting off some steam. Nobody else wanted to go with me, but I figured I'd run into someone I knew and took off on my own. I ended up cruising down a street not too far from the garage where I'd abandoned my old car. A club I liked was just around the corner.

I found a spot big enough for my Chevy in front of an all-night liquor store. Posters in the windows advertising the weekly specials blocked any view of the goods inside, but three derelicts leaning against the iron bars held several samples. Thanks to the jammed car door, I had to slide across the seat and get out directly in front of the drunks. It didn't matter, really, because I was halfway in the bag myself, having started drinking before I left work.

I pulled the collar of my coat around my neck and took off at a brisk pace—not because I was afraid, but to ward off the December chill. A more sensible person might have used the word "rough" to describe the neighborhood. I simply took it in stride. I knew I shouldn't have been out there alone, especially after midnight, but the allure was just too strong. I felt fairly sure that some of the regulars I hung out with would be in town. That wasn't necessarily a given, since they were transients of a different sort than the bums on the corner. My friends worked for Mister Barnum and Mr. Bailey.

Okay, so maybe I wasn't the best judge of character, but their lives with the circus seemed a heck of a lot more exciting than mine.

I got to the club, walked through the door, and stopped inside the entrance to scan the room. The band's equipment was set up in a corner; but the players sat drinking in some chairs beside the stage. Most of the tables were empty at that hour, but the hard core partiers could still be found at the bar. I recognized a familiar face on one of the stools and headed that way.

"White Russian," I said to the bartender as I sidled up beside my friend.

"Hey, Travis," I said. "What's happening?"

Travis was a carnie. His small, close-set eyes sat beneath blonde brows on a protruding ridge of bone. His large nose looked as if it had been broken at least twice. He squinted at me for a few seconds, then gave a quick nod as if my name had hit him in the head.

"Yo ... Janet. You got a light?"

"Yeah, sure," I said, and reached into my purse.

He held out his hand. "You got a cigarette to go with that light?"

I laughed, and pulled a Marlboro from my pack.

Travis lit up, then took a long drag. He eyed my purse as he reached for his beer. "Got anything stronger in there?"

"Not tonight."

"Damn." He scowled, looked toward the door leading to the alley, then back at me. "This place is too quiet."

The bartender handed me my drink and I sucked half of it down at once.

"Whoa," Travis said, "Take it easy before you get sick."

"Don't worry about me," I sniffed.

"It's not you I'm worried about," he said, waving his hand in front of his clothes. "I ever tell you what it's like to run a Ferris wheel?"

"Nope."

"Take my advice, Janet. Don't ever ride one. Kids puke on 'em all the time. When they do, we kick everybody off and wipe it up with a rag. Then we run the ride empty for a minute so people won't remember which seat it was."

I made a face and took a smaller sip.

The band started back up, making further conversation impossible. I swiveled around and leaned back against the bar to listen. When I finished my drink, I waved over the bartender and switched to Sambuca. The anisette flavor tasted good on my tongue as it mingled with the creamy cacao. I lost track of how many more I polished off before the band finished up their last set.

When they started turning off the lights, I stumbled getting off the stool.

"Whoa!" Travis said, grabbing my arm. "You sure you can make it home?"

His fingers hurt, and I shook him off. "No problem."

"Where you parked?"

"Just down the street."

"Come on. I'll walk with you."

In all honesty, I don't remember getting from the club to my car, but I do recall what happened once I got there. Travis glared at the liquor store windows and said, "Damn, man, those bars remind me too much of my time in the joint." He turned to look at me. "I ever tell you the real reason I joined the circus?"

I shook my head.

"Makes it harder to track me down."

He turned towards my car, but staggered and fell against me. After steadying himself on my arm he looked down at my purse. "You sure you ain't got nothing else in there I can have?"

"I'm sure."

He moved closer. "Don't shit me, Janet."

A surge of fear cut through the cobwebs in my head. I'd convinced myself that the people I hung out with were my friends, but I suddenly realized that given the right circumstances, some of them could actually hurt me.

"I'm telling you the truth." I glanced at my car. "Thanks for walking with me, but I need to get going."

I backed toward my Chevy, climbed in the passenger's side, and somehow got the key in the ignition without taking my eyes off Travis. The ride back to Oakland passed in a blur.

I thought I did a pretty good job of keeping quiet when I got home, but the next morning when I walked into the kitchen, my mother scowled at me.

"You need to take better care of yourself."

"I'm fine."

She crooked a finger at me and said, "One day you're gonna get hurt."

I turned my back as she left for work, but her words stabbed at my conscience like a hot poker. I didn't care so much about myself, but I couldn't help but worry that some day I might harm someone else and have to live with what I'd done.

I crossed to a cupboard in search of breakfast. The sound of the apartment door opening again after it had just shut made me turn. There stood my mother, her face as white as the flakes on her shoulders. I hadn't realized it was snowing.

"What's the matter?" I asked.

"It's your car," she said, her eyes wide. "There's a cross in the frost on the hood."

We stared at each other for a moment without speaking. I'm sure that she, like me, was remembering a time not too much earlier when she claimed to see angels flying over my car while I was driving. As she turned to leave again, she shook her head and said, "Someone is looking out for you, Janet."

I closed the cupboard empty-handed and leaned on the counter. I wanted to rush out the door and see the cross for myself, but my thoughts kept me glued in place. I was as reckless as they came: hanging out with the wrong people, taking stupid risks, and—I rubbed my throbbing temples—maybe drinking more than I should. Visions of angels and a cross on the hood of my car didn't make sense.

Still, if those things really happened, I allowed myself to wonder … could God actually be starting to like me?

Chapter 5

Lucky Lady

Once I got the hang of being a waitress, I picked up a second job working part time at a truck stop. Manny's Diner was over in Mahwah, New Jersey, but don't bother looking for it. They built a highway right through the place in the late eighties.

The only reason I picked Manny's was for convenience, being less than half an hour from my mom's apartment. When you look at what happened to me there, it kind of makes you wonder if I didn't end up in Mahwah on purpose. You see, *Mahwah* comes from the Lenni Lenape Indians. It means "meeting place," which Manny's certainly was for plenty of over-the-road truckers. It also means "place where two paths meet," which is exactly what it turned out to be for me and Cowboy.

I was filling salt shakers just before the lunch rush when one of the other girls let out a low whistle.

"Would you look at that?" she said.

I raised my eyes and had to hush the little hum that jumped to my throat. I knew full well that Robert Redford would never eat at Manny's, but the guy settling in at the counter could have played his double in *Butch Cassidy and the Sundance Kid*.

The fellow was about five-ten or eleven with narrow hips, broad shoulders, and none of the extra weight around the middle that most of the truckers carried. He wore a big, round buckle on his belt and a pair of brown cowboy boots with his faded jeans. The wide brim of his cowboy hat shaded a pair of gorgeous blue eyes.

I put his age around twenty-eight—eight years older than I was then. I could tell before I even spoke to him that this guy was a man's man. Lots of fellows still had pony tails in the late seventies, but he'd trimmed his brown hair short. There was just enough bristle on his cheeks to make me wonder if he'd forgotten to shave that day or if he was just trying to look sexy.

He needn't have bothered. My heart hadn't beat that fast since I stopped scrubbing floors for a living.

I was no fool. I knew that a lot of the truckers that came in to Manny's were looking for hookups with the girls that worked there. But I'm the one who paid a hundred dollars to have a curse taken off me, remember? I didn't know love growing up, and a part of me absolutely craved that. So when this good-looking guy sat down at my station and flashed me a smile that would charm a quarter from a panhandler, I felt that old curse disperse like fog in a sunbeam.

"Hi," I said as I placed a set-up in front of him. "I'm Janet."

"No kidding," he said with mock surprise, then nodded at my name tag.

I looked down and gave an embarrassed snort. I didn't usually ask the customers their name, but found myself saying, "So, what's yours?"

"Folks just call me Cowboy."

"No kidding," I said with the same mock surprise he'd used on me.

We laughed together.

"First time I've seen you in here," I said.

"First time I've been here, but if I'd known you were here, I would have stopped in sooner."

I rolled my eyes at the corny line, but inside I was quaking. No one had ever talked to me like that. Especially no one that looked like him.

"So if you're a cowboy, do you ride horses?" I asked, knowing it was a stupid question, but wanting nothing more than to keep the conversation going.

"Nah, just trucks."

I glanced at the parking lot. A boxy bread truck sat right out front. "What kind?" I asked.

"Eighteen wheeler. My rig's just down the street."

I looked at the Wonderbread logo outside and felt a strange sense of relief. Disconcerted, I pulled my order pad from my pocket. "So, what'll you have?"

He ordered a burger and fries, and we kept on chatting between his meal and my other customers. I tried to talk him into a piece of pie, but he said he had a load of bananas that he had to get to upstate New York before they started rotting.

Given a lasso, I would have roped him to the seat, but all I could do was try not to look as disappointed as I felt when he got up to pay his check.

"Good talking to you, Cowboy," I said lamely.

"Same here, Janet. You take care." He actually tipped his hat.

I watched as he started toward the exit. The view from behind was as good as the front, which didn't help my plummeting mood. I could feel that old evil eye boring into me, when suddenly it blinked.

Cowboy pulled his hand back from the door, turned around, and tilted his head.

"You like country music?"

"Me?" What did I know about country music? I'd grown up in a Polish family. "Sure," I said.

He nodded. "There's a great country-western bar over in Paramus. You wanna meet me there tonight?"

I would have said yes even if he'd asked me to square dance.

* * *

The rain left streaks like tears on Manny's big plate glass windows. It seemed like forever since I'd seen the sun—or Cowboy. It had only been a few days, really, but my mood matched the weather. Then Mike, one of the regulars, looked up from his plate of meat loaf and said, "Hey Janet, Cowboy's in town."

I felt a rush of adrenaline—an instant high. I'd become a Cowboy junkie, and I was badly in need of a fix. If I'd had a choice, I never would have fallen for a long-haul trucker. His life was more transient than the carnies I hung out with, but that just made our reunions all the more sweet.

It had been two years since that day he first walked into Manny's. I was managing the place now while still working at The Owl and I. When Cowboy was in town, nothing could get me down. I walked around humming all the time. When he was on the road, I counted the hours until the next time he passed through Mahwah.

I'd heard that artists go through periods when what's happening in their lives affects the work they produce. They might have a blue period or a red period, and that's what they became known for. My time with Cowboy was my truck-riding, country-western period, and everyone knew I was crazy about the guy.

Never in my stunted dreams growing up did I ever picture myself sitting in the cab of a big rig with a movie-star look-alike. The first time Cowboy took me on one of his runs, it was all I could do not to reach over and blast that big air horn out of sheer exhilaration. Instead, I restrained myself and simply rested my hand on his leg.

"Like it?" he asked as he merged the truck onto the highway. I noticed that cars seemed to scurry out of our way.

"I love it."

He nodded, pleased, then jerked his head toward the windshield. "Hey, I know that guy!" He pointed at a red tractor trailer in front of us.

As Betty Boop stared back from the other truck's splash guards, Cowboy reached down and plucked a microphone plugged into a small radio. "How 'bout ya Red Rover ... you got a copy on Cowboy?"

A voice came back immediately. "Kick it in, good buddy. What's your 20?"

"Right at your back door, Rover."

"10-4. Beware you got a Kojak with a Kodak at yardstick 154. I'm gettin' off at the next cash box and find me a pickle park. How 'bout you? Come back."

"Not today." Cowboy glanced at me. "I got me a seat cover."

Red Rover chuckled into his microphone, then said. "I'm gone."

I listened, fascinated. CB radios had become the rage in recent years, even among car drivers, but this was my first time to hear actual truckers in action.

"You follow all that?" Cowboy asked as he nodded at the radio.

"Most of it. What's a seat cover?"

He winked. "Means there's a pretty lady in my passenger seat."

"Get outta here." I waved him off.

"You wanna try it?" He held out the mike.

I pulled back. "I don't think so."

"There's nothin' to it, but you gotta have your own handle."

I bit my lip, feeling like a kid. An excited kid.

"What's it gonna be?"

I shook my head. "I don't know ... "

"I do," Cowboy said. "From now on you're my Lucky Lady."

I blinked at him in surprise, then I realized that he had no idea how ironic the nickname was. I'd chosen to spare him the dreadful details of my home life. After all those years of terror and abuse, I was the last person in the world I'd ever call Lucky. But sitting on top of the world next to my real life Cowboy, I couldn't argue that the handle now fit.

Given my choice, I would have quit both of my jobs to join him full time on the road, but I had to earn my own way. Our time together in the truck came in infrequent one-week bursts. In between, we hit the local country-western joints whenever he passed through.

I quickly learned why country music held such appeal. The songs we listened to in honkytonks across New Jersey and New York told the story of my life. This was real cry-in-your-cups stuff, that—just like Cowboy himself—touched a part of my heart that had only known darkness. I memorized all the lyrics. When we weren't racking up *Motels and Memories,* my every waking hour was filled with *Daydreams About Night Things* and *What a Man My Man Is.*

Cowboy liked to drink as much as I did, but he also liked to dance. He had to teach me everything, but he never seemed to mind, even when I tripped on his toes. I got pretty good at the Texas Two-Step, but what I really liked was the slow dancing. If they could bottle the feeling that I got from being in his arms, I wouldn't have needed to drink at all.

Now, as my pulse quickened at the news that Cowboy was back in town, I flashed back to the last dance we shared. He'd held me close as Glen Campbell belted out his latest hit, *Rhinestone Cowboy,* from a juke box. Swaying together, I felt as if my heart would burst if I didn't say the three words that were still such strangers to my ears.

So I said them.

"I love you."

Cowboy pulled me closer and showed me that life really could be a dream by answering back, "I love you, too, Janet."

That's why Mike's announcement that Cowboy was in town surprised me, and snapped me back to reality. Why hadn't he called to let me know?

I approached Mike and asked, "Have you seen him?"

A guy in a black *Peterbilt* ball cap sat across the booth from Mike. He looked up at his table mate and said, "You're not talking about Cowboy that drives the rig with the produce?"

"That's him," I answered out of turn, smiling at the image of my boyfriend. The stranger shook his head. "Watch out for that one, Honey. Fella's got a girl in every truck stop."

I saw the shadow that passed over Mike's face across the table. His eyes clearly signaled *don't go there,* but his friend wasn't looking.

I gripped my order pad so tightly that my fingernails turned white. "It can't be the same guy," I said. "I'm going home with him soon to upstate New York."

Ever since we'd confessed our love, Cowboy and I had been talking about how our lives might come together instead of always heading off in different directions. What I didn't mention to Mike and his friend was that when I started planning my visit, Cowboy started making excuses.

"That right?" The man gave a small laugh and sliced my dreams out from under me with one sharpened sentence: "Then you'd better give his fiancée a heads-up that you're comin'."

Mike put his face in his hand and I stood there, legless, as the room began to sway. In the distance, I heard Glen Campbell telling me how long he'd been walkin' these same old streets—singin' the same old song ...

For two years I'd ridden the rig and danced in the honkytonks with Cowboy, hanging my every hope—my very happiness—on his affections, only to find that he'd been singing the same old songs to countless other women. For me, the tune had been a completely new one—a chart-topping, blockbuster of a hit. But Cowboy had snowed me, making me believe for the first time in my life that I actually knew how it felt to be loved.

The Lucky Lady's streak had run out. The handle no longer fit.

I stumbled away from Mike and his friend, deaf to all but the lyrics still taunting me from that last, unforgettable dance. Glen Campbell just wouldn't let it die as he whispered that he really didn't mind the rain, but a smile could hide all the pain ...

Which just goes to show you that songwriters don't know everything. For, like I learned that dreary day in Mahwah, New Jersey, it's damn near impossible to smile with a broken heart.

Chapter 6
Wake-up Call

I got over Cowboy like I got over all the other hard times in my life: I drank until I couldn't feel a thing. In the meantime, I changed jobs at The Owl and I restaurant to something far more suited to me than waiting tables: I became a bartender. Perfect, don't you think?

But I was 21 now and legal in any state. Starting out, I didn't know much more than how to mix my favorite White Russians or hand over a bottle of Bud. The other bartender, Frank Donovan, showed me how to mix fancy cocktails and fill a beer glass just right. After quitting time, he and I would pour drinks for the rest of the staff and help ourselves as well. If you've ever worked in a bar, you know that's just what everyone did; it was part of the life.

Christmas Eve that year gave us the perfect excuse to party even harder than usual. It had been snowing all night and nobody was in any hurry to go out in the cold. When the last customers walked out the door, the owners, cooks, and waitresses joined Frank and me at the bar to celebrate. Finally, around three A.M. we turned out the lights and headed to our cars.

I slipped a little in the icy parking lot and flailed my arms to keep my balance. Somebody behind me laughed and I waved them off as I fumbled with my keys.

"Yo, Janet, if you ever fix that door, the rest of your car's gonna fall apart," Frank yelled.

"Screw you!" I called over my shoulder and slid across the seat.

"Merry Christmas to you, too!" he called back.

I could see Frank's lights in the rear view mirror as I pulled out onto Maple Avenue. Snow completely covered the lines on the road, but I could find my way home even in the thickest fog. I'd proved that many a night after one too many drinks.

The Owl and I sat just down the hill from a bend in the road. I gave the car some gas to get up the incline and felt the back end fish tail. I gripped the wheel, pressed harder on the pedal, and headed into the curve.

If God looks out for drunks and sailors, He must have been busy over in New York harbor that night. Things might have turned out differently if it hadn't been icy. Or if I'd stopped after three drinks

In all fairness to God, at least He didn't let anyone else get hurt when I plowed head-on into a telephone pole.

Metal mated with wood in an ear-shattering shriek. The windshield exploded into a shower of ice crystals as my body slammed into the steering wheel. Don't waste your time wondering if I was wearing a seat belt—I wasn't into making smart decisions at that point in my life.

The blow was a thousand times worse than my most memorable beating. I slumped over, only dimly aware of pain in my face and chest, but I very clearly remember thinking, *this is bad.*

Then I heard Frank's voice by my side.

Janet! Are you okay? … Holy Shit!"

Lucky for me, I passed out after that. I came to only for a few brief moments in the back of an ambulance.

They took me to Fair Lawn Hospital because it was the closest one, but they didn't do me any favors. The place was small and badly understaffed. Maybe the doctors were home nestled all snug in their beds, but I lay there for two hours with visions of what a mess I'd made of my life dancing in my head.

I could see blood on my clothes, but I was too afraid to feel around with my fingers. Fully conscious now, I watched the faces of those around me. Some looked away immediately; others stared at me in fascinated horror. I began to panic, wondering what I'd done to myself. My heart and mind raced like they hadn't since I was 14 when I found a doctor who'd give uppers to any girl who wanted to lose weight. Being a big-boned Polish girl, size became an issue for me, and I didn't care that I might get hooked on speed. When the police arrested the doctor, my source of Black Beauties dried up. It was just as well, since they made me hyper as Hell. I sometimes went days without sleeping, running around like a crazy person until I'd crash from exhaustion.

But that was crashing in the metaphorical sense. I'd gone and done it for real this time. I'd survived, but messed myself up royally—exactly what I feared would happen back when I considered jumping off that overpass in West New York. Now, lying there thinking about my mother getting a phone call from a hospital on Christmas morning, I almost wished I'd gone ahead and jumped when I had the chance.

Someone finally figured out I needed more help than they were able to give me in Fair Lawn. Back I went into the ambulance for a ride over to Valley Hospital in Richmond. All this waiting gave the alcohol a chance to wear off, only to be replaced by more panic and pain.

Things got a little crazy at the new place. Nurses and doctors crowded around me and everyone seemed to be talking at once. I saw a flash of scissors and felt my clothes being peeled away.

"We're going to take you into surgery now," said a disembodied voice as a plastic mask descended over my face. I think something stronger than a White Russian came flowing through that mask, because I was out before we left the ER.

I didn't awaken fully until the next morning on the ward. It hurt to breathe, as if someone had been sitting on my chest all night. But that pain was nothing compared to my head, which felt like an over-ripe watermelon.

A doctor about my father's age stood beside my bed studying a chart. I got the feeling he would have rather been home opening presents with his family than reading off the laundry list of damage I'd inflicted upon myself. I could hardly blame him for his lack of good cheer.

"Your chest is badly bruised, but you didn't break any ribs," he said.

When I tried to speak, my mouth didn't work.

The doctor held up a hand. "Two of your lower teeth came through your chin. I sewed up the laceration, but I couldn't save the teeth."

I attempted a question, but my words came out garbled.

"Don't try to talk. You broke your jaw, and I had to wire it shut."

I managed a moan and tilted my head back into the pillow.

"You'll be able to talk eventually, but I want you to give everything a rest for a day or two."

I held out my left hand and made a spooning motion over it with the right. My eyes asked the question: *Will I be able to eat?*

His answer left me reeling. There'd be no need for diet pills from this doctor. According to him, I'd be drinking my meals through a straw for the next three months.

Narcotics took the edge off the pain, but there was no magic cure for the shame that hung in the air heavier than the smell of antiseptic and bandages. My mother and my sisters showed up just after the doctor left. They touched my arms and said nice words, but seeing my mother cry hurt worse than my jaw. Later, Frank and my friends from the bar stopped by. They smiled and joked to make me feel better, but behind their laughter I sensed a touch of guilt mixed with relief that it was me lying there instead of them.

I held in my tears in front of my visitors, but alone in the darkened room that night I let them flow until they soaked the pillow. The broken jaw was painful and a major inconvenience, but it was temporary—I'd have to look at the scar where my teeth came through my face for the rest of my life.

With that thought, something inside me snapped.

I'd truly believed I'd be dead by 30. I'd come within inches of fulfilling my prophecy, but suddenly I didn't want the rest of my life to be only 9 more years. My photos might be marred from there on out, but a scar on my face was a small price to pay for a second chance at living.

Like a light bulb turning on at the bottom of a dark well, I realized that I could no longer maintain such a reckless existence. I didn't want the shame of my drunk driving to be the picture that I or others held of me. Yet, I knew no other life than the one I'd lived. I'd grown up in a home where fear and superstition ruled—taught to believe I was powerless … a victim. I inhabited a hostile universe.

But that accident woke me up. The scar would be my constant reminder that I'd hit rock bottom and survived. I had no idea how to climb out of the darkness, but if peace were out there somewhere, somehow I would find it.

Chapter 7
A Voice in the Night

"Hi, my name is Janet," I said, wishing they would have skipped right past me. But I'd sat in the circle enough times to know that I had to at least introduce myself, if nothing else. Even though I'd forced out the required tag line at each of the previous meetings, it still hurt when I heard myself say, "and I'm the adult child of an alcoholic."

"Hi, Janet!" came the reply from the group.

I acknowledged their welcome with a nod, then passed to the woman on my left. As she introduced herself with the same words, my mind drifted back to how I'd ended up in this sterile meeting room at Valley Hospital.

It was obvious after my accident that I couldn't continue on the same reckless path. I didn't know how to make things different, but something had to give. Maybe I sent that thought out to the universe. Or maybe it was the fact that with my jaw wired shut it was easier to read than to talk. Whatever the reason, I found a bunch of books that struck really close to home. The more I read, the more I discovered that my family's lunacy actually had a name for it: *Dysfunction*, with a capital D. For the first time in my life, I began to see that not everyone had grown up in the kind of household I did.

About the same time that I was doing all that soul searching, my father reached his own crisis point. Years back when we lost the house, he'd ended up on the street, living in his car. Eventually, the family helped him out by finding a residence home in Paramus that would take him. You'd think that would have been the end of it, but my dad was his own train wreck waiting to happen. If his drinking was out of control in the privacy of his own house, it didn't stop just because strangers were now watching him.

Once he got old enough for social security and the checks started coming in, he had extra money to spend on booze. When that ran out, he'd call my mother or one of us kids. I was as bad as everyone else, always bailing him out. We started getting calls from the home. They'd say, "Please do something about your father." We lived every day with the threat that they were going to toss him.

Then when I started reading more about dysfunction, I found out there was a name for me as well: *Enabler*. According to the books, I had to learn to put my foot down—to say "no," which definitely wasn't part of my vocabulary. The whole issue of *boundaries* seemed really important, but I had none. Absolutely zero. I was a people pleaser of the highest order, who now found out I was supposed to say, "No, I'm not giving you money for alcohol. No, you gotta be a big boy—don't call me; I can't be taking care of you."

You can learn the fancy words and read all the good advice, but doing something with it is another thing altogether. As a first-class victim, I only knew how to take the trash that other people dished out, not how to take control.

I guess that's why the pamphlet somebody gave me a few months after my accident caught my attention. The big letters on the front spelled out *ACOA—Adult Children of Alcoholics*. Inside it had this laundry list of 13 characteristics common to people whose parents drank too much. Thirteen being an unlucky number, I identified with every single trait, starting with the very first one: "*You guess at what normal is.*"

On the back they had the 12 steps that helped you become a functioning member of society. Once again, the first item on the list jumped right out at me: "*We admitted we were powerless over the effects of alcoholism or other family dysfunction, that our lives had become unmanageable.*"

Did you catch that last word? *Unmanageable ...*

I'd never pictured myself going to a self-help group, let alone pouring out my darkest secrets to a bunch of strangers, but for the first time, I sensed there might be a way out of my problems. The 12 steps weren't just useful advice from some self-help book. They were real live actions to undertake—things I could actually *do*.

The pamphlet said that ACOA was a sister program to AA. Sure, I questioned whether I was a contender for the parent group myself. I knew I wasn't too far from qualifying. But I honestly felt I was doing enough at the time to keep from pinning that "alcoholic" label on my own shirt. Yes, I was still drinking ... maybe not quite as much as before, but to my credit, I'd quit working as a bartender and stopped hanging out so much with the rowdy crowd. In fact, I left

The Owl and I restaurant altogether and started working at Manny's full-time. I made a deliberate choice to remove myself from that bar environment.

My work life was a bit more stable, but I still had family problems to deal with. So, after fielding yet another pitiful phone call from my father, I decided to see if the 12 steps would work for me. I gotta tell you, that initial meeting was a real eye opener. First of all, no one flashed me that who-the-hell-are-you look when I walked in the door. Nor did anyone smother me with sweetness-and-light chit chat while waiting for things to get started. Instead, everyone just gave me a friendly nod and let me hide behind my skin.

That was a relief in itself, but the truly amazing part came after the introductions. The group began to share their personal stories one by one (not me, thank God ... they let me just sit there), and I came to the most wonderful realization: Those people were as screwed up as I was.

So after that first time, I went back. And I kept going back. The 12-step programs all have these little phrases, and that's one of them: "Keep coming back." They might sound a little hokey, but I kind of liked them. I could get through a week if I just took it "one day at a time." Stuff like that gave me strength while I was starting to figure out the kind of person I wanted to be. Those little phrases gave me something to hold onto.

So there I was, back for my umpteenth meeting, and I still wasn't real comfortable with the whole sharing thing. It helped that I could identify most of the faces now. I'd actually made friends with the woman to my right. Charlotte's name might not have been Irish, but her red hair gave her away. In her mid thirties, she was about ten years older than me. She worked as a nurse, which was perfect for someone with such a caring soul. She had four kids—less than half as many as I hoped to have some day. But even with her job and her family, Charlotte still found time to get together with me for coffee.

Charlotte and I shared a lot of the same history, but like me and the woman on my left, she chose not to share it with the group that evening. So then it came to the guy two seats away. I'd never seen him before, but he looked like any fellow you'd see walking down the street.

"Hi," he said to the group. "My name's Hal."

"Hi, Hal," I repeated with everyone else.

"What I remember most about growing up," Hal said, "is there I was living in this fancy house in a nice, normal neighborhood, thinking all the time that nobody would believe what it looked like inside."

That got my attention, and I leaned my ear closer as Hal continued.

"I mean, if people really knew what was going on in there ..." He shook his head. "I was terrified that people would find out and judge me based on what my family was like."

I blinked, feeling like a ventriloquist. My lips weren't moving, but my words were coming out of this Hal guy's mouth. But he was no dummy—his next thoughts showed that he'd traveled a good bit farther down the road to recovery than I had.

"I learned a lot by going to these meetings back where I just moved from," he said. "Talking about all the stuff you've buried is hard, but that's when you start to heal. We've all swallowed a shitload of pain, and until you bring it back up and address it, it just eats away at you like an ulcer."

Okay, I thought as I stared at my shoes, *maybe I'll start talking* ... next time.

Hal passed the floor to the next guy and they went around the room like that. Each person had survived horrific situations, yet those who'd been going to the meetings for a while were now putting their foot down and saying, "This is unacceptable." I wasn't there yet, but I could see the faintest glimmer of light.

When we got all the way around the circle, they started to wrap things up. George, the moderator for the evening, held up his hand to stop people from leaving.

"In two weeks we have another weekend coming up at the Holy Spirit Retreat Center. Anybody wants to go, see me tonight to sign up."

With that, everyone started stacking the chairs.

"Are you going to the retreat?" Charlotte asked as we walked toward the exit.

"I don't know. What's it all about?"

"It's something most 12-step groups do—going on retreats. We go to the Holy Spirit Retreat Center about four times a year."

"Yeah, but what do you do there?"

She smiled. "Reflect, mostly. The place is run by some Carmelite friars, but you don't have to be Catholic to go. The Carmelites are known for their silent, solitary lives, so we go to the retreat to get some of that for ourselves. It's a gorgeous setting ... really peaceful. I think you'd like it."

"Peaceful, huh?" I stopped at the door and let the word sink in. I'd taken the step of attending ACOA and had survived so far. Going on a retreat didn't seem any more threatening. Now that I'd decided to start talking at the next meeting, a weekend of silence might do me some good.

"Come with us, Janet. See for yourself."

"Why not?" I said, and turned back to sign up.

* * *

If you've ever driven to New York City from the south on I-95, you pass through a part of New Jersey that's all gritty and gray. The view of Newark airport and all the factories makes most people think the whole northern part of our state is like that. If people would just get off the highway and drive a few miles to the west, they'd have a completely different picture.

The Holy Spirit Retreat Center is only 20 miles west of Manhattan and less than that from where I lived. As close as it is to a major metropolitan area, arriving there from the east is like being transported to heaven. Passing along the front of the property is the kind of road that people from the Bronx take when they want to go for a scenic Sunday drive. The road cuts right through the mountains—a real back-to-nature paradise that makes you want to pull over, roll down the windows, and suck in all that fresh, clean air.

The retreat center originally belonged to a New York businessman who had more money than I'll ever see in my lifetime. The estate sits on top of a hill between two mountain ridges. The 32-room mansion dates back to the early 1900s, as do the two smaller houses you pass on the driveway that winds through the grounds.

I had to hand it to my fellow ACOAers: as a getaway for the weekend, the place had the Motel 6 over in Paterson beat by a mile. Stepping through the front door of the main house, I suddenly knew what it felt like to be rich. I'd heard not to expect anything fancy from the bedrooms, but the main entry made my jaw drop. A crystal chandelier shined down on stylish furniture, polished wooden floors, a huge stone fireplace, and thick blue drapes at the windows.

"Wow," I said aloud

Charlotte stood beside me. "Nice, isn't it? And you haven't seen the dining room yet. I'll show you the rest after we settle in."

I followed her up the elegant main staircase, running my hand along the curving, hand-carved banister as we climbed. On the second floor I stopped when a series of photographs on the wall caught my eye. They featured a serene looking priest with a high forehead and round, wire-rimmed glasses.

"That's Titus Brandsma," Charlotte said, doubling back when she noticed I was no longer behind her.

"Who was he?" I asked, still staring at his picture. There was something about him ...

"He was a Carmelite, like the priests here, but he was Dutch."

She went on to tell me how Father Brandsma had been imprisoned by the Nazis in a concentration camp in Amsterdam, then later moved to the infamous Dachau for speaking out against the Nazis' treatment of the Jews. Ultimately, he was killed by lethal injection, and was martyred within the Catholic Church. I couldn't help but think of my parents, imprisoned in the Polish work camps. As hard as their lives were, they'd had it easy compared to those like Father Brandsma.

"His faith was so strong," Charlotte said, "that in the middle of all that horror, he'd walk around singing and humming. It drove the guards crazy."

I looked at the picture of the brave priest in a new light. While I was nowhere in his league, I sure identified with his story. Throughout my life I'd found special comfort in humming. I'd always believed that as long as I could hear my own voice in the dark, everything would be okay. Father Brandsma had actually given hope to others with his singing, letting those who needed strength know that you could kill the body, but you couldn't kill the human spirit.

I followed Charlotte down the hall, hoping that I, too, would always be able to hum through life.

* * *

Much of that weekend I was free to wander the retreat center at will—to enjoy the silence and reflect to my heart's content. The estate sat on 30 acres of land that backed up to a wilderness preserve. Walking around the grounds, I didn't have to worry about running into any living souls except my fellow 12-steppers and a few squirrels and rabbits.

I was pretty new to the whole concept of quiet reflection. I'd never before bothered to try and still my restless mind. Instead, I carried all the destructive thoughts and images from my childhood straight through to adulthood, giving them free rein to run around inside my brain. Their constant negative chatter formed the very foundation of my belief system.

Thankfully, the priests at the retreat center had a few tricks up their robes to help people like me. They taught a technique called visualization and recommended I wander down to the garden and try it out. I did as they said and found a quiet spot in the shade of an enormous tree.

Growing up, I hadn't gone to church much, but I was no stranger to prayer. I'd spent a lifetime pleading for God to help me—please help me. Now, sitting in the shade of that thick canopy of branches I did my best to quiet the chatter in my mind. I pictured Jesus there with me under that tree, just as he'd sat in the garden of Gethsemane, and you know—I swear I sensed his presence.

The experience really floored me.

I shared what happened with Father Paul, one of four resident priests who provided spiritual direction to any guest who requested it. To my relief, he didn't laugh or seem to doubt me. With his gray hair and kind eyes, he had a grandfatherly air about him. I found his quiet voice and gentle nature as soothing as the soft brown tones of his robe. After just a few minutes in his presence I opened up to him as if I'd known him for years.

When Father Paul discovered that I lived nearby, he invited me to come back the following week to chat with him again. I hesitated for a moment. As director of the retreat house, he represented a father figure, and the voices in my head tried to protest. But maybe that little bit of reflection had opened up some room for a new voice. I surprised myself by agreeing to return.

* * *

Charlotte knew what she was talking about when she said that the retreat center was peaceful. When not wandering the woods, I gravitated to the small chapel that used to be the estate's pool room. The dark wood paneling gave the place the look of a British college, but it wasn't the walls that made me feel like a stranger in a foreign country. I'd never known such all-encompassing peace, and I soaked it up like a wilted flower soaks up water.

That weekend, guests were invited to attend Mass in the little chapel. All the members of my group went, and I took a seat beside Charlotte. I enjoyed the prayers, the hymns, and the sermon more than I'd imagined. When it came time for Holy Communion, I rose to join the other Catholics at the altar.

Charlotte put a hand on my arm and said softly, "Hold on a second, Janet, you can't go up there."

"But I'm Catholic," I answered back.

"Yes, but you were never confirmed, were you?"

The chapel suddenly grew warmer. "No, but I was baptized as a baby."

The guy on my other side whispered, "They get so many visitors from different denominations here, that they don't let you take Communion unless you've been confirmed."

I sank back into my chair, fighting back the urge to rush out the door. Until that point, I'd enjoyed every bit of the Holy Spirit experience, yet here was a piece that was unavailable to me. Suddenly, I was five years old, sitting in the front yard watching the kids going to church across the street. I was an outsider once again. Maybe it was because my mother had experienced so much deprivation in her own life and passed that on to me that I felt the pain twice as much.

I watched the practicing Catholics take the small white wafers and place them on their tongues. I sat there, cheeks burning with shame as I admitted to myself how little I knew about Catholic traditions. One thing I did know for sure that day: those at the altar were blessed. I was a wretch.

After the Mass, Charlotte walked with me toward the dining hall. "You know, most churches offer adult confirmation classes."

That was news to me and I perked up immediately. "They do?"

"Sure. You should check with the church in your town."

"How long does it take to get confirmed?"

"I'm not sure, but there's no hurry. We come here all the time."

Charlotte was sensitive enough to feel my pain, but she didn't know me as well as she thought. I'd spent enough time on the outside looking in. If my local parish offered adult confirmation classes, I wasn't going to waste a second before signing up. I vowed in that moment that I'd be back there at the altar with the rest of the good Catholics before any of them could say *amen*.

* * *

"Come in, come in, little bird."

Father Paul came around from behind his desk and greeted me with a gentle kiss on the cheek. As usual, I flushed. How anyone could call me a little bird was beyond me, but I hungered for his familiar greeting like a starving sparrow.

"How are you, Father?" I sat across from him and smiled at the mess on his desk. As usual, it looked as if someone had emptied the contents of a filing cabinet onto it.

"I'm well," he said, shifting a stack of papers to the side. Today he'd chosen to wear his black suit and he tugged at the white collar as he leaned back. "Have you had a good week, Janet?"

I had, in fact, had an especially good one, and it felt even better to me now. My chats with Father Paul were the highlight of each week.

"So good," I said, "that I can hardly wait to tell you about it."

"Splendid," he said, leaning forward to rest on his elbows. "Did something happen at work?"

I shook my head. Father Paul knew that I no longer worked at Manny's. He'd shared my excitement when I took a job as cook at The Union House Restaurant. This was a fancy place where people came to eat a nice meal, not just to hang out and drink. Yes, The Union House had a bar, but it wasn't their bread and butter like it was at The Owl and I. The job turned out to be a good fit.

"Something happened at church, then?" Father Paul asked, seemingly enjoying this little game of *20 Questions*.

"No, but last Sunday's homily was really good."

I'd been confirmed in the church and continued to attend services weekly. I enjoyed my new status as a practicing Catholic, even though I still struggled with my image of God. The topic came up frequently during our weekly chats. My interpretation of the Catholic God was that of a male patriarch sitting high on a throne. Other than Father Paul, any fatherly figure was still abusive and scary as Hell.

"All right," he said, giving up. "Tell me what made this week so special."

"It was something somebody said at my 12-step meeting."

Father Paul knew all about my meetings, as well as my family's history. From the beginning of our relationship I'd felt free to open up and talk with him about my past. His comments that life didn't have to be that way had helped me to continue moving forward instead of slipping back to my old ways. This week I'd taken a major step in the right direction.

I leaned forward and said, "A man spoke up and said that drinking is like chocolate."

Father Paul tilted his head. He knew how much I liked chocolate.

"The guy said you can't have just a little of either one. It's like being allergic."

"And you agree with that?"

I nodded. "That analogy really hit close to home. Ever since my accident, I told myself I could continue to drink and still be okay, but that guy was right. It just doesn't work for me."

"So what are you going to do?" Father Paul asked.

"I've already done it," I said. "I had my last drink five days ago, and I haven't looked back."

Father Paul came around the desk again and hugged me. "God bless you, little bird. I'm very, very proud of you."

And standing there in the warmth of his love—I gotta tell you—I knew that if God was anything like Father Paul, I might just learn to trust Him.

* * *

I lay in my bed, a book propped on my stomach. Suddenly I jerked, unaware that I'd drifted off. I blinked back the cobwebs, but found myself reading the same paragraph three times in a row. It wasn't the book—the life of St. Francis fascinated me—but it had been a particularly busy day at work.

My job at The Union House had lasted over a year, but it turned out to be only a stepping stone to something even better. It seemed I was destined for bigger things in the food industry, for I was hired by a company that ran corporate cafeterias. They put me in charge of food services for Russ Berrie, a large company that made stuffed animals.

I'd ended up managing Manny's truck stop and worked my way up to head chef at The Union House. Now I ran the show in Russ Berrie's cafeteria. I was finding out that I kind of liked being the boss.

But all that responsibility was tiring. I laid the book on my night stand and turned out the light. Sleep came so fast that I thought I was still awake when I heard the man's voice. I wasn't awake, though, because that voice was so loud it definitely woke me up.

"You're going to be a Catholic nun," it said.

Shocked more by the message than the voice itself, I sat bolt upright and answered back, "No way! You're in the wrong house!"

I looked around. When my eyes adjusted to the darkness, I could see that I was alone. But there was no doubt in my mind that I'd heard a man's voice. I hadn't been dreaming; it wasn't just in my thoughts. It came from outside me—in the room. I shook my head. Had he really said I was going to be a nun?

I waited a full minute for the guy to admit his mistake, but all I got was the silent treatment. I lay back and stared at the ceiling. As tired as I'd been before, there was no way I was falling back to sleep after that little bombshell.

A thousand thoughts buzzed around my brain. Me—a nun? That just wasn't my plan. I was going to get married and have ten kids! Yes, I went to Mass regularly now, but my time as a practicing Catholic represented only a small fraction of the last 27 years. Even though I volunteered for the church in a soup kitchen and at a homeless shelter these days, Catholicism wasn't my whole life.

I flashed back to my drinking years, hanging out with carnies in places I never should have been. I thought about my jobs … Bartenders didn't become nuns! Or what about my days with Cowboy—not to mention the nights—riding an 18 wheeler and hanging out in honkytonks? That particular memory brought an instant stab of pain to my chest. It had been years since he jilted me, but even if Cowboy had walked in the door at that moment, he'd break my heart all over again. What kind of nun carried a torch for a truck driver?

My past was littered with events that would make the Pope turn as white as his robes.

I rolled over, laughing at the thought of me in a habit. My family would choke. Becoming a nun was the farthest thing from my mind.

I closed my eyes, but I kept hearing that voice. Maybe I'd made it up.

But no, the voice had been real. I had no doubt that I heard it correctly. It was dead wrong, though. I had a corporate kitchen to run, and if I didn't get back to sleep, I'd be useless in the morning.

I willed my mind to settle down, but a single thought kept me from falling back to sleep:

What if the voice was right?

Chapter 8
Crossroad

Charlotte set her fork down and looked at me sideways. "There's something different about you, Janet."

"What do you mean?" I continued chewing my dinner, but I knew what she was going to say. I'd noticed a change in myself as well. A sense of peace had wrapped itself around me like a warm sweater in the week since I'd received my calling.

That's right. When a voice wakes you in the middle of the night to tell you you're going to be a Catholic nun, that's pretty much a *calling*, in my mind. I hadn't decided what to do about it yet, but something inside me had definitely changed.

"I don't know," Charlotte said. "You just seem so … "

"Peaceful?"

She cocked her head. "Yeah. That's it. What's going on?"

I shrugged my shoulders. I wasn't ready to have people start laughing at me yet. "Nothing special. I guess things are just going well at work."

"Yeah?" She didn't seem to buy it. "Well, whatever you're doing, keep it up. It suits you."

I nodded and went back to chewing. I felt bad about not coming clean with my friend. At least I hadn't really lied. Things were, in fact, going particularly well at work. The folks at Food Concepts, my parent company, were talking about making me a district manager. I had to hide a smirk when I realized that the pay raise itself would probably be more than what a nun earned—if they were paid anything at all.

The next day as I bustled around the big kitchen at the Russ Berrie plant, I thought about Charlotte, Father Paul, my family, and everyone else in my life. I didn't have the nerve to tell any of them about the voice I'd heard, let alone that I was actually giving the idea some thought. And why shouldn't I? All of the nuns at my parish church were wonderful, kind women. Didn't they do good things for the community?

I dumped a heavy sack of potatoes onto the steel countertop as I wrestled with the choices I faced. Everyone respected nuns. They lived lives of service— lives that actually meant something. Hadn't I been reading about St. Francis? He was a religious man who gave up everything to serve the poor. It didn't seem like a bad way to spend the rest of my life.

I picked up a peeler and started scraping potato skins into a large sink. The monotonous motion allowed my mind to continue its persistent train of thought. I recalled Charlotte's observation from dinner the night before. What was up with the peace I'd been feeling lately? The only other time I'd felt such a feeling of calm was in the chapel at the retreat center. Hadn't I been searching all my life for a sense of comfort like this? Maybe the sudden serenity was some kind of sign.

I nodded as I worked. Signs were a big thing in my family. It probably went back to the gypsies my mother used to talk to. Years ago she'd seen that cross on the hood of my car and the angels flying overhead. At the time I thought they meant that somebody might be looking out for me. Could they have actually been pointing to my future vocation?

With my hands working as fast as my mind, I had the entire bag of potatoes peeled in record time. I laid down the peeler and picked up a knife. I chose a large potato from the pile and set it on a cutting board. In one expert slice I split the potato in half. I was about to make another cut crosswise, when my hand froze in mid-air. I stared down at the potato, then picked it up and turned it over in my hand. I looked left, then right, then back at the potato.

Sure that my thoughts had turned me into a crazy woman, I walked over to my colleague Barbara and thrust the potato at her.

"What does that look like to you?"

She took a step back and glanced at me cock-eyed, then looked down at the potato. When she did a little double-take, I knew I wasn't losing my mind.

"It's a cross."

"Yeah, that's what I see, too."

"In the rot."

"Yeah."

"Hey, Harriett," Barbara called across the kitchen. "You gotta see this potato!"

Before I knew it, the potato was a celebrity. Somebody even grabbed a camera and took a picture of the rotted cross for posterity.

I didn't need a photograph to prove what I'd seen. That cross was a sign—a giant neon notice meant just for me—embedded in a potato. I wasn't ready to drop everything and take my vows just yet, but now I knew for sure that I had to at least check this nun business out.

* * *

I knew that Father Paul, like Titus Brandsma, was a Carmelite priest. Priests belonged to Catholic orders. St. Francis was the original Franciscan. Then I found out that nuns belonged to orders as well. If I was really going to be a nun like the voice said, I'd have to choose an order. This was 1986, and you couldn't just sit down and Google "which nuns are best for me?" Luckily, there were books about these things. I grabbed whatever I could get my hands on and started studying.

I didn't even bother with the cloistered Carmelites. Quiet reflection is good in small doses, but I could never keep my mouth shut for days on end. To make things worse, some of them lived so simply that all they ate was rice. I wouldn't even survive a week.

The more I read about the Franciscans, however, the more my interest grew. I learned about a retreat house in Graymore, New York, where they worked with drug and alcohol issues. If anybody was well versed in that particular subject, that would be me.

So I did a little more checking. I discovered that it was the priests in Graymore who did all the counseling. The nuns only ran the retreat center. I had tons of respect for all of them, but that male domination stuff didn't sit too well with me.

I decided that if I was going to be a nun, the traditional conservative route wasn't going to cut it. I'd have to find a more progressive order. After all, I might have given up drinking, but I still enjoyed my cigarettes. I wondered what the Franciscans would think about that?

What started out as mild curiosity turned into months of secret research. My searching led me to an order called the Sisters of Charity. Here was a group of nuns who didn't stay behind their convent walls; they got out in the community and worked directly with the needy. Progressive in dress as well as their actions, they wore regular street clothes if the spirit moved them. When I found out that their headquarters was in nearby Morristown, I called to set up a visit.

The Catholic Church wasn't hurting for money when they built the impressive mother house for the Sisters of Charity. I experienced the same feeling of awe when I stepped into the lobby of the massive main building as I did when I first saw the mansion at the Holy Spirit Retreat Center. The ornate architecture and the all-pervasive serenity took my breath away. The mother house served mainly as an administrative building, but I learned that nuns lived there as well. The thought that I could someday call such a place *home* defied my dreams.

The mother house was one of several buildings spread across the 200 acre campus of The College of St. Elizabeth. They had their own train stop in Morristown and called it Convent Station. My guide walked me through the beautiful chapel, then explained more about the congregation's mission as we continued our tour by car. From what I could see, these were intelligent, caring women. Best of all, there didn't seem to be any of the "Yes, father; No, father" kowtowing like some of the other places I'd looked into.

Everything about the visit placed the Sisters of Charity at the top of my list. Then we came to a large brick building called The Villa.

"This is where our retired nuns live," my guide explained.

I followed her inside, where she led me to a large room. I suppose I should have been pleased that the Sisters of Charity didn't try to hide anything from me, but The Villa would not have made my list of highlights if I'd been leading the tour. I found myself surrounded by a dozen elderly women in various stages of dementia. Most of them sat in wheelchairs and stared vacantly into space. The air of serenity I'd experienced earlier turned thick with sadness and despair.

I don't know about this, I thought. I was almost thirty—the age I never thought I'd live to see—and I'd actually survived. It was nice to learn the nuns would take care of me in my old age, but my sights were focused on new beginnings—not ending up like these poor souls.

As if to accentuate that I was facing a lifelong decision, the tour ended rather appropriately at the convent cemetery. The perfectly aligned gravestones were as simple as the nun's lives. The dearly departed had a choice of only two styles of markers: a large rectangular block of stone or one with a slanted face. Each showed nothing more than the sister's name and date of death.

I would have been further depressed by the graveside tour, but my guide saved the day with a story. She told me that one of the nuns buried before me had died while in her novice year. This depressing fact did little to raise my spirits until I learned that the young nun had been quite the poet. Her beautiful verses about her relationship with God had attracted the attention of the Vatican. The nun was in the process of being beautified—considered for sainthood by the Pope.

By this time, I'd read all I could get my hands on about the saints—not just St. Francis, but Joan of Arc, St. John of the Cross, and my personal favorite, St. Therese. The thought that a girl from New Jersey could become a saint gave me something new to think about. To me, becoming a saint wasn't something you did for the glory; it simply meant that you'd reached the pinnacle of selfless service to others. If she could do it, why couldn't I?

But to become a saint, I first had to decide if I really wanted to be a nun. Several times I drove back to Convent Station and sat in the parking lot in front of the mother house. I'd look at the sky and ask aloud, "Is this where you want me to be, God?"

I didn't get any responses as clear as that voice in the middle of the night— rather a gut feeling that the Sisters of Charity were a good fit. But even that far into my search for the right order, I still couldn't make up my mind. Was I willing to give up everything for a life of poverty, obedience, and chastity?

I was definitely conflicted. After all that searching, I still hadn't even confided in my spiritual director, Father Paul. Right about the time I decided to share my discernment process with him, he called me to his office.

"You wanted to see me, Father?" I asked from the doorway.

"Yes, yes. Come in, little bird."

I noticed that he looked troubled. At first I worried that I might have done something to upset him. Then, as he began to talk, I realized that the creases on his forehead had nothing to do with me. He explained that the center's long-term chef, who everybody knew and loved, had been caught ordering extra meat and selling it to another institution. They had no choice but to fire him.

"As you know," Father Paul said, "we can't conduct our retreats without full kitchen service for our guests."

I nodded. I'd personally enjoyed many a delicious meal in the center's formal dining room. With room to feed over a hundred guests, the chef often had his hands full. I wondered why Father Paul was telling me all this.

"I'll be moving on soon," he explained, "and I want to make sure that I leave the center in the best possible hands. I'd like you to consider taking over the position as Holy Spirit's head chef."

I stared back at him, stunned.

"What do you think?" he urged.

It's true what they say: timing is everything. Maybe there was a reason I hadn't told Father Paul about my calling. Had he known I was considering such a major life change, he might never have offered me the job. Now I faced a new decision: take the vows of a nun, or become the head chef at the Holy Spirit Retreat. Either one would mean a pay cut from my current position, but no matter which way I decided, it wasn't about the money.

My stomach churned as I thought about my options. Just to become a nun I faced a daunting application process. I'd need letters of recommendation and psychological testing. There would be interviews and background checks. But now Father Paul was offering me a great job with none of those hassles.

Over the past few years I'd started to learn about boundaries—how to say "no" when appropriate. But could I really say no to this offer? Did I even want to? Other than cleaning houses, all I'd ever done was work with food—first at The Owl and I, then at Manny's, The Union House, and now at Russ Berrie. I pictured myself bustling about the large corporate kitchen, and suddenly, the image of that rotted potato flashed before my eyes.

The cross had been in a piece of food. I was a food service professional now being offered a dream job in food service in a beautiful spiritual setting. Was that what the sign had meant? Was I supposed to take this wonderful opportunity that had landed in my lap, in spite of what the voice had said? Surely God knew how much I loved being at the Holy Spirit Retreat Center …

I was tired of all this thinking. I raised my eyes, looked directly at Father Paul, and said, "I'll take it."

Chapter 9

Metamorphosis

The drive from the retreat center to Teaneck was short. I could leave my job and be home in less than 30 minutes. Most people tried to leave their stress at work, but for me, the stress began when I walked in the house.

I stopped in the foyer and looked left, then right. I seemed to be the only one home. I slinked across the living room and turned down the hallway. Just as my bedroom door came into view, I heard the ominous growl. I froze, too frightened to take another step.

There, at the far end of the hallway—an equal distance from my room— stood my nemesis. With his long black hair, Blackie was appropriately named, but with his glinting white teeth and sadistic eyes, to me he was Satan in a dog suit.

Blackie pulled back his lips and dared me to take another step. We glared at each other with mutual hatred, but there was no doubt who would reach the bedroom first.

"Sister Elizabeth!" I called. She was usually home from work this time of day. When she failed to answer, I tried my other options.

"Sister Mary! Sister Frances!" The two nuns were both retired and should have been around.

My heart raced as I tried my last, desperate hope. "Sister Anne!"

Why I bothered with her, I don't know. She was the one who took care of the dog. She knew he terrorized me, but she never did anything about it. In the silence of the house, Blackie seemed to sneer.

What makes you think you belong here?

I backed up ever so slowly and returned to the living room—the very spot where months earlier I'd been welcomed with a small ceremony in my honor. Blackie either missed that part, or else he was part of the test.

I wasn't a nun yet. I wasn't even a novice. I had simply been accepted into the community, given a full year to live with the Sisters of Charity and check them out, just as they were checking out me. I sank onto the couch and frowned. This was my time to decide if I was made for the life of a nun, not to see if I played well with dogs.

I'd taken the job as the retreat center's chef and loved it, but that hadn't stopped me from thinking about my calling. Father Paul had been getting ready to leave, so I finally confided in him that I was seriously thinking of becoming a nun. He advised me to take my time with the decision, which is exactly what I was doing. Every day at work I stayed an extra hour to sit in the chapel. My time there only deepened my conviction.

One of my biggest stumbling blocks was the concept that when a nun took her vows, she was actually marrying God. The only picture I had of marriage was my parents', and that looked like something Picasso would have painted. I had no doubt that I could do good things as a Sister of Charity, but my Husband-to-Be still scared me to death.

The more I prayed and read the Bible, the more my ideas about God began to change. God supposedly knew every hair on my head. Jesus said that not a sparrow fell from the sky that He didn't know about it. I wasn't supposed to fear a thing, because to God I was worth more than an entire flock of sparrows. These were loving words, just like Father Paul's. If God was truly loving, I realized, then my vision of Him had to be flawed.

Having grown up believing that God didn't like the Nohavecs, it was a huge shift to think that He actually loved me. I began to see that the universe wasn't as hostile as I'd been led to believe. My mother and father had created that reality for me. It turned out that the universe—created by a loving God—could be as loving as I allowed it to be. I gradually understood that if I became a nun, I could help others come to that realization as well.

So I went ahead and applied to the Sisters of Charity, especially after I found out about the pre-novitiate year. It offered the best of both worlds: I could experience life as a nun, yet continue to work at the retreat center. My membership would be provisional. I would have few responsibilities other than to live among the sisters and to ask myself if this was the right place for me.

I hid nothing in my application, nor when I took their psychological tests. The sisters knew all about the things I'd done, the jobs I'd held. They also knew I hadn't been a practicing Catholic all my life, but the letter of recommendation from my parish priest helped a lot. He let them know that I'd become a valued member of the church and that my desire to become a nun was sincere.

My acceptance came in the form of an official letter. Only after I had that piece of paper in my hands did I break the news to my family. Their reaction was predictable: *You're gonna do what?* Pure astonishment and disbelief.

My brother laughed and said, "Do they know about— "

"They know everything," I said, cutting him off.

One of my sisters couldn't keep quiet. "But did you tell them about the time you— "

I sliced my hand across the space between us. "I've already been accepted."

I don't think they thought I was serious until I moved to the convent. They all came to the little entrance ceremony in the living room—even my dad—as did Father Angelis, the priest who'd recommended me so highly.

If your image of a convent is a big Spanish-style place, this was nothing like that. A convent can be any building where nuns live in a communal setting. In Teaneck, there were only five of us in a modern, ranch-style house.

My new home sat on the grounds of St. Anastasia Roman Catholic Church. It was simple, but comfortable. Like any house, it had a kitchen, a living room, and a dining room. There were private bedrooms for each of the full-fledged nuns plus me. I would have liked to have been relaxing in my bedroom at that moment, but I was sure Blackie was still lurking in the hallway.

Resigned to my fate, I leaned my head back against the sofa and closed my eyes. So far, I enjoyed communal life. I got along well with all the sisters, especially Elizabeth, with whom I shared a bathroom. The five of us seemed to have the same desire to help others, but I felt a special kinship with Elizabeth. She and I had one major thing in common. I glanced over my shoulder ... She hated that dog as much as I did.

* * *

Back in the 1960s, about 200 women a year chose to join the Sisters of Charity. By the time I came along, that number had dwindled to three. Needless to say, the older nuns were very happy to have me. They encouraged me to get around and spend time with the sisters in any activities I liked.

"This is going to be your family now," they'd say.

I'd drive over to the mother house at Convent Station with big boxes of cookies and hang out in the TV room with the nuns who lived there. That's how I met the sister who played the violin. She offered to give me lessons, and I agreed.

Every week I traipsed up to her room on the third floor. I never did get any good at the violin, but you couldn't walk those halls without noticing all the beautiful artwork. Museum quality portraits in ornate, gold frames lined the corridors and anterooms. It was obvious from the subjects' attire that most were nuns, but the brass plaques at the bottom gave their names and little else. I asked around to find out more about them.

Everyone knew the history of Elizabeth Ann Seton, a nun featured in several of the more prominent paintings. She'd founded the American Sisters of Charity and was the first person born in the United States to become a canonized saint.

As for the rest of the paintings, few of the current residents had any idea who the people in them were. As one of the intern novices, I'd been asked to do a project to familiarize myself with the order's history. Now I knew what I wanted to do for my assignment. I asked permission to create an archive of the mother house artwork. I proposed calling it "The Art that Adorns Our Walls."

My superiors loved the idea. I had no idea what I'd gotten myself into.

I started working on the project the very next weekend. I stood alone in the quiet hallways and started making notes. First I copied the information from the brass plaques, then I studied the artwork itself—the women's habits, their smiles, and their eyes. That's when the pictures started to talk to me.

If that sounds crazy to you, imagine how I felt.

Standing there in front of the canvases, those old nuns came back to life. With some, I sensed their personalities as if I'd known them. Others told me all about themselves in their own voices. As I got deeper into the project I'd see their spirits walking the mother house halls just like the current day residents.

As shocked as I was by these events, they didn't scare me. I never made the connection between what was happening and seeing my dead grandparents as a child. With nothing in my recent personal experience to explain such strange goings-on, I chalked them up to my new environment.

I'd been doing a lot of reading about mystical occurrences in my studies. Joan of Arc heard voices. A nun from the Passionist order reported levitating during rapture. Padre Pio could be in two places at once. There were countless examples of events far more unusual than seeing a few friendly apparitions and hearing voices. I knew that some people would have a hard time believing such things, but to me—especially with what I was experiencing now—they were completely credible.

After many nights and weekends of effort I finished my project. The multi-page report I turned in to my superiors included previously unavailable information about the subjects of the mother house paintings. I brought the portraits to life on paper, but I never told a soul that their spirits had come to life for me.

* * *

The Sisters of Charity wanted to make sure that my motives were sincere. They wanted to know that deep in my heart I believed that being a nun was a worthwhile way to spend my life. Mid-way through my trial year they gave me a meditation to practice. They told me to face an empty chair and pretend that Jesus was sitting in it.

I chose a day when the house was particularly quiet. I closed my bedroom door, sat on my bed, and faced the chair in the corner. I was used to closing my eyes when I prayed, so I shut them.

Jesus, I asked silently, *what do you want me to do?*

The priests at The retreat center had taught me how to visualize. I was supposed to create a vivid image in my mind, but they never warned me the results would be so dramatic. When I opened my eyes, there sat Jesus—an apparition so real I could reach out and touch his robe and long hair. My first weekend at the retreat center I'd sensed his presence under the tree, but this was different. He was sitting there as real to me as any living person.

Most Catholics would have fallen to their knees or burst into tears at such an apparition. To this day, my instinctual reaction fills me with regret. Instead of seizing the greatest opportunity of my life and talking with the Master of masters, I gasped and turned away. I sat frozen in the chair, my mind racing. I had followed my calling and was actively pursuing the path to become a nun. I'd given up my familiar possessions and a good deal of freedom to live in a convent with the sisters. In that moment of panic, I was petrified that Jesus would ask even more of me. I couldn't handle having to say, "No, I can't do it."

My only consolation is that Jesus, being who he is, understood that I meant no disrespect—I was simply terrified. I had asked him what he wanted me to do, never dreaming he would show up in person to tell me. When I finally looked back, he was gone. I stared at the empty chair and became aware that my mouth felt like cotton. I got up to get some Sprite from the kitchen, but wobbled a bit and had to lean against the dresser for a moment. When the shakiness passed, I walked to the door, opened it, and began to step into the hallway. Blackie's bark snapped me fully back to reality.

"Whoa! Easy, boy!" I held up my hand and Blackie looked at me as if I were his mid-day snack. He lowered his head, but kept his eyes locked on my throat. The hair on the back of his neck stood on end, as did mine.

I backed up and slammed the door shut in one swift movement. I settled for a cup of tap water from the bathroom, then stood in the middle of my bedroom, fuming. I was sick and tired of being the victim, fed up with having no control.

The image of Jesus flashed before my mind as did a now-familiar story from the Bible. If God protected Daniel in the lion's den, surely He'd protect me from Blackie. I was damned if I was going to let that evil dog keep me prisoner in my own bedroom.

I yanked the door open and Blackie let loose a barrage of menacing barks. I slammed it shut again and growled. Jesus may have been watching me, but God helped those who helped themselves. I picked up the phone and dialed the church office across the parking lot.

"Sister Anne?" I said when she answered, "Please do something about your dog."

* * *

Even before I went to live in the convent, I volunteered at a homeless shelter over in Paterson. My duties often included spending the night there, and the nuns fully supported me. After all, they sent missionaries to El Salvador and other garden spots. The part of Paterson where I volunteered wasn't much different than a third world country. Imagine the worst inner-city ghetto you can think of, and that's what it was like.

I was working a night shift when someone started pounding on the door. I looked up from the desk where I'd been dozing and checked my watch. It was two o'clock in the morning. The neighborhood was so bad that we locked the door at night. The shelter had about a thousand regulations, and one of them said you weren't supposed to open the door after a certain hour, no matter what. But this was the middle of winter. Whoever was out there might freeze to death if I didn't answer.

I broke the rules and opened the door. There stood this pitiful woman about 45 years old, who barely came up to my chin. I could tell from the bruises on her face that someone had done a number on her, and fairly recently. Her eyes told me that the same bastard had probably been doing it to her for years. I recognized that look right away—I'd seen it in my mother's eyes more times than I cared to count. Life had beat the shit out of that lady. She had no soul left.

I stepped to the side and motioned for her to come in. She walked past me without a word and I locked the door behind her. All the beds were full that night. The best I could offer her was a blanket on the floor in a corner. She curled up there and closed her eyes. I felt bad, but I sensed her relief to finally be safe.

I couldn't help but think that I could have ended up just like that woman. Luckily, I'd found out that even if you fall as far as you can go, you can always climb back up. Now, looking down at her, I knew that God had sent me another signpost. If I became a nun, I could give others more than just shelter ... I could give them hope. More than anything, I wanted to put the light back in people's eyes.

That woman helped me to make up my mind. In spite of my problems with Blackie, it had been a good year. I liked the communal life. It was a good fit. If the Sisters of Charity would have me—which was a pretty sure bet, considering the numbers—I would go through with my plans.

I went back to my desk and dozed, waking every so often to check on all the women. We were supposed to keep it nice and dark so people could sleep. That night I kept a light burning ... in honor of my latest guest.

To Hell with the rules.

Chapter 10
Saint Janet

In all my time as a nun, I only wore a habit once. I put it on to pose for a picture ... with a cigarette hanging out of my mouth. What can I say? Novice year was tough. I had to let off steam somehow.

If you get the sense that I had a bit of a rebellious streak, the older nuns sensed it too. It started at the ceremony my very first day as a novice. It was New Year's Day—a pretty good time to begin a whole new life. Family members weren't invited to this one; it was mostly an internal thing.

They said lots of nice words and welcomed us into the sisterhood. I was proud to be part of it—very sure in my decision. So there we all were, standing around afterwards, and one of the older nuns brought out this little blue felt box. The others smiled and nodded; they knew what was inside it.

"This is our pin," the sister said proudly. "The pelican is the symbol of the Sisters of Charity. She's feeding her young, which is symbolic of our service to others."

Another nun chimed in. "You'll each be given your own pin when you take your first vows."

The meaning in her words was clear: we had to earn that pin first.

I peered into the little box, then leaned in closer to make sure what I was seeing. My lips twisted and I glanced at the other girls. Didn't they see it, too? The pelican was feeding her babies all right, but she was tearing off her own skin to do it.

"That's the most co-dependent pin I've ever seen!" I blurted out. "If I ripped off my flesh to feed my babies, I'd die! We have to take care of ourselves if we want to help others."

The room grew deadly quiet. If anyone had captured the look on the nuns' faces after my surprising outburst, the picture would have won a Pulitzer. I'm sure someone was wishing they could hit the rewind button and back up to the beginning of the ceremony. They'd re-do it without Sister Janet and everything would be fine. But it was too late; they were stuck with me. The ceremony was over, and novice year had begun.

My sainthood seemed a very long way off.

* * *

They welcomed four of us that day. The other three included Mary Anne, who transferred from another community; Nancy, a big tough girl who worked a lot with teenagers; and one girl who didn't make it through the year. As novices, we weren't full-fledged nuns yet. That wouldn't happen until we took our first vows.

Once I entered this stage of my formation, I was able to continue volunteering, but I said goodbye to the staff at the retreat center. Even though I was no longer working, my days were full from morning to night. We had morning prayer, meals, and meetings; Mass, more prayer, and time with the community.

My new home was a white wood convent on the grounds at Convent Station. They stuck the novices at the bottom of a hill, as far as possible from the mother house. Other nuns lived there as well, but they kept us separate, in a different wing of the building.

There were some nice women in that group. I'd escape through a side door and visit with them every chance I got. They'd all been through novice year and knew how bad it was: twelve months of intense, unrelenting scrutiny. Everyone said we were like hot-house tomatoes—always being watched. And no one watched us more closely than Sister Alexis, the novice directress.

Girls used to enter the convent as young as 15. Sister Alexis was probably only in her mid-forties when I met her, but she'd been a nun longer than I'd been alive. I don't know what happened in *her* childhood, but that woman had a ton of excess baggage. Unfortunately, she buried it just deep enough that it kept creeping back to the surface. If you struck a bad chord with her, she'd stand there and squirm as if she were trying to push that stuff back down. She was a ticking time bomb, prone to explosions, and you never knew just when she'd go off.

Sister Alexis made Blackie look like a pussy cat.

The directress had a lot of anger inside and she would take it out on me. When she wasn't yelling or accusing me of things I hadn't done, she would give me the silent treatment. This was a lady who was supposed to be helping me, yet she had no idea of how to deal with people.

I'm sure the incident with the pin didn't help much, but she watched me like a hungry wolf from day one, circling and hovering and waiting for me to screw up. She lived in the same building, and I had to meet with her for my daily assignments. She'd send me to committee meetings, to events for the older nuns, or to do whatever little chore struck her fancy. At the end of the year, I would either pass or fail. My fate rested in Sister Alexis' hands.

Every week we'd travel to Marion Shrine in Ossining, New York, for inter-novitiate discussions. Because there were so few of us, they'd pool the novices from other communities to form a larger group. The morning after one of these excursions, Sister Alexis confronted me.

"Where did you go last night?" she demanded.

The question caught me off guard. "Nowhere, Sister. I was asleep in my room."

"No you weren't," she said, now standing mere inches from my face. "You snuck out of your room and went off somewhere!"

I took a step backwards, totally confused. The woman was living in Fantasy Land. "I never left my bed," I said. "And even if I had, I couldn't have gotten past the front door without somebody seeing me."

"You left!" she said, smoothing her skirt over and over as if wiping her hands. "You tied your bed sheets together and used them to climb out the window."

"I'm telling you the truth," I insisted. "I was there all night long."

"You're lying!"

I might have been a rebel, but I was no liar. I took a long, slow breath as we locked eyes.

"You know, Sister Alexis," I said, "I think I'm gonna have to go to a 12-step program just to deal with you."

The novice directress breathed audibly through her nose. She flexed her fingers as if she wanted to attack me. Luckily, there were no heavy objects within reach. Had she been armed, I never would have made it to take my first vows. Unable to find a suitable come-back, she spun on her heel, stalked off, and didn't speak to me for two weeks.

At least with me, she only played mind games. My fellow novice Nancy had an even harder time than I did. The two went at it constantly. One day Sister Alexis, unable to express her anger in words, shoved Nancy. Pushed her hard.

They had to call in a mediator after that one, but nothing changed. Sister Alexis still called the shots. I spent many a day wondering if I should pack it in and go back to the real world. But I knew that if I left, it would be for the wrong reason. As a whole, the Sisters of Charity were some of the most selfless, dedicated women I had ever met. I couldn't base my leaving on the actions of one irrational nun.

So I stuck it out and worked my tail off. One of the reasons they kept us so busy was because there were so few of us. They wanted us to be as visible as possible, especially to the older nuns.

In the summer, the novices were often assigned to spend a day with the retired sisters who lived in The Villa. One morning Nancy and I picked up two of them for a trip to the beach. Sister Eugenia and Sister Mary Agatha were both pushing ninety, but they were as sharp as women half their age.

The four of us had a great time. We took them to Spring Lake on the Jersey shore, just south of Asbury Park. We ate some fresh seafood and walked along the boardwalk. The older nuns enjoyed soaking up the sun, but Nancy and I enjoyed getting away from Sister Alexis even more.

On the way back, Nancy reached over and turned on the car radio. I glanced in the rear-view mirror. The two sisters didn't seem to mind, so we tuned the station to 95.3, WPLJ, one of our favorites. Just as we were approaching Bloomfield, the DJ announced a special promotion at the local MacDonald's. Anyone spotted there at 5:00 with a WPLJ sign would win 95 dollars. I looked at the clock on the dashboard. It was almost five and we were only a few miles away.

Nancy and I looked at each other with raised eyebrows, then nodded like cohorts in crime.

"Sisters," I called over the back seat. "The radio station is having a contest. Do you mind if we stop at MacDonalds and try to win some money?"

"How much money?" Sister Mary Agatha asked.

"Ninety-five dollars," Nancy answered.

"Ninety-five bucks!" Sister Eugenia clapped her hands. "We could go to Atlantic City!"

"What are you waiting for girls?" Mary Agatha asked. "Count us in!"

We took the detour and scribbled a quick sign on a piece of paper. The four of us, including Sister Eugenia in her habit, sat there for almost an hour proclaiming, "We love WPLJ" with our little hand-made placard. Unfortunately, nobody showed up to give us our prize.

It's just as well. We had a hard enough time explaining to Sister Alexis why we were late. It would have been even harder sneaking Sister Eugenia off to play the slots.

* * *

The word *joyful* didn't come up too often in my early years, but the day I professed my vows, that word took center stage. It was a joy to be accepted—to have survived novice year and receive a passing grade from Sister Alexis. It was a joyful day for the community to have three new nuns entering the order. And I was joyful—no, downright *jubilant*—to walk down the aisle of the mother house cathedral with my family and friends as my witnesses.

To plan for the most important day of my life, I spent a weekend at the Holy Spirit Retreat Center. I holed up in the middle house by the gardens, and there I wrote my vows. Like any bride, I took my task seriously, trying to come up with just the right words. I was free to say whatever I felt in my heart, as long as I included the three vows themselves.

I had no problem with poverty and chastity, but that third one—obedience—gave me some trouble. Growing up with a father who ruled our home like a tyrant, I valued what little free will I had. Submitting to authority—even God's—was a tough issue, but if I was going to be a nun, I couldn't pick and choose among the vows.

I invited my family, Charlotte, other friends from my 12-step meetings, and people from the detox center where I'd been volunteering for the past year. The cover of my invitations showed a road with a bend that curved out of sight, just like my own journey had taken many turns.

When the big day came, the other two novices and our guests filed into the cathedral at Convent Station. Many of the established nuns showed up as well. I wore flat shoes and a navy blue suit—blue being the color of the Sisters of Charity's habit. Unlike most brides on their wedding day, I skipped the heavy makeup.

Father Angelis presided over the ceremony. I tried to pay attention as he delivered his homily. I picked up on words like *service* and *dedication*, and I sang along with the hymns that followed, but I was too nervous, thinking about the part yet to come. Before I knew it, the moment was upon me.

I walked to the altar and knelt. Actually, I pretty much slammed myself down thinking, *this is it*. The whole thing was pretty daunting—marrying God. This was a huge step. But don't get me wrong: by this point I had no doubts that I was doing the right thing. All of my uncertainty had been washed away in the last year as a novice. This wasn't a case of "I'll just try this out and see how it goes." When I opened my mouth to repeat the words I'd memorized, I knew there was no turning back.

"God," I said aloud, "I offer myself to Thee, to do with me as Thou wilt. I vow poverty, chastity and obedience to the rule of the Sisters of Charity. Take away my difficulties, that victory over them may bear witness to Thy graciousness, Thy power, and Thy love. I come before thee in humility. I am Yours. Amen."

I climbed onto my shaking legs, crossed to the side of the cathedral, and signed the official book. It was a done deal. I was a full-fledged nun.

I glanced back at my parents. I'd never seen them smile so proudly. I said a quick prayer to God that my father would behave himself at the reception.

We all went down the road to the Xavier Center. They had a big room downstairs, and there we ate, talked, and celebrated as I opened all my gifts. My friends gave me cross necklaces and small religious statues and plaques. I was grateful for the envelopes with money inside. My stipend as a nun would only be a hundred bucks a month.

When the party was over, I walked out of the building. I glanced across the street at the cemetery and paused. I'd spent whatever free moments I could grab in the past year wandering the grounds there. It wasn't that I had some kind of morbid fascination with graveyards; it simply gave me a place to get away from Sister Alexis.

I flashed back to how I used to read the nuns' names on the markers and imagine what they'd been like. I would look up from my thoughts to find their spirits wandering the rows around me. Just as when I'd seen them in the halls of the mother house, their presence never scared me. I chalked the visions up to the spiritual life I was now leading. Mystical experiences weren't so unusual for the saints I studied. There were plenty of examples of religious people talking to spirits and hearing them talk back. People on the outside might call them ghosts and consider the cemetery haunted. I intuitively understood that the spirits were nothing more than former residents who came back to visit a place they loved.

I wouldn't say I loved Convent Station, but I did get a lump in my throat as I left there that day. My new home was a convent in New Brunswick, about 45 minutes south, across the river from Rutgers University. The sisters liked you to experience a variety of communal experiences. I'd already lived in a small house as an intern and a mid-sized convent as a novice. Now I'd get a taste of a larger community, sharing a three-story building with 32 other nuns.

When I arrived in my new room that evening, I laid my bags on the bed. The four walls felt claustrophobic after such a big day. A train passed by so close it made the floor shake. I grabbed my Marlboros and climbed the stairs to the roof. I gazed up at the stars, then lit a cigarette and watched the smoke drift slowly skyward. The realization that I'd actually done it—I'd given up my car, my belongings, and even my family—finally began to sink in. I was a nun, with no attachments at all.

The feeling was liberating.

I reached into the little pocket on my skirt and pulled out the one gift I'd bought for myself. I stared down at the plain gold band in my palm. Not all the nuns chose to wear one, but if I was going to be married to God, I wanted that symbol as my constant reminder. I picked it up and slipped it onto my ring finger.

That's it. I'm all Yours now.

A lone star drew a silent streak of light in a long, curved path toward the horizon. I watched it until it disappeared, then I stubbed out my cigarette on the wall. I realized that not only did I feel free, there was a second component to my feelings that I hadn't expected: I felt safe for the first time in my life. Not even a passing train could shake the thought that hit me as I descended the stairs to my room:

I'm not gonna get hurt anymore.

Chapter 11

Rebellion

I stepped into the lobby of St. Elizabeth's Hospital and blew warm air onto my hands. I turned my wrist and read my watch. After nearly two years of making the commute from the convent in New Brunswick, I had the timing down to the minute. It usually took me three quarters of an hour. Today, with the weather, I spent over an hour on the road.

I stamped my feet, leaving snowy outlines of my shoes on the black rubber mat. I wiped the soles back and forth, but I still trailed wet footsteps on the tiles as I crossed to the elevator.

A voice greeted me when I stepped out into the detox center. "Good morning, Sister Janet."

I looked up to see the night clerk putting on her parka.

"Good morning, Gloria," I said. "You'd better zip that up. It's nasty out there."

"So I hear. A couple of the regulars tried to convince the staff they needed to be admitted last night."

We shared a knowing look. Our unit helped alcoholics and drug addicts clear the toxins out their systems before moving on to rehab, but some nights the street people just wanted a warm place to sleep. Or to hide from the police. One of my main duties was to screen out the fakers from the ones who sincerely wanted to break free of their addictions.

The medical staff dealt with the physical effects of detoxification: the nausea, hallucinations, insomnia, and anxiety that made the first few days of withdrawal a living Hell for our patients. I helped with the mental side, taking psycho-social histories, leading group discussions, and trying to get those who showed promise into longer-term programs.

The phone rang and Gloria grabbed it. She looked over at me as she listened, then hung up.

"We've got another one, Sister. Down in the ER."

"I'm on my way."

I hung my coat on a hook in the staff room, picked up a clipboard with a questionnaire, and headed downstairs.

A wiry black man in a tattered brown coat sat hunched over the desk where we screened our patients. I sighed when I recognized him by his constant scratching. I'd spent a lot of time with George during past hospitalizations. The last time we said goodbye, I'd hoped to never see him again.

I could fill out the form for George without even asking him the questions. There was no doubt he was an addict. I knew what kind of drugs he was taking, how much, and how often. I also knew that he truly wanted to stay clean. But every time we discharged him, he went right back to the drug-infested environment he called home.

I stared at George and sighed. He wasn't the only one. Not by a long shot. At times I wondered if they shouldn't install a revolving door on our ward.

Did my work here make any difference at all?

I sat down across from George and studied the web of red veins in his yellow eyes. Bruises snaked onto the backs of his hands like inky black tattoos. I felt his mood like a passing car's radio that was turned up too high—his pain hitting my chest in rhythmic waves. He scratched behind his ear and I fought the urge to do the same.

"Good morning, George." I said softly.

"Mornin', Sister."

"I'm sorry to see you back again."

"I'm sorry too, Sister."

"Anything changed since the last time?"

He shook his head and scratched his shoulder. "No, Ma'am."

"Do you have any knowledge of having HIV?"

He lowered his eyes. "I don't think so, Sister."

I pushed the clipboard across the desk and handed him a pen. Just as he reached for it, a commotion across the room made both of us look up. A young black girl stood inside the entrance to the ER. Strands of stringy hair stuck to her wet face. She wore only a windbreaker and thin jeans—hardly the kind of attire for such a cold day. To make matters a thousand times worse, she was barefoot.

An ER clerk leaned over the counter that stood between her and the girl and pointed toward the exit. The girl stared back. Most of the seats in the waiting room were full, and all eyes focused on the mini stand-off. I wasn't the type to butt in when it wasn't my place, but when I heard the clerk say, "You have to leave," I went ballistic.

I shoved my chair back and stormed across the lobby. "Excuse me," I said to the clerk.

She looked at my nametag. "Yes, Sister?"

"You can't send this girl outside."

"But she has no reason to be here. She's not sick."

I looked down at the girl, who seemed even smaller up close, then glared at the clerk. "You gotta be kidding me!"

The clerk shrugged.

I pointed at the girl's feet. "She doesn't have any shoes!"

"I know, Sister, but the rules say—"

The whoosh of air through my clenched teeth stopped the clerk mid-sentence.

I leaned in close and said, "Last time I checked, this hospital was run by the Sisters of Charity. This girl may not need emergency treatment, but she could sure use our charity. You are not going to throw her out in the cold!"

The woman shrugged again. "Whatever you say, Sister."

I led the girl to a seat in a corner. We shared a wordless nod before I went back to finish George's paperwork. I returned to the ward on trembling legs. I hated confrontation, but the nuns were allowed to tell the employees what to do when the situation called for it.

Later that day, when I was summoned to my superior's office, I knew right away what she wanted. I stood in the carpeted office and reminded myself that any praise for looking after the girl's best interests should go to God and not to me.

"I understand there was a scene in the emergency room this morning," the senior nun said.

"Yes, Sister."

"I understand your motives, Janet. We're here to serve the community."

"Yes, Sister."

"But I'm afraid you were out of line."

I looked up in surprise. "I'm sorry?"

"We may be a hospital, but we're also a business. Our paying patients don't want to share the waiting room with derelicts."

My head bobbed and I blinked. Then I realized that the ER clerk must not have told the whole story. "I'm sorry, Sister, but the girl was barefoot."

"That's exactly my point," said the nun. "It wouldn't look good."

I swallowed and choked on a drop of saliva.

The nun stepped forward. "Do you need some water, Sister?"

"No," I waved her off as I coughed and cleared my throat.

"I know how you feel," she said, "but we have rules, and we expect everyone to follow them."

Actually, I thought, as I left her office, the woman had no idea how I felt. *Crushed* came kind of close. *Disillusioned*, even closer. It was a feeling that was becoming more and more familiar with every passing day.

I returned to the unit, trying my best not to let the actions of a few drag my thoughts to a place they'd been lingering a bit too often lately. Most of the sisters I lived and worked with continued to impress me with their dedication and kindness, but some seemed callous and unbending. I couldn't help but question how such an attitude fit in with a life of service and love of God.

In spite of the reprimand, I knew I'd done the right thing. I'd actually surprised myself by standing up to the ER clerk and couldn't wait to tell my counselor about it. It was thanks to her that I was learning to say *no* more often. My superiors certainly had no trouble with the word. Even getting permission to see a counselor had initially been in doubt. I'd heard that of one of the three Sisters of Charity provinces outright forbade their nuns to get counseling.

Lucky for me, my province was more progressive. They were always asking, "Are you happy here? Are there things you need to talk to someone about?" Maybe they knew what I'd been hesitant to admit to myself: that sooner or later I had to deal with the issue of my father. As a novice, I'd complained about Sister Alexis and her baggage, but I was still lugging around a few suitcases of my own.

So I finally gave in and sought help. The sisters even paid for it. They recommended a secular counselor named Connie, who worked a lot with nuns. I met with her regularly now, digging through all that garbage from my childhood. She knew her stuff, that lady, and ever so slowly she was helping me to see that my self-worth was God-given. It came from inside, not from always saying *yes*, just so people would like me.

So I wondered what Connie would say about me standing up for the girl in the ER. I'd gone out on a limb and said *No, this isn't right.* And I got shot down. I didn't understand it, so maybe Connie could help: If the rules couldn't be bent when common sense and compassion prevailed, what was going to keep *me* from breaking?

* * *

If you asked me to describe the perfect nun, I wouldn't even hesitate. She would be someone just like Sister Cathy Roe. Vibrant and upbeat, Cathy was holy, but she wasn't pious. If she didn't like something, she let you know it. I saw a picture of Janet Reno recently and she reminded me of Cathy with her glasses and short brown hair. They had the same kind of look, but Cathy had a lot more spunk. She was gutsy, too. She worked in one of the toughest areas in Paterson, where you'd hear a bang and know right away it wasn't a firecracker.

Cathy ran Eva's Soup Kitchen before it grew to the huge place it is now. I was volunteering there with her the day someone broke into her car. All the homeless men were lined up waiting for a meal. The line snaked outside and went right past Cathy's VW. When she came out and found her window bashed in, she looked at them and said, "Help me out here, guys. I know you saw who did this." But not one of them spoke up. They put up the Big Wall of Silence.

Sister Cathy gave her whole life to those men—she fed them every day. Talked with them. Comforted them. When they refused to step up on her behalf, that really cut her. I saw the look on her face. But she straightened up, turned around, and went right back to work.

She was the kind of nun I wanted to be: brazen, brave, and devoted. And she had her own apartment. She lived right in the heart of Paterson so she could be there when they needed her. I thought it would be great to live there, too, but not just because I looked up to Sister Cathy.

Because I was just plain tired.

In the two years since I'd taken my vows, my schedule hadn't slowed a bit. I held a full-time job, attended morning and evening prayers, and daily Mass. I also went to classes for my state certification in alcohol and drug counseling, and I volunteered during whatever hours were left over. When I finally did get to bed, the blasted train woke me every time it roared past my room.

I had no problem with the things the sisters asked of me. I'd signed up willingly for a life of service. But I was rapidly wearing out the little Ford Escort they gave me to get back and forth in. I commuted almost an hour each way to St. Elizabeth's. When I volunteered in Paterson, that drive took an hour and a half, which is the same time it took to get to Convent Station for my frequent trips to the mother house. And to my *own* mother's house—if I could find the time.

So I didn't think I was being unreasonable when I asked to move in with Sister Cathy.

The answer was a resounding *no*. I was too new. I needed the communal experience that the convent in New Brunswick offered.

Okay. I could see that. But the Sisters of Charity had communities all over, including several that were a lot closer to my work and classes. "It would really make things easier," I told the nuns.

"I'm sorry, Sister Janet, but the answer is still no."

You want to talk about unbending? Those women could have withstood a hurricane. They had "no" down to an art form.

Being turned down a second time, I said, "Look, I understand you're saying no to me, but I've been going through a rough stretch at work on top of all that driving, and I don't know how much longer I can handle this. I'm looking into my soul here, and I'm telling you that all this running back and forth is really tough."

But these nuns were even tougher. The answer after that impassioned plea? You guessed it: a big fat *no*.

I found out later why they might not have wanted me to move in with Sister Cathy. It turns out she was sick and didn't tell me. She had cancer, but she kept on working at Eva's Kitchen, even later, when she lost all her hair. God may have had bigger plans for Cathy Roe, but He took her way too early, if you ask me.

But as for why I couldn't live in any of the closer convents, I couldn't figure that one out. After I bared my soul and explained how I felt, it seemed as if they were saying no just on principle ... making me be obedient just because I'd taken that vow.

I went back to work and back to volunteering, and I continued going to morning and evening prayers. Quiet reflection is a big part of religious life, but all that time I spent in silence only made things worse; it gave me time to think. I began to question whether obedience to people who thought they knew what was best for me was really what was best for me.

Thanks to the counseling, I was starting to come into my own. More and more I felt driven to listen to my inner voice, rather than to someone outside of myself. I was slowly healing my issues, and I didn't know if I wanted to spend the rest of my life being told what to do by people who might have issues of their own.

Within religious communities there are people you can just look at and know they're in love with God. People like Sister Cathy. But I discovered a few who were so dogmatic they left me no room to breathe. They weren't content, and they certainly didn't seem loving. The real problem wasn't them, though. It was me. I realized I felt that same discontent in myself, and I didn't want to end up looking like a nun who didn't love God.

My love for God was never in question. It was simply the lifestyle—one which I found more and more restrictive. It would be painful to leave the Sisters of Charity, but I knew I could do it, if that's what it came to. The agonizing piece was breaking my promise to God. I didn't know if I could do that.

If I was going to leave, it had to be before I took my final vows. That day was rapidly approaching, and I was getting nowhere with my mental tug of war. The one place where I'd always done my best thinking was at the Holy Spirit Retreat Center, so that's where I headed.

As I drove up the familiar winding driveway, I felt an immediate lift in my spirits. The place had closed for remodeling two years earlier, right about the time I took my first vows, and it still hadn't reopened. It seemed strange not to see people wandering the grounds, but I was glad for a bit of privacy.

I parked my car and walked toward the main house. Seeing the chapel at the end of the south wing, I suddenly recalled the words of Father McKenna, one of the priests I'd befriended years back. He said to me more than once, "Don't enter religious life, Janet. You can be of much more service on the outside."

Coming from someone on the *inside*, I guess I should have paid more attention. But my mind was pretty well made up at the time.

I walked around to the front and tested the door, but it was locked. I pressed my face to the window and peered inside. The place had looked good before, but now it was downright gorgeous. Someone had poured a lot of money into the renovations. There were fancy furnishings, new drapes, and new carpeting, but they'd left some things the same. I could still see the tribute to Titus Brandsma at the top of the staircase.

I pulled back from the window as a sudden realization hit me. I'd wanted to be able to hum through life, just like Father Titus … but I hadn't hummed in a very long time.

I didn't know if God would forgive me, but in that single moment of insight, I knew that I couldn't remain a nun and remain true to myself.

Chapter 12

Broken Vows

How does a woman divorce God?

The decision was so agonizing that I ended up in the very emergency room where I screened patients every day. I'd been visiting my mother, feeling even more dragged down than usual, when suddenly I couldn't get air in my lungs. The diagnosis was a bronchial asthmatic attack brought on by stress. They admitted me, put me on a ward, and hooked me up to an I.V.

I was supposed to lie in the bed and de-stress while the antibiotics did their job. Instead, I laid there stewing about my vows and craving a cigarette so badly I would have traded both lungs for a smoke. Of course, it was probably all the extra Marlboros I'd burned through to *relieve* my stress that had landed me on my back, but that kind of reasoning didn't do anything to stop my cravings.

Being a nun in a smoke-free hospital run by nuns meant only one thing: I couldn't put a cigarette to my lips in the five days of my admission. I didn't dare. When they finally released me, I was still pretty sick. I crossed the hospital parking lot, moving slowly and panting like a dog on a hot summer day. I climbed behind the wheel of my car and instinctively reached for my cigarettes. Then reason prevailed and I pulled back my hand. I knew that I could either give in and light up, or build on my five-day streak.

It was the longest I'd ever gone without smoking. I'd tried several times in the past to quit, even going so far as to lock myself in my room at the convent. I vowed that I wouldn't open the door and go out for a smoke, but I caved in within hours. This time was different. I'd had five days of breathing nothing but clear air. My lungs were just starting to heal. If I was ever going to quit, now was the time.

In fact, it turned out to be the worst possible time. The self-induced pressure over giving up my vows caused me constant anxiety. Without my cigarettes, I felt as if I'd lost the one companion who could help me to cope. I chewed Nicorette gum, sucked on hard candy, and kept a straw in my hand to fool my fingers.

Quitting smoking was brutal, but it didn't come close to the difficulty of telling the world that I no longer wanted to be a nun. Lying in the hospital being cared for by those loving sisters, you'd think I might have changed my mind. But in spite of the most sincere intentions, not all marriages last forever.

The mechanics of being released from my vows seemed almost too easy after making such an agonizing decision. I went to the head of my province and said, "I think I'm gonna leave."

She clasped her hands over her heart in that typical "mother superior" pose, looked at me for a moment, then said, "May I ask why?"

"This just isn't working," I said. "I'm not humming in life, and if I don't look content doing this, then I'm in the wrong place."

Even to my ears the words sounded weak.

She didn't seem to understand the humming part, so I told her that I'd made certain requests that were denied and that I didn't think being a nun was a good fit for me.

I honestly thought she'd try to talk me out of it. At the very least I expected her to issue a well-practiced "no." Instead, she simply nodded and gave me a year to reconsider. She told me that if I wanted to return at any time during the next twelve months, they'd welcome me back with no hard feelings.

After one year as a pre-novice, one year as a novice, and two years as a nun, that was that. No gnashing of teeth. No wailing. Just a polite, "We're sorry to see you go" from the head of my province.

After that came the paperwork. When I first entered the convent, I signed all kinds of papers: things like my Last Will and Testament and forms that sent my salary from the hospital straight to the Sisters of Charity. (I pledged a life of poverty, remember?) To undo it all, I simply signed more forms.

With some religious orders you have to seek dispensation from the Pope. The Sisters of Charity granted it themselves. I signed the most official looking form of all, and I was no longer a nun. They gave me a thousand dollars to go and start my life again.

Like I said, the mechanics were easy. The mental part was a whole other issue.

In my mind, I wasn't just leaving the convent—I was leaving God. He had called me to enter religious life. I answered that call and I took those holy vows. Every other nun I knew was dedicated to the max. What was wrong with me? I was letting Him down big time, and that made it brutally hard to live with myself.

The Provincial may not have tried to change my mind, but plenty of others sure did, both before and after I signed the forms. Co-workers, friends, and other nuns called me when they heard the news. They knew about the one-year grace period. Some invited me out for coffee … "just to chat."

"Don't make this decision so fast," they'd warn. "Give it more time."

"You're making a terrible mistake," others would say.

Some would beg, "We want you to stay."

But my favorite of all: "You make a really good nun, even if you're not exactly conservative."

I could understand why they were confused. I'd seemed so joyous when I took my first vows. And I was. But the reality of religious life and a year of therapy had changed me.

Every time someone questioned my decision I suffered a stab of guilt straight through the heart. I didn't need the extra pressure they loaded on me; I was doing a fine job of tormenting myself. My thoughts kept up a non-stop debate that left me staring at the ceiling when I'd try to sleep. I'd made up my mind, but that didn't keep me from waffling.

Like a new widow still getting used to her loss, it took me a while to take off my ring. Signing some paperwork was one thing, but removing that symbol of commitment represented a finality I wasn't quite ready to deal with. When I finally worked up the nerve, I placed the ring in the blue felt box right next to my pelican pin. I still didn't care for that self-destructive bird and her babies, but I couldn't blame the pin for my leaving.

When I shut the jewelry box, it was like closing the lid on a coffin. Looking at that band of pale skin on my finger proved more than I could handle, so I opened the box and put the ring back on. I tried again later, then faltered a second time. Off and on it went. Off and on …

Like I said: waffling.

I moved back in with my mother until I could find a place of my own and used part of the thousand bucks for a down payment on a car. I could have kept my job at the detox center and earned a real salary, but it felt too awkward. Everybody there knew me only as Sister Janet.

Then I found out about the retreat center.

At the same time that I left the convent, Holy Spirit finished their renovations. I stopped by for a visit, and the director, Father Fergus, asked if I wanted to come back and work for them. I guess God couldn't have been too mad at me with divine timing like that, especially when they asked me to run the whole kitchen.

I took the job and started within a month of returning to civilian life. Being back at Holy Spirit was a Godsend; it helped me to heal on several levels. I was out of the inner city, surrounded by nature and bathed in blissful solitude. When I wasn't working, I spent as much time as I wanted in the silence of the chapel or walking through the woods. Working in a retreat center kept my link with the Church—something that was vitally important to me in those first few months. Most important of all, I enjoyed the loving company of people like Father Fergus and Father Leonard Broghan.

Father Leonard was my new Father Paul. Kind and compassionate, he made visitors feel welcome and comfortable, as if the retreat house were their home. He and I spent hours talking about my leaving. Although he was committed to his calling, he knew the ups and downs of living a religious life. He understood my turmoil because he'd struggled with his own personal choices. He'd started out as a diocesan priest with a parish, but for whatever reason, he didn't feel fulfilled. He made the difficult decision to leave his congregation and join the Carmelites.

"Yeah," I said one afternoon after the lunch crowd cleared out, " but you didn't let God down. You're still a priest."

He threw out his hands. "Okay, Janet, we'll just give you a veil and you can be our nun. There's no difference to me."

Can you see why I loved him?

As far as Father Leonard was concerned, by being part of the ministry of Holy Spirit I was still living a life of service. He showed me that in returning to the world, I wasn't abandoning my promise to God. I was changing the context within which I would fulfill it, but my commitment to that promise—to serve humanity and to make a real difference in the world—remained constant and complete.

I started to breathe again. And I threw myself into my work—my new ministry. As people enjoyed the good, healthy food we prepared for them, I'd come out of the kitchen and walk among the guests, sharing a smile or friendly conversation to ease someone's burden, just like Father Leonard had eased mine.

It took me a long, long time to forgive myself, but when the end of my one-year grace period rolled around, I no longer agonized over what to do. I simply stood back, and let the date pass quietly by.

Chapter 13

Open Mind

If I got anything at all from my father, it was a strong work ethic. When you say you're gonna do a job, you do it right. I usually showed up at the retreat center around seven in the morning and left after the evening meal. If I had to work on weekends because of a retreat, I took a couple of days mid-week to compensate.

I never minded the long hours, but my days of counseling taught me that you had to have some balance in your life. I made an effort to spend time with friends every chance I got. I found out that a woman I knew from ACOA had a bookstore in Ramsey, the same town where I was now renting a room. I hadn't seen Nancy in a long time, and something told me to stop by and say hello one Thursday afternoon.

Nancy's store specialized in New Age books. I'd heard the term *New Age*, but I didn't know what it meant. I stood on the sidewalk outside The Open Mind Bookstore and scanned the window display. Not one of the titles looked familiar. Many of the colorful covers included fanciful drawings of the sun, twinkling stars, and strange symbols that meant nothing to me.

I stepped inside and got a nose-full of sweet-spicy incense. My ears filled with snake charmer music that slithered from a boom box by the cash register. A quick glance at the shop revealed not just books, but boxes of shiny, multi-colored stones, odd-shaped crystals, and swirly silver jewelry. Posters on the walls showed angelic beings unlike any I'd ever seen in a Catholic church.

I don't know if it was the cloying smell of the incense, the strangeness of the music, or the unusual inventory, but I felt oddly uncomfortable. I considered leaving before anyone saw me, then the curtain of beads at the back of the store parted, and Nancy stepped through. She hadn't changed a bit, still able to brighten a room with her flowing red hair and powerful presence. Now that I had a sense of what *New Age* meant, I saw that my old friend fit perfectly in her surroundings.

"Janet!" her face lit up in instant recognition. "It's been a long time."

I returned Nancy's greeting and we did some quick catching up. Like everybody else in northern New Jersey, she'd heard I left the convent. She was nice enough not to press me about it, and I quickly turned the conversation back to her by asking about her shop.

She told me that most booksellers wouldn't carry the titles she sold. This was 1992, and your average Joe didn't know a whole lot about metaphysics. She'd gone out on a limb to open the store, but I could tell by her glow and the way her words sped up as she talked that she'd found her passion.

She showed me around the store and I simply nodded and smiled. It would have been polite to buy something, but it all seemed a bit too strange. When we got back to the register, Nancy pointed to an announcement taped to the wall.

"We're having a psychic development circle tonight. Why don't you come?"

Feeling a bit foolish, I asked, "What's a circle?"

Nancy snorted. "You sat through how many 12-step programs, and you don't know what a circle is?"

I shrugged. "Well, that's what I thought, but this is all new to me. The only psychic I ever went to took every cent I had to get rid of the curse hanging over me."

Nancy gave me one of those *you-really-weren't-that-dumb* looks and said, "A curse, Janet?"

I shrugged my shoulders and told her how I'd put the little pouch under my pillow to try and get a boyfriend.

"And did it work?" She was outright laughing at me now, but I deserved it.

"Not exactly." I didn't feel like going into the whole Cowboy saga.

Nancy pouted on my behalf, then reassured me. "There won't be any talk about curses tonight. We're just a bunch of open-minded folks trying to learn more about the world beyond our five senses."

I had to admit that the idea of psychic development intrigued me. Hadn't some of the Catholic mystics I'd read so much about shown special psychic abilities? I let myself consider joining the circle, until I remembered I had a dentist appointment that evening. When I told Nancy, she looked skeptical.

"On a Thursday evening?"

"No, really. He has a lot of patients who work during the day."

"Maybe you could reschedule," she said.

"Maybe … "

"You really should come, Janet," Nancy urged. "Some awesome stuff happens at these circles."

I didn't know if I was ready for the new age, but Nancy's enthusiasm was contagious. Whatever it was that got her so excited, I felt it rubbing off on me. I said goodbye to my friend, then went to call my dentist before I lost my nerve.

It was just a simple phone call. It couldn't have taken more than thirty seconds. But there are times when we look back and wonder how our lives would have changed if in any one instant we'd turned right instead of left, said *no* instead of *yes*. I had no idea when I cancelled that appointment that my life's path was about to bend in a completely new direction.

* * *

To my surprise and relief, everyone in the group looked fairly normal. No one wore flowing robes or pointed hats; no forked tongues waggled behind their welcoming smiles. The psychic development circle started out pretty much the same as a 12-step meeting, just as Nancy had said. Twelve of us sat in chairs arranged in a large circle and introduced ourselves. The moderator, Robert, started with a prayer, then he went around the room one by one and asked each person to give what he called "messages."

I listened as those before me made predictions about others in the room. I began to squirm as my turn grew nearer. How did I know who was going to get a new job or whose relative was going to get married? When the person to my right finished and all eyes focused on me, I wished I'd gone and had my teeth drilled, instead.

Having watched the others, I knew I was supposed to close my eyes. After that I'd be expected to come up with something prophetic. If nothing came to me, I wondered if I should just make it up.

I closed my eyes, painfully aware of eleven pairs of eyes focused on me. I could feel my heart beating faster than normal, but when I started to get dizzy, all thoughts of the others in the room disappeared. A little bit of lightheadedness would have been okay, but within moments my head was swirling like a bad case of bed spins. My body began to buzz as if electrified and sparkly colors danced behind my eyelids.

"I don't know what's going on," I said aloud, "but something's happening to me." The sensations frightened me, yet at the same time, they weren't altogether unpleasant.

"Go with it," Robert said. "Just let it flow."

It was an easy thing to say, but far more difficult to do as the voltage coursing through me increased to the point where my limbs were shaking. I suddenly became aware that someone had entered the room. I sensed a tangible human presence, and then I saw her: a small woman in a purple dress, surrounded by a blindingly bright light. A burst of fear-laced adrenaline made my heart beat even faster.

I'd seen the spirits of the deceased nuns at the convent, but that made sense to me in the context of a religious experience. I'd seen my grandparents' spirits as a child, and that somehow made sense because they were family. I had no idea who this woman was or what she wanted, and the sparkly energy was a whole new experience. My ears roared with words that I could barely make out.

"I'm hearing *Ma … roni,*" I said. "or maybe *Moroni.*"

Was that her name? It felt right, if not strange. I could hear the group encouraging me to stay with it, and I hung on for what could have been seconds, minutes, or hours. Just when I felt I couldn't take much more of the swirling and shaking, the woman and the sparkly lights vanished. In the sudden, deafening emptiness I opened my eyes and looked at the others as if seeing them for the first time. They stared back at me with wide eyes.

"What in the world just happened?" I asked, still buzzing.

"You seemed to be in some kind of trance," Nancy said while the others murmured among themselves.

Even Robert lacked an explanation. "That was a bit out of our league," he said.

"What was that word you were saying?" Nancy asked. "Something like *Moroni?*"

When I told her about the woman in purple, she nodded. "She must be some kind of angel."

"Or a spirit guide," Robert added.

I gave them a weak smile. With all the others sitting there it didn't seem polite to tell the group leaders that I thought they were crazy. Why would an angel or a spirit visit *me*? Especially now that I was no longer a nun.

The group broke up soon after. I don't think anyone wanted to compete with the show I'd put on. Nancy walked with me to the door while I continued to shake. My teeth chattered as if I'd been standing out in the cold.

"Are you going to be all right?" she asked.

"I hope so," I said and shook out my arms. "I still feel like there's all this energy flowing through me."

"That should dissipate soon. Why don't you come with us to the diner where we hang out after the circle and we can talk about this some more?"

"Maybe to talk, but the last thing I feel like doing is eating," I said, patting my stomach. "Too bad I can't bottle this high; it would make a great weight loss drug."

Nancy looked concerned. "I don't know whether to apologize or to be envious that you had such a unique spiritual experience."

"I don't know either," I said. "but I really want to know more about what happened."

She recommended that I return to the circle the next week as well as to the church service that she and Robert led one Sunday a month.

"You lead a church?" I asked.

"Yes. We're both Spiritualist ministers."

I had no idea what a Spiritualist was, but after such a shocking introduction to the new age, I didn't have the nerve to ask. Feeling overwhelmed, I picked out a couple of books that I hoped would help explain what had happened to me in the circle and called it a night.

The next day I went to the library. There I found a couple more books on psychic phenomena to add to the pile. Unfortunately, nothing in them answered my nagging questions. I wanted to know *why* the experience happened. *How* it happened. Was it a good thing or should I be worried? Somehow I knew I'd touched on something big, and even though I was still a bit frightened by the power in those sensations, I wanted to feel them again.

I went back to Nancy's bookstore the following Thursday and sat in the circle again. I felt somewhat like a celebrity with everyone chattering about me and wondering the same thing I was: Would I have a repeat of the strange trance? The answer turned out to be a resounding *yes*. I felt the energy coursing through my body, saw the same sparkly lights and the woman dressed in purple.

"What the heck is happening to me?" I asked.

"It's nothing to be frightened of," Robert said. "You may be experiencing some type of mediumship."

"Mediumship?" I had no idea what he was talking about.

"Communicating with spirits," Nancy said. "You're bringing through this Moroni woman, just like a medium does."

Robert nodded. "I think you should try meditating on your own and see what happens."

Nancy rested a reassuring hand on my leg. "You might want to write down what you sense and see if anything else comes to you while you're at it."

I was no stranger to meditation, having spent full days of silence in my time at the convent. There seemed to be no harm in taking their advice, although I did feel a few pangs of good old Catholic guilt—so much so that I hadn't shared any of what I'd been up to with Father Leonard.

Thinking of Nancy and her store, I forced myself to keep an open mind and to accept whatever happened. To my amazement, each time I sat down to meditate I felt the energy flow as if flipping a switch. The woman in purple appeared, always surrounded by a beautiful light. Soon I began to hear thoughts like a melody running through my mind.

Armed with paper and pen as Nancy suggested, I wrote what I heard as fast as the ideas came to me. This Moroni woman seemed to want to teach me things. She showed me strange symbols that I somehow sensed were meant to heal people. Other days she would share her philosophy about God as having both fatherly and motherly energy. Moroni's God was benevolent and caring and had nothing to do with all the bad things that happened in the world.

Later I would read what I'd written and shake my head. Where was all this stuff coming from? Everything I was hearing and experiencing was about as far from my life as a Catholic nun as I could get. The only consolation was that Moroni's messages were always loving and helpful.

I called Nancy and told her what was going on. She got all excited and claimed that what I was doing was called automatic writing—channeling messages from the spirit world. It was just more scary New Age stuff, as far as I was concerned.

I began to question God. "Are You sure You want me doing this?" I asked. If not, I asked Him for some kind of sign to let me know I should stop. I stayed alert for His warnings, but instead of being told to cut out the nonsense, I found myself drawn back to the circle, back to the meditations and writing, and back to my books.

If I were truly meant to stop, I never would have found the book that finally turned the light on for me. As I read *We Don't Die: Conversations with the Other Side,* I felt a growing excitement. The author, George Anderson, called himself a medium—the same term Nancy and Robert had used in the circle. According to

George, a medium served as a middle man between disincarnate spirits and their loved ones.

George made mediumship seem like the most natural thing in the world. In his book he related story after story of communicating with spirits who had once been ordinary men and women. Suddenly I had a name to put to my experience with my dead grandparents and the spirits of the nuns. Was that mediumship? Was I a medium like Robert and Nancy said? They had talked about mediumship in regards to angels and spirit guides, but the kind of mediumship George Anderson described was highly personal and very evidential. These weren't otherworldly beings, but good old John and Mary who once lived in Kansas and Wisconsin.

I tried to hold my excitement in check. "Remember, God," I said in my prayers, "If You don't want me to keep this up, then close the door."

The next Thursday I approached Nancy. "What else can you tell me about mediums?"

She shrugged, and I had to remind myself this was all normal stuff to her. "They communicate with spirits and give messages, just like we do at our church services."

I must have looked puzzled, because she pulled an announcement off the wall and showed it to me. "Remember I told you about our monthly Spiritualist service? It's coming up this Sunday."

I searched my mind and vaguely remembered her mentioning it. "Tell me again what a Spiritualist is?"

"First of all, note that it's spelled with a capital S."

I looked at the flyer and nodded.

"We believe that the spirit and consciousness continue after death and that it's possible to communicate with that spirit through mediumship."

What she was describing was exactly what George Anderson wrote about in his book, only he didn't mention Spiritualism specifically. It would be some time before I found out that Nancy and Robert's version of Spiritualism was quite a bit different than the mainstream. They practiced a sort of "anything goes" mediumship, mixing in their New Age methods as they saw fit. True Spiritualism, I later learned, was anything but new, having been around in America since the mid-1800s.

I wanted very badly to see what the service was all about, but first I had to squelch the protests in my mind. I prayed and meditated and found more reasons to attend the meeting than to stay at home and hide: George Anderson was a medium, and he'd had a strict Catholic upbringing. Catholics had been talking to spirits for centuries, in the form of saints and God. The Spiritualists said it's not just saints and God; you can talk to your dead relatives, too.

I realized there wasn't a single faith that didn't believe we go on to something else. The Spiritualists' beliefs seemed to fit in perfectly with all religions. But not all religions allowed you to question things. The folks who met at The Open Mind bookstore were all about questioning. They wanted to prove that life went on—that just like George Anderson said: we don't really die.

I wanted to prove it, too, and to find out if the experiences that started when I was a little girl were not something to be frightened of after all, but a gift that I could develop.

I gathered my courage and went to the Sunday service in a rented VFW hall in Oakland. Unlike the development circle, I didn't have to say a thing. I hid out in the back row and took it all in: the prayers to a loving mother-father God and the spirit messages from the ministers to those in attendance. The pastor's name was Marla. She'd been part of a larger Spiritualist church in Florida named the Sanctuary of Light. When she moved to New Jersey, she started her own branch of the church in Oakland. As she, Nancy, and Robert talked about the guides and angels who came through, I couldn't help but wonder, *could I do that, too?*

As I continued to attend the weekly development circles and the monthly services, I could see that mediumship was a gift, but it was also a skill that could improve with training and practice. My initial experience in the circle had shown me that I could be a channel for spirit energy, but I needed to fine tune the voltage.

Nancy and Robert taught me that everything in the universe is energy. Humans vibrate at a certain frequency and spirits vibrate at another, far higher frequency. They're around us all the time, but just like radio and television waves, we can't see them because they're out of our range. Mediums are like radio receivers, able to tune in to frequencies that others can't. I merely needed to practice tuning in to that frequency on demand.

As nervous as that thought made me, I couldn't deny a growing urge inside me. I'd seen spirits off and on since I was a little girl, and now it was as if they were trying to get my attention. They seemed to be waiting for me, and I could no longer close the door in their faces. I reassured myself that it was okay to proceed. God hadn't held up a stop sign.

On the contrary, the red carpet was laid out in front of me. Within six months of attending my first Spiritualist service, Marla, Nancy and Robert—three ordained Spiritualist ministers—asked me to join them at the front of the hall and deliver spirit messages.

Chapter 14

Finality

It's one thing to tell someone, "There's a spirit guide here who says you're gonna have a great life." It's another thing to say, "I have a man named Albert who died from a bump to the head … Is this your uncle?"

The people who came to Sunday services at The Open Mind were used to getting airy-fairy messages that sounded exciting but came with no proof; they touched on the psychic, but didn't have a thing to do with mediumship. Once I started deliberately tuning into spirit, the stuff that came out of my mouth astounded everyone—including myself.

I would stand in front of the congregation and try to sense the presence of spirits. Immediately I'd see or hear them—the dead relatives of people in the room. These weren't spirit guides or angels, these were Mom and Pop and old Uncle Harry. Rather than simply tuning into my guide, Moroni, or the spirits of some former nuns wandering around a cemetery, I was suddenly touching people on a very personal level—reuniting them with loved ones they'd given up for dead.

At first I got things right about 50% of the time, but even that was exhilarating. Problem was, if I said, "I see a woman with a patch over her eye. Do you know who this is?" and the person said *no*, my confidence would crash. I'd shut down and switch right over to psychic mode. It's a lot easier to say, "You're coming into money" than to give evidential proof that you're talking to a spirit.

People responded with so much enthusiasm to my messages that Nancy set up hours for me to practice giving readings in her bookstore. I would sit one-on-one with anyone who showed up and tune in to their departed loved ones.

The feeling I'd sensed earlier that the spirits had been waiting for me proved true. Once I opened that door, the spirit people lined up and took a number.

Rarely when I sat with someone did I have to say, "I'm not getting anything." Instead, I'd come out with names, places, and other irrefutable evidence that their dead relatives hadn't really died. The response from the sitters when I got a good hit electrified me. They would look at me with astonishment and many times they'd cry, but they were always tears of happiness to realize that their loved ones were still around.

Back then very few people had any idea what mediumship was. Nobody I knew had ever heard of Spiritualism. Yet there I was, fully immersed in this whole new arena. I would put in a full day of work, then once a week hurry over to the bookstore to give my readings. I continued to sit in the development circle and I attended the Spiritualist services. In a way, I felt as if I were living a double life. I certainly didn't tell anyone at the retreat center what I was up to, and I didn't care to share it with my family.

So one Tuesday night when a little voice told me to stop and see my father, I decided to keep the spirit people to myself. I'd heard he was in Hackensack Hospital because he'd fallen. His injuries were nothing life-threatening, so I hadn't rushed right over. You gotta remember, this is a man who used to show his affection with his fists on a near-daily basis. I actually hadn't planned on visiting him at all, but like I said, this voice literally spoke to me and said very clearly: *Go visit your father.*

I walked into his room and stopped at the foot of his bed. He didn't look like he'd hurt himself. I took a deep breath, then said, "You doing okay, Pop?"

He narrowed his eyes, glared at me, and barked, "It's about God damn time somebody from this family showed up."

I recoiled and stood there for a moment, staring at this man who had played such a critical role in shaping my early years. My response, when it burst forth, proved beyond a doubt that at 35 years old, the scared little girl had finally grown up.

"You son of a bitch!" I said. "You have no right to say that to anybody. You owe every member of this family an apology for your sorry behavior. You have some kind of expectation that we should all be taking care of you, when you never took care of us. You were supposed to show us how to be strong. Instead you beat us all down till we broke. To expect us to be loving at this point without an apology is totally unrealistic."

My father gaped back at me. When he opened his mouth, his words had lost all their venom. "You don't understand, Janet. I had a terrible life. I told you about the orphanage and the work camps. Nobody ever helped me one little bit."

I flashed on the image of Titus Brandsma, humming away at Dachau and inspiring others right until they stuck a needle in his arm. My father's excuses ran off me like raindrops. "So you took it out on us?" I jabbed my finger at him. "You weren't a nice guy, Pop."

"I got screwed out of that property, Janet, and nobody helped me."

By now I was trembling. I realized I was kidding myself if I expected him to say, "I'm sorry I wasn't a good father."

"You've always had it backwards, Pop. You were supposed to be the adult— to love and protect us. So when do you call us? When you want some booze. That's not about love."

I could see in his eyes that he would have killed for a bottle right then. Like me without my cigarettes, there he was stuck in that hospital bed with nothing to kill the pain, which is what the drinking had always been about for both of us. We stared at each other until he turned away from me. Had anyone made the slightest noise in the hall at that moment, I never would have heard the pathetically soft "I'm sorry" that came from his mouth.

If you think I jumped for joy at the apology, you didn't understand his words. What he really meant was, *I'm sorry for myself that I had such a lousy life.* But a forced apology is better than nothing, I suppose.

When I told him I had to go, he asked if I'd come back and see him again.

"Yeah, sure," I said. And that's what therapy does for you.

* * *

I was checking the inventory in Holy Spirit's kitchen when somebody yelled out, "Call for you, Janet!"

I picked up the phone, wondering who would be calling me at work. A woman identified herself as a nurse from Hackensack Hospital, then asked, "Are you Miro Nohavec's daughter?"

"Yes," I said warily.

"Miss Nohavec, we need to inform you that we've placed your father at the Rosary Hill Home."

"What are you talking about?" I demanded. Rosary Hill was a hospital for terminally ill cancer patients. They only took people who had less than six months to live.

"You don't know?" she said.

"Know what?" I asked.

There was a slight pause, then the woman muttered, "I can't talk to you," and hung up.

I walked to the nearest chair and sank onto it. This had to be a joke. My father was dying? But nobody would joke about that. I recalled our conversation from the day before. I'd called him a son of a bitch … thoroughly blasted him. If I had found out just 24 hours earlier that his days were numbered, I never would have spoken my mind.

And then I remembered the voice.

Go visit your father.

I'd gone to visit my father, and it had been cathartic.

That's when I knew for sure that angels do exist, and they help us to heal.

* * *

One of my most fervent prayers is that when my time comes, I'll go quickly. I don't want to linger in pain, but if it comes to that, I want to go somewhere like Rosary Hill. The nuns there truly love their patients, and you can't beat the setting. The beautiful red-roofed buildings sit atop a wooded hill in Hawthorne, New York. The place felt a lot to me like the retreat center, except you went there to die.

My father may have hurt his back in a fall, but his real problems were lung cancer, heart problems, and—no surprise—cirrhosis of the liver. I gotta give it to my family, they really rallied when they got the news. Everybody went to visit my dad at Rosary Hill. Suddenly we're all doing whatever he asked, giving him whatever he wanted. If he asked for lobster, we'd bring it in and wheel him outside to eat it.

Yeah, I know. Other people would have closed the door and said, *Die in Hell, you bastard.* That's not what we chose to do. We chose to be there and to spoil him for the last six months of his life. We did it because that's who we were, not because he was this great guy who deserved it. I'd learned through therapy that we're free to make choices in our lives, which is a pretty big deal when you grow up believing you're powerless. I could treat him like he'd treated me my whole life and end up just like him, or I could be the kind of person I wanted to be.

I chose not to be like my father.

My reaction was loving because that's who I was now. That loving aspect came from enough counseling and 12-step programs to show me how lucky I was to have survived that dysfunction. I learned that you can run from the pain and avoid it your whole life, or you can stand and look at the things that scared you so much. You can only become as light, infused by God and grace, if you look at all the stuff that's buried inside and shine a great big flashlight on it.

In his final hours, my father could hardly breathe. He looked up at me with this utter look of terror. I looked back at him and said, "You're not gonna go to Hell, Pop. You had it here."

Before he took his final breath, I forgave him, but it had nothing to do with his behavior. Once again, I had to model what I believed as a person. That's a touchy word—*forgiveness*—but it's never an excuse for bad behavior. Forgiveness is letting go of the anger, which in a way separates you from the event. What my father did will never be right.

Our family had never been through a death. Nobody knew what to do, and we didn't have the money for a funeral. "We'll have a memorial service at the retreat center," I told my mother. "And we'll get him cremated."

She shook her head and said, "I don't know how you're so strong."

I knew, but I couldn't tell her. I drew my strength from a loving God who was 180 degrees out from her God—the scary one who never liked the Nohavecs.

Father Leonard, God bless him, led the memorial service in the retreat center's chapel. We talked about the tragedy of my father's life and the difficult time he had. We said he was a hard worker and that he tried to provide food and housing for his children. I mean, what else could we say? He did come here to build a dream. He truly intended to create success for himself, but it never worked out.

When the ashes arrived, we all just looked at the urn, like, *what do we do with this now?* We ended up dumping them in the woods at the retreat center in the middle of a blizzard. Like my father, we did the best we could.

I went back to work and busied myself in the kitchen, but I kept having to shut myself in the walk-in freezer. My therapist had told me I had to compartmentalize my grief—to let it all out, then pull myself together and do what I had to do to function. So I'd stand there in that frozen box where no one could hear me and sob until my throat was raw.

There are plenty of people who don't get what they need from their family. Lord knows I was one of them, but I'd always held out hope that my father would change. When he died, the finality of his death cut me like one of the big butcher knives lying outside the freezer on the counter.

I dammed up my tears until the next time I could let them out, just as I'd been counseled. And it was excellent advice. For how else do you function, knowing that you'll never have a father who loved you?

Chapter 15

Kindred Spirits

The weathered statue of an angel caught my eye, and I stopped walking. I'd seen plenty of winged cherubs in Nancy's book store, but this one was much larger and sat in the front yard of a small white cottage in Lily Dale, New York. The expression on the angel's face mirrored my feelings exactly. His head rested peacefully on his forearm and he had the most serene smile on his lips. If this little statue could talk, he would have let out a long, satisfying *ahhhhhhhh*.

Being out of my car after a seven hour drive was enough to make me sigh like that, too, but that wasn't why I felt so at peace. My *ahhh* came from inhaling the extraordinary air. Yes, it was pure and clean as you'd expect it to be at the edge of a lake, miles from the nearest big city. But more than that, this air held a special energy—an all pervasive sense of love and acceptance that hit me the moment I drove through Lily Dale's gate.

I'd heard about the place some time back from a group member at The Open Mind. She said it was the largest Spiritualist community in the country, if not the world. Lily Dale was founded by free-thinking Spiritualists back in 1870, when such notable believers as Sir Arthur Conan Doyle—the guy who created Sherlock Holmes—and women's rights activist Susan B. Anthony promoted its principles. The Spiritualists wanted a place where kindred spirits could get together to openly discuss life after death and the spirit world without being judged.

I wanted the same thing now. I hadn't been ready to take the leap when I first heard about the town, but I kept the idea of visiting tucked away in my pocket. Now, with my interest in mediumship growing stronger by the day, I'd worked up the nerve to make the trip. Had I known how welcoming Lily Dale was, I would have come a whole lot sooner.

More than a hundred years after it opened, the community was still small and quaint enough that most people parked their cars and walked everywhere. I'd left my car in front of the Maplewood Hotel, and joined the smattering of tourists wandering the rutted lanes and soaking in the sights. With so little traffic, the only sounds came from wild birds, the occasional barking dog, and friendly neighbors calling out a greeting.

You have to be a Spiritualist to own property in Lily Dale. Many of the houses I passed displayed a sign showing that a medium lived there and was available for readings. I'd had no idea there were so many mediums in the country, let alone living together in this one small community. I felt a thrill of excitement as I passed the assembly hall, the museum, a gift shop, and a library with more books on Spiritualism than I imagined could exist. Bulletin boards at the post office and cafeteria announced lectures, classes, workshops, and daily demonstrations of mediumship.

I ended up at a building that looked like a small chapel with a sign that read "Healing Temple." According to the posted hours, a service was scheduled to begin in just a few minutes. I stepped inside and chose a seat somewhere near the middle, for once in my life not hiding in the back. Soft, meditative music played through the speakers, and I closed my eyes as I waited, just like those around me.

Exactly on the hour a woman who'd been standing off to the side stepped to the front. She welcomed visitors and gave a brief introduction to Spiritualism. I was familiar with most of what she said, but her version seemed somehow more structured than what I was used to hearing at the monthly services back home. At the conclusion of her remarks, the woman invited the official healers to join her at the front. A half dozen men and women in white shirts and dark slacks or skirts came from the back and took their places behind strategically placed chairs.

Just like taking Communion at Catholic Mass, the guests in front of me stood and went forward row by row for their healing. When my turn came, I took the next empty seat and greeted the healer with a nod. He was a balding man in his fifties with kind, blue eyes. Without a word he held his hands out, palm down, over the crown of my head. I closed my eyes and immediately felt the healing energy flow through my body from his hands like a cascade of warm, soothing water.

I could tell without looking when the healer shifted his hands to a spot just above my shoulders and held them there for a minute or two. He then moved to my side and placed one hand in front of me and the other in back like a pair of bookends. He never touched my skin, but the warmth he radiated filled me with the same sense of well-being as an hour-long massage.

My few minutes in the healing seat ended too soon as far as I was concerned, but others were waiting. I reluctantly stood and returned to my original seat. Most of those who'd gone before me had simply left the temple when their turn was over, but I wasn't ready to leave. I faced the front and closed my eyes again, content to simply *be*.

After two years of tiptoeing around my family and colleagues, I'd found a place where I could develop my gifts and discuss my new interest openly. I loved Lily Dale already and said a silent prayer of thanks to its founders. Sitting there that first day, I felt as if I'd come out of my spiritual closet and could finally breathe.

* * *

I got out of bed the next morning, gave a long, lazy stretch, and looked around the simple room. In keeping with its 19th century feel, the Maplewood Hotel had no TVs or telephones. They didn't have air conditioning, either, but I didn't need it with the cool mountain breeze that wafted in the window. I pushed the curtain further aside and looked out on the lawn. A lone woman sat in the gazebo by the lake. Her head tilted slightly upward, her eyes were closed, and her hands rested palms up in her lap as if waiting for rain. If this were anywhere else, she'd look a little strange.

I turned back toward the room to get dressed, then cocked my head as an image from the night before flashed before my eyes. Had I been dreaming? No, I clearly remembered being awakened by the presence of a spirit at the side of my bed. I hadn't realized how far I'd come in my acceptance of the spirit people until that moment, for I recalled saying hello to the man, then rolling over and going back to sleep.

People had told me the Maplewood was haunted, and my experience proved it, but this was Lily Dale. You had to expect there'd be spirits wandering around like that. I'd run from so-called ghosts as a child, thinking they were scary and something to be avoided. Now I knew that a haunted place was simply one that spirit people liked and came back to visit from time to time. The Maplewood was charming. Why wouldn't they want to drop by?

I dressed and ate a quick breakfast. By its very nature Lily Dale encouraged a more leisurely pace, but this particular morning I didn't care to linger over my food. After such a positive experience in the healing temple, I'd decided to have my first reading with a medium. I was looking forward to reversing the roles and being a sitter for once.

With dozens of mediums from which to choose, I let my intuition guide me. As if pulled by an invisible string, I found myself drawn back to the cottage where I'd seen the blissful angel. A sign next to a fountain announced that the medium, Alice Ainsley, welcomed walk-ins, so I knocked on her door.

I had no idea what to expect as I waited for someone to answer. When a white-haired woman appeared behind the mesh of the screen door, I felt a surge of relief. If age had anything to do with skill, I'd chosen well. At the very least, the woman's calm energy and welcoming smile put my mind at ease.

"Good morning," she said. "May I help you?"

"Yes, good morning," I said. "I'd like to have a reading, if you're available."

"Certainly, my dear. Come in." She opened the door and we introduced ourselves as I stepped inside.

She led me to a small sitting room where two cushioned arm chairs faced each other next to a wall of book shelves. I took a seat, wondering what would happen next. I'd been practicing my mediumship based on what I learned from my friends at The Open Mind, which was limited, at best. The people at Lily Dale lived and breathed Spiritualism. The place was Mecca for a medium, and I found myself buzzing with anticipation. Alice had the air of someone who really knew her stuff.

She sat across from me and studied me with narrow eyes. After a moment she made a little *mm hm* noise and nodded as if she'd figured out the answer to a riddle.

"I usually begin by asking my clients if they have any questions about mediumship," she said, "but I sense that you're a medium, yourself. Is that right?"

Her words took me aback. "I guess you could say that." Even though I'd been giving readings in Nancy's bookstore, I still had a hard time seeing myself as a medium, let alone a Spiritualist.

"Oh yes," Alice nodded. "You have a gift. You've been seeing spirits since you were a child."

How would she know that? I wondered as Alice closed her eyes and began to sway ever so slightly.

"So let's see now, Janet … yes … mm hm … There's an older gentleman here with a little dark goatee like this," Alice stroked her chin. "He's dressed completely in black, from his shoes to a tall black hat."

I stiffened as a long buried memory stirred in my stomach.

"I get a grandfatherly feeling from this man. Does this mean anything to you?"

"Yes," I said. It meant more than she could imagine. Suddenly I was five years old again, with my father's father standing beside my bed. I had to remind myself that I was grown up now, and that my grandfather's spirit was no more frightening than the visitor in my hotel room the night before.

"He tells me that he did construction work for a living."

I nodded, speechless. Like father like son.

"This man, he—oh, my … I get the sense that he took his own life."

"Yes, he did," I said, amazed at her accuracy. There was no way Alice could have made up such details.

Then, as if my grandfather had stepped aside, she went on to bring forth my father's sister, Mary. Aunt Mary and I shared a special bond because she'd once considered entering a convent. Alice stated correctly that Mary had become a chef, instead.

"It's all true," I said, shaking my head.

I suppose I shouldn't have been so surprised that Alice was communicating with my dead relatives. After all, I was seeing the spirits of other people's loved ones more and more often. But somehow it seemed more fantastic to hear about my own family from a stranger.

The thing that impressed me most was Alice's accuracy. She left no question that my grandfather and my aunt were there in the house with us. And then, like a skillful archer, she brought forth one final spirit with perfect aim.

"I have your father here," Alice said, "and he wants you to know that he's sorry."

A small groan slipped out with my breath. The woman was good. I wasn't impressed so much by the fact that she brought through my dad – I was familiar enough with mediumship that I didn't need to be convinced that my father was still around. It was the evidence in her words that struck me. A less credible medium would have told me she had my dear departed dad and that he missed his little girl. Alice had no way of knowing that my father owed me an apology, and that made her message all the more healing.

No other spirits came through, but those who had were enough for me.

"Everything you gave me was so detailed," I said, "So … "

"Evidential," Alice said with a knowing smile.

"Yeah," I said. "Things that nobody else could know."

She nodded patiently. "There's no sense in giving any other kind of reading, my dear. I'm sure you know that the sole purpose of mediumship is to prove the survival of consciousness."

I thought about the so-called messages I was used to hearing in the services back at home. I'd been to several Spiritualist churches in New Jersey by now, and it wasn't uncommon to hear things like, *I've got your grandmother here. She says you're gonna move.* Alice was right: Where was the proof in that? I was still guilty of falling back on psychic messages, myself, from time to time—especially if someone didn't respond well to my words. I never made things up, but I wasn't always as evidential as Alice had been with me.

"How long have you been a medium?" I asked.

"Longer than you've been alive, I'd guess, but don't worry," she said, as if sensing my unease, "you're going to do very well as a medium."

I shook my head. "I don't know. I'd like to get better, but I'm not so sure the people I'm working with know what they're doing. Nobody there has had much experience with the kinds of things that have been happening to me."

I described the frightening trance state I'd experienced my first night in the psychic development circle. I told her about Moroni, the automatic writing, and the readings I'd been giving in the bookstore.

"I just feel like I'd give better readings and understand things more if I had a good teacher. Someone experienced like you."

Alice looked pleased, but she shook her head. "You already have the best teachers in the world, Janet."

I tilted my head, confused.

"The spirits on the other side," she said. "Your guides. You simply need to sit in the quiet and ask them to teach you."

Everything Alice said made sense. Moroni had taught me a new way of looking at God, and I hadn't even asked her for guidance. If I gave Alice's suggestion a try, maybe someday I'd be as credible a medium as she was.

I paid her modest fee, and she led me to the door. My eyes fell on the little statue outside in the yard, and I felt a rush of gratitude to the real-life angels who had led me to her house. A bad experience could have easily soured me. Instead, I was looking forward more than ever to going home and working with my guides.

Alice intuitively sensed my excitement. "Remember what I said, Janet. You have a gift that will only get better the more you work at it. Once you've gained all you can from the spirit world, if you feel the need to learn more you should go to Great Britain."

I gaped at her. "To England?"

"Yes," she grew serious and looked left and right as if she were about to share a great secret. "There are some good teachers here, but the best mediums in the world are all in Great Britain."

I thanked her for the advice and for the incredible reading. Then, before she could sense my thoughts, I made a hasty exit. Everything had been going great until Alice dropped that last little bombshell. Study in England? Who was she kidding? The farthest I'd traveled in my entire life was that very trip to Lily Dale—a whopping seven hours from my house. The mere thought of flying, let alone across an ocean, made me wish I'd skipped my breakfast.

Alice was a nice woman, and she was a heck of a medium, but she was crazy if she thought I was going to get on an airplane.

* * *

Once I started asking the spirit people for advice, I got better and better at tuning in. I took every chance I got to practice, giving readings at Nancy's shop and another metaphysical bookstore, and I started a message circle of my own once a week.

It was Nancy who gave me the confidence I needed to move to the next level.

"You've been doing free readings for a while," she said. "and there's a demand for you now. You should start charging a fee."

Something inside me chafed at asking for money. I made a good salary running the kitchen at the retreat center. But at the same time, all the mediums in Lily Dale charged for their readings. It gave them a sense of legitimacy. I'd always strived in all my jobs to be as professional as possible. I realized that if I charged a fee, I could afford to rent a place and pay for a telephone line to schedule appointments. I pictured myself in my own office and got a little shiver of excitement.

When things are meant to be, they all fall into place. A woman I gave a reading to at the bookstore owned a massage school in Brookhaven near my home. When she heard I was looking for an office, she agreed to rent me a small room in the basement for a hundred bucks a month. I didn't care much for the boxes stacked up under the stairs or the little bug that skittered away when I turned on the light, but I couldn't beat the price.

I didn't know how much people would be willing to pay for my services, but I settled on $25 for a reading. I figured I'd break even on the rent if I could get four clients. I was willing to pay for the phone out of pocket if no one else came.

I needn't have worried.

I printed up some business cards and hung a sign in the window of the massage school. Other than that, I did no advertising, but somehow word got around. I think it was the demographics. The area had no shortage of Catholics—many of them fine, upstanding people who had always wanted to see a medium, but for whatever reason had been too frightened to do so. You wouldn't have caught them dead in a metaphysical bookstore, but when they heard there was a former nun giving readings in a private office, my new phone started ringing off the hook.

I could tell the Catholics right away. They were the ones who stood back and wouldn't come in until they asked, "Did you really used to be a nun?"

Only after I assured them that I had, did they step through the doorway. Then they'd sit on the edge of the seat, ready to bolt in case the floor opened up.

That's exactly what the twenty-something guy named Mark did one evening when he showed up for his appointment. I hadn't been working in my new office very long, but I recognized the look of a good Catholic right away: scared and skeptical.

"I heard you were a Catholic nun."

"That's right," I said as I sat down and pointed to the chair where he could sit.

"We don't usually come to people like you," he said, sitting as far forward on the chair as physically possible without tipping it over.

"I understand where you're coming from," I said, "but I can tell you that you're safe here, and that I truly believe in what I do."

My words didn't seem to help him relax, but he didn't get up and leave, either. I knew there was no sense in trying to convince him that he wasn't going to burn in Hell for visiting a medium. All I could do was give him a reading and let him see for himself.

I'd gotten so used to working with the spirit people by that point that I only had to ask for their presence and they'd show up. It was no more difficult than flipping a switch and *click*, there they were. So I flipped the switch, and right away I had company.

"There's a young guy here," I said, actually seeing the fellow. "He comes to me like a brother."

Mark's muscles went rigid.

"He wants me to tell you about a leather jacket. A black one, I have to say. He's really insistent about this. You have his jacket, he's telling me."

Mark eyes widened and he gave an almost imperceptible nod. His head didn't move, really. It was more like his whole upper body just sort of rocked a little.

"He was in an accident," I said. "A fiery one … there's something about being trapped in a car that was on fire."

Mark's chest rose and his nostrils flared. His eyes became little black marbles.

I concentrated on the grisly scene in my mind's eye. I could see Mark's brother sitting in a half-crushed car that was completely engulfed in flames. The image might have been unbearable, were it not for my insider's view.

"I see him surrounded by spirit people. They knew he wouldn't be able to get out, and they came to take him with them before he could suffer."

I glanced at Mark and saw that his eyes were tearing up.

"Your brother did not experience pain," I stated with a confidence that came from seeing with my own eyes. "His body may have been trapped, but his spirit was already on its way when the fire got to him." I leaned forward and looked directly into Mark's moist eyes. "I *know* that your brother is okay. He's here now with us and he's fine."

Mark slumped back against the chair. His hands rested limply in his lap, all the tension gone from his body. The difference between the young man who had walked into my office minutes earlier and the one sitting before me now was nothing short of stunning. I could see him processing this new version of a horrific event that had surely been playing in his head like an incessant nightmare. The details I had given Mark about his brother's last moments—details that a complete stranger had no rational way of knowing—had a visibly calming effect on my client. He looked peaceful, and I knew that he hadn't looked that way in a long, long time.

It was in that moment that I knew my purpose in life. The thought ran through my mind as clearly as any message I had ever received from spirit: *This is what I'm supposed to do.* Until that point, I had continued to ask God if I was doing the right thing by giving readings. In Mark's face I saw that mediumship was my way to help people heal.

I knew from losing my father that people didn't talk much about death. My family certainly didn't. Until Pop crossed over, the topic had never come up in our house. We were totally unprepared for the loss, and we didn't know how to deal with the grief. I was lucky to have a counselor to help me work through things, but people like Mark simply shut down.

By using my gift, I could show others that there is no death, merely a transition to a world we can't perceive with our limited senses. As painful as it is to say goodbye, death is only a temporary farewell. As I said goodbye to Mark—a changed man from the burdened brother who had dared to come to my office—I realized that he never would have believed me if I hadn't given him irrefutable evidence.

The proof was in the details. It was the facts that gave a medium credibility. If I wanted to live a life of service, to help others heal by using my gift, I had to be as accurate and evidential as humanly possible. I was good, but I knew I could be better.

The best mediums in the world are all in Great Britain.

Alice Ainsley's words echoed in my ears and my stomach lurched. Then I looked at the chair where Mark had sat so precariously. I shook my head, ashamed at my insecurities. My clients walked through their fears to have a reading with me. I owed them the same courtesy.

I reached in my desk drawer, pulled out the Yellow Pages, and turned to *A* for *Airlines*.

Chapter 16

New Directions

I called the airlines about flying to England, but don't think I just jumped on a jet and zipped right over. Besides my fear of flying, there was the minor problem that I didn't have the slightest idea where I was supposed to go. I found out about schedules and pricing, but that was as far as I got. The airlines certainly couldn't tell me where mediums went to school in Great Britain, and unfortunately, neither could Alice Ainsley, the medium back in Lily Dale.

I asked around at my church, the Sanctuary of Light, and at The Open Mind bookstore. Someone had heard of a college for mediums near an airport in Stansted, England. I got on the phone and tried the international operator.

"I'm looking for a special school in Great Britain," I said. "Near a place called Stansted. Is there some sort of college around there?"

It's a wonder she didn't hang up on me. I tried the same line of questioning with several other operators but didn't get anywhere. Disappointed, but hopeful, I figured that when the time was right, I'd find it.

In the meantime, my involvement with Spiritualism was picking up speed and growing like a rolling snowball. In addition to giving readings in my office, I started sitting with clients once a week at a place called The Wise Man in the next town over from Brookhaven. The Wise Man was a metaphysical bookstore like The Open Mind, but quite a bit bigger. Its owner, Richard, didn't fit the New Age stereotypes. He was a retired accountant.

Richard let me use a room at the back of his store for my readings, then I started leading psychic development classes in the same space. There weren't too many New Age bookstores at the time, so those who knew The Open Mind knew all about The Wise Man. Information went back and forth between the two stores, and I had no trouble filling my classes.

Those were exciting times. I woke up every morning energized about the day ahead. I loved my job at Holy Spirit, where I continued to feel as if I made a difference. Then, after a full day's work, I'd spend hours more giving readings or leading classes. Once a month I attended services at the Sanctuary of Light.

One Sunday, Reverend Marla approached me with a proposal that I never could have imagined three years earlier when I was living in a convent. She offered to ordain me. I'd agonized over every decision in my spiritual path to that point, but this one came rather easily. I knew that I was good at what I was doing, and the Spiritualist philosophy was fitting better every day. Being ordained meant that I would officially be able to minister to the community, which is exactly why I practiced my mediumship.

In the back of my mind, I already knew that some day I'd have a Spiritualist church of my own. Sundays at the Sanctuary of Light seemed a bit disorganized to me and they were still held only once a month. I'd sit there at the services and see things I'd do differently if I were running the show. By accepting Marla's offer, I could give more credibility to this whole new world of mine. I could start turning my fuzzy ideas into real, firm plans.

As always, I prayed about the decision, and ultimately I agreed. I met with Marla and did the coursework she recommended. I learned about counseling and we discussed the questions people might come to me with. I took part in the services, giving demonstrations of mediumship, and I volunteered for the church. And with that, three years after leaving the convent, at the age of 37, Marla declared me ready.

The ordination ceremony took place in Oakland, New Jersey. Dressed completely in white and surrounded by roses, I knelt on my kneeler from my Catholic days and dedicated my life to service. I chose the roses in honor of my favorite saint, Therese, who held a bouquet of roses in most of her portraits and statues. I had no doubt that she was with me as I took this next step in my spiritual journey. She had continued to guide me, even after I left the Catholic Church, and I still prayed to her regularly. I prayed to God and Jesus, of course, but Saint Therese was always right up there.

As proud as I was, I made the deliberate decision not to tell my family or my colleagues at the retreat center that I'd been ordained. I was well aware that Spiritualism wasn't exactly mainstream. This was 1994. If you went to the hospital and somebody asked you what religion you were, nobody said "I'm a Spiritualist."

Back then it had a kind of cultish feel that carried a bit of stigma. Even the term *metaphysical* came with some baggage, yet broken down into its component parts, the word simply meant *beyond the physical*.

I felt no shame that I communicated with spirits. On the contrary: my work brought people greater comfort than anything I'd ever done as a nun. But my journey as a Spiritualist, and now as a Spiritualist minister, was my own. I'd left the Catholic Church, where I had to *do this* and *believe that*, and had chosen a more personal path. I didn't need others to believe what I believed, for I believed it in my heart.

If I had any doubts about my new ministry, they were completely dispelled one evening in the back room of The Wise Man. I welcomed a burly man named Joe and asked him to have a seat. I'd never met the guy before, but he told me that I'd given readings to his daughter and ex-wife. Joe looked nervous, but he admitted that after the things I'd said to his daughter, he wanted to check me out for himself.

I flipped the switch, and right away a couple of spirits stepped up to the plate.

"I have a woman here named Mary," I said. "She was very sick at the end, I have to say."

Joe nodded, wide-eyed. "My mother-in-law's name was Mary. She was like a second mother to me, and you're right—she was in really bad shape when she died."

"I get the feeling this is a fairly recent passing," I said.

Joe bit his lip. "Just two months ago."

"Well, Mary is here, and she wants to thank you for everything you did for her. She says you went way beyond the call of duty."

Joe puffed a column of air through his lips.

"There's another relative here," I said. "Someone who died from cancer."

"My brother passed a couple months ago, too, of cancer," Joe said, wiping his forehead.

"And why am I hearing *Bobby*? Who's Bobby?"

"Bobby was his partner."

I raised my eyebrows, but said nothing more. I could feel Joe's pain, losing two close relatives in the same number of months. I tilted my head and listened for more.

"Your brother's telling me that he's okay with where he was buried … What does he mean by that?"

"Aw, Jeez," Joe's head dropped as if his neck muscles had given out, then he slowly looked back up at me. "He wanted to be cremated, but I just couldn't do it. I had him buried instead, against his wishes."

I closed my eyes for a moment and listened to his brother's response. I smiled as I regained eye contact with Joe. This was the part of my work I liked best—putting people's minds at ease in a way that no one else could. "He's okay with that," I repeated. "He knows that you were motivated by love."

Joe's eyes grew moist. "You don't know what this means to me."

But I wasn't ready to stop yet; I was on a roll. I kept seeing trains and told Joe that I had a man who was apologizing for leaving him so early. Joe confirmed that his father had died young and had worked for Lionel Trains.

"And why is my arm hurting me?" I asked as I cradled my forearm.

"Whoa, Janet, you're blowing my mind here." Joe explained that he'd broken his arm twelve years earlier and it had never healed right. To prove his point, he raised his arm halfway to his face and said, "I can't even touch it to my nose. See?"

I then brought through his mother, who talked about Joe's kids, her grandchildren, and his uncle, who described a business he'd had in Brooklyn.

"I can't believe this," Joe said when the reading was over. "What a gift you have."

I knew he was right. I thanked God after every reading for allowing me to communicate for the spirit people—for letting me be their instrument.

Like so many of my clients, Joe was a changed man as he got up to leave. The smile on his face was reward enough, but his parting words to me were priceless: "You must be a saint," he said as he shook my hand in both of his.

I laughed, embarrassed by his praise, but also at the irony of his words. Years ago, when I heard about the nun from New Jersey who was in the process of being canonized, I'd dreamed of one day becoming a saint, myself. To me, sainthood had always represented the pinnacle of selfless service to others.

A lot had changed since then, except my primary motivation. I might never be recognized by the Vatican, but like I said: my path was more personal these days. Saint Janet had become Reverend Janet, and my client's recognition was good enough for me.

Chapter 17

Nigel

I stared out the small, rectangular window, still not comfortable looking *down* at the clouds. I'd gotten used to the noise of the engines after the first few hours, but every time the plane hit a bump I had a talk with St. Therese. I still didn't know how something that big got off the ground, and couldn't stop worrying that gravity would catch up with us at any moment. My only comfort came from the thought that if I hadn't been meant to fly to England, I never would have found the Arthur Findlay College.

I'd almost given up on ever finding the British school for mediums. Then a friend mentioned a church in western New Jersey whose pastor was from England. Once I heard that, I wasted no time heading west. I sat in on the church's service and watched the English minister demonstrate. Right away I could see that she was credible, and I felt a shiver of excitement. Here was the evidential mediumship that Alice had been talking about.

After the service, I asked the pastor if she knew anything about a school for mediums in England. It was like asking a New York baseball fan if he knew anything about the Yankees.

"You must mean Arthur Findlay College," she said. "They offer year-round courses on psychic science and Spiritualism. It's the best in the world."

"That's probably it," I said, still unsure.

"It's also the headquarters for the SNU," she said, "The Spiritualists' National Union. They have their offices on the same grounds as the college in Stansted."

"Stansted! That's the place!" I felt as if I'd won the lottery.

I went home and called the international operator. She had no trouble connecting me with Arthur Findlay College, now that I had an actual name. I spoke with a representative from the school and smiled at her clipped accent. She might talk funny, but she was well versed in the various courses. Every one of them sounded interesting, but I chose a week-long class on advanced mediumship.

Before I could lose my nerve I applied for my passport, arranged for time off from the retreat center, and cleared my private readings calendar. Now, as we landed at Heathrow airport, I marveled at how things had come together for me to take this major step in the development of my mediumship. Everything had fallen into place perfectly, and my plane hadn't fallen out of the sky.

I claimed my luggage and headed toward customs, gawking at all the strange signs. Everyone except me seemed to know what they were doing. I followed the crowd like a sheep in a herd as the line snaked slowly forward. My brain felt muddled. The fact that the clock read seven o'clock didn't fool my body, which told me it was two A.M. back home.

With my first-ever stamp in my passport, I stepped outside. I looked around and realized that I didn't have a clue where I was going as far as distance or direction. When I asked a skycap how to get to Stansted, he pointed me toward a bus several lanes over. Watching the cars coming toward me on the wrong side of the road with no one on the driver's side, I was more than happy to settle for public transportation.

I arrived in Stansted several hours later and hailed a boxy black taxi. The driver loaded my luggage into what he called the *boot* while I sank into the back seat, drained.

"Arthur Findlay College," I said as he got behind the wheel.

He glanced at me in the rear-view mirror and gave a twinkly smile. "Spooks' College, is it? Alright then, Miss. Off we go."

A short ride later, my heart sank as the taxi pulled up to the campus. The "best mediumship school in the world" was a bit more run down than I'd expected. In all fairness, they've completely refurbished the place since then. It's magnificent now, but I didn't think so at first glance.

Luckily, the aging furnishings and a little peeling paint couldn't hide its innate stateliness. The mock Tudor style building with the pitched roofs, multiple chimneys, and a bell tower gave the place an Ivy League feel. Like the Holy Spirit Retreat Center, Arthur Findlay College had once been a private estate, known as Stansted Hall. It was built in 1871 and bought in 1923 by Arthur Findlay, a prominent businessman and ardent Spiritualist. He approached the Spiritualists' National Union in 1945 with the idea of turning his property into a Spiritualist college, and ultimately bequeathed it to the SNU.

I soon discovered that the school truly did have world-class status. I scanned the roster as I signed in and saw that 70 people had registered for that week's course. The column labeled "Nationality" showed many from England, of course, but also students from Italy, Sweden, Germany, and from as far away as Africa.

The course would be led by an instructor named Nigel Baxter. The man's name had meant nothing to me when I signed up for the class, but once I arrived at the school, I started hearing murmurs. From the sounds of it, I'd ended up with one of the best mediums in the school, but also one of its toughest task masters.

"He's absolutely brutal," I overheard a woman say.

"Ruthless," replied her partner.

My first view of Nigel the next morning didn't exactly scare me off. He wasn't much taller than me, had next to no meat on his bones, and was exactly what you'd expect of a British teacher: very proper, very neat. His thick, wavy brown hair and tortoise shell glasses gave him a bookish look, but the closer I got to him, I sensed a strong personality. He had this unmistakable energy that said *"I'm in charge here"* loud and clear.

The first order of business was to separate the 70 students into smaller sections based on our level of expertise and knowledge. Nigel would take a handful of students for the hands-on classes and the rest would work with his assistants. I filled out a questionnaire about my mediumistic ability and handed it in. A short while later Nigel called me to sit with him.

"You're Janet Nohavec?" he asked.

"I am."

"Right." He scanned the questionnaire. "Well, Janet, I just need to go over a few of the things you've marked here."

"Okay."

"I see that you've checked *yes* to all of the questions."

Maybe it was his accent, or maybe the disdainful look he gave me, but I had to pinch my lips together to keep from smirking.

"That's right. I did."

"Then perhaps we should go over these one by one."

"Whatever you want," I shrugged.

"Right. Let's see, then. Are you clairvoyant?"

"Yes," I said. I could see the spirit people.

He made a checkmark beside mine. "Are you clairsentient?"

"Yes." I could sense spirits' presence.

He made another checkmark. "And are you clairaudient?"

"Yes," I said. I heard them, too.

"Do you sit in development circles?"

"Yes."

"Have you experienced trance?"

"Yes."

He peered over the top of his glasses at me, then gave a funny little chuckle. "Right."

He laid the questionnaire in front of him, aligning it perfectly with the edges of the desk, then announced, "I'm going to put you in my group." An unspoken *we'll see how good you really are* hung in the air between us.

Class started shortly thereafter, and I had to admit, Nigel knew his stuff. From the very first lesson he was a total professional. He stressed the strong discipline required to become a credible medium, then introduced a concept that no one at home had ever discussed. According to Nigel, mediums needed to follow a system when communicating with spirits. We'd get far more consistent results, he said, if we asked the same questions of the spirit people every time—a kind of *name, rank, and serial number* routine. Those on the other side wanted to communicate with us as badly as we wanted to hear from them. By using a system, everyone would know what to expect.

After a couple of hours of theory, our small group moved to a larger hall for a group lecture. I couldn't get enough of the good, practical information being taught. The sessions ran all day, starting just after breakfast, and ending well past supper. We paused only long enough for meals and tea breaks, but I never grew tired.

On the second morning with the smaller group, Nigel announced that we would venture beyond theory into hands-on practice. He reviewed what we'd covered the day before, then suddenly he zeroed right in on me.

"Alright, Janet, get up there and do what I told you."

I bristled at the brusque command. I stood deliberately slowly and we locked eyes. "I'll get up there and *apply* what you taught me," I said, "but I'll do it *my* way."

With that, the gauntlet had been thrown.

I had demonstrated my mediumship countless times at services in New Jersey. I was used to standing in front of small groups by now and summoning the spirit people. But those groups had always let me know by their expectant faces that they looked forward to hearing what I had to say. Nigel looked like he wanted to hear what I had to say as well … just like a lion looks forward to eating its prey.

I strode to the front of the room as if I had all the confidence in the world, but only my pride kept my feet moving forward. Nigel had the power to do the one thing I feared most: to ridicule me in public. Suddenly I was little *Pupa* with a patch over my eye, afraid of my classmates' name calling. Growing up, you didn't get singled out if you were invisible. As I turned to face the lion, I wondered what I'd been thinking when I chose to be a medium.

If I'd brought anything to England from my previous practice, it was the power to focus. I pushed all thoughts of Nigel to the back of my mind and called on the spirit people. Thankfully, they weren't about to let me embarrass myself. I really turned it on that morning, I have to say, and gave a kick-ass demonstration. I brought through the loved ones of several of my classmates, and when I sat down, they smiled with encouragement.

When the class let out, Nigel pulled me aside. "Well, Janet, I must say that you do have some talent."

I nodded, feeling vindicated by his compliment.

"But clearly you need a lot of polish."

I let out an amused laugh, but Nigel pressed on.

"One can see the potential of what you have," he said, "and if you give me a few years, I dare say I can straighten out your mediumship."

"Straighten it out?" I gaped at him, recalling the many readings I'd given at home already. I was changing people's perception of death. One man had called me a saint. My mediumship was good enough for them. "I have a full practice back in New Jersey," I told Nigel. "I don't need you."

He merely smiled. I fumed. Like cowboys in a duel, we turned our backs and walked off in separate directions.

That afternoon, I gathered with the full group in a lecture hall. The schedule called for a demonstration of mediumship by Nigel and the other tutors. It would be my first chance to see the British mediums in action. Still smarting from my encounter in the classroom, I slouched in my seat.

When the first medium took the stage, I slowly sat up straighter, surprised at the level of detail she brought forth right off the bat. By the time the second tutor had finished, I was sitting on the edge of my seat. Nigel went last, and as much as it pained me to admit it, he was absolutely brilliant. I was witnessing mediumship on a level far beyond anything I'd ever seen: dates, full names, addresses, and even phone numbers from the spirit people!

As we filed out of the auditorium, I thought about my practice back in New Jersey. Yes, I could go home and continue to give readings exactly as I'd been doing. But after seeing these mediums demonstrate, I knew I would never be able to settle for less. If I was going to dedicate myself to this path, this was the level of detail I wanted to provide.

That night at dinner, my thoughts were consumed with the day's events until I noticed the dinner plate in front of me. I'd never seen or smelled anything like it—certainly not in our Polish household growing up. One of my tablemates noticed the look on my face and leaned over.

"It's kidney pie," she said.

"Kidneys?"

She forked up a few small morsels. "Yes. They're quite tasty."

I pushed the meat around my plate, then picked out a piece of potato.

"By the way," my neighbor said. "That was a brilliant demonstration you gave in class today."

"Thank you," I said, but after seeing the Brits perform, I no longer felt satisfied.

"What did Nigel say to you afterwards?"

"He thinks I could use some work," I admitted.

She shook her head in commiseration. "He's a tough old bird, that one is."

My classmate was right: Nigel earned his reputation, but now I saw that he had a reason to be so demanding. I grimaced, recalling how I'd told him that I didn't need him or his teaching. And I'd thought *he* was arrogant! There were definitely weaknesses in my gift, and if Nigel could help me correct them, I was going to listen to whatever he said.

I pushed the food around my plate. The kidney pie looked awful enough … I wondered how it would taste to eat crow.

* * *

Other than learning violin at the convent, I never had the benefit of music lessons growing up. I missed out on having a teacher stand over me and make me practice the same piece over and over. Nigel made up for that. I'd stand at the front of the room and apply one of his techniques, only to have him say, "Do it again. Do it again. Do it again."

I wanted to kill him.

But much as I hated to admit it, he was right. I had some bad habits to break. He called me right away on my old trick of resorting to psychic predictions if someone said "no" to my questions. In the back of my mind, I knew I was guilty of that. Then he pointed out another personal pattern that I was completely unaware of.

It came to light in the middle of a demonstration that I thought was going well. I stood in front of our group, my focus intense. "There's a lady here who used to do something with music," I said, squinting as I tried to fine-tune the link.

"I'm not quite sure what she's doing … playing an instrument or something …"

In spite of my concentration, I heard several of my classmates laughing.

I looked up to see Nigel shaking his head and scowling. "For God's sake, Janet, look at your hands!"

I glanced down and saw my fingers running up and down an imaginary keyboard. Even I had to laugh. "I guess she used to play the piano," I said sheepishly.

"The spirits are using your central nervous system to communicate," Nigel informed me. "You need to develop your mind, Janet, not your body. You're not their puppet."

I wasn't sure how "Screw you, buddy" would go over in the hallowed halls of Stansted, so I kept my mouth shut.

On the fourth day at Stansted we had a scheduled meditation period. I'd gone back to my room for a few minutes and arrived late at the chapel. I was surprised to look up and see Nigel at the podium. I slid into a pew and noticed that the woman beside me had tears in her eyes. I'd felt that way in Nigel's classes a time or two, myself, but as I tuned in to what he was saying, I saw a side to Nigel that he kept hidden when he taught.

He was reading a poem whose words were beautiful enough by themselves, but the way the lines rolled off his tongue, he made them sound like music. The same man whose acerbic demeanor had brought out my claws with his criticism stunned me now with his poignant delivery. In that chapel I sensed a deep sensitivity that I never would have imagined he possessed.

Later that evening, I stopped by the college bar to have a drink.

"Sprite, please," I said to the bartender. I looked to the right and there sat Nigel, sipping a clear drink adorned with a slice of lime. Had I not heard him in the chapel earlier, I might have turned the other way. Instead, I walked over and sat down beside him.

"That was a beautiful poem you read today."

"'Tis a lovely one, indeed."

"What was it?"

"You don't know it?"

I tried not to take offense at his tone and merely shook my head.

"It's entitled *I Am There* by James Dillet Freeman. One of your astronauts liked it so much that he took it with him to the moon."

"Get outta here."

"Actually, I just got here," Nigel said, and raised his drink.

"No, I—"

"I know what you meant, Janet. I was having you on."

"Right," I said, and took a sip of my Sprite.

We sat quietly for a few moments, then Nigel broke the silence. "I heard that you were once a nun. Is that correct?"

"Yes," I said, surprised how word got around. "I was."

He nodded thoughtfully, then said softly, "And so you've become a Spiritualist."

"That's right," I replied, not sure where he was going with this line of conversation.

He swirled the ice in his drink, then said, "It suits you."

Neither one of us needed to say what we both understood. Spiritualism was more accepted in England than it was in America, but still it was far from conventional.

We stayed in the bar and talked for a long time about our backgrounds, our beliefs, and even our dreams. Nigel asked if I had considered starting my own church, and I told him that I had. In fact, it was all I'd thought about on the long flight over.

"I want to create a spiritual oasis," I told him. "A place where people from every faith and every perspective feel welcome."

Nigel nodded thoughtfully. He told me that he had his own church in Plymouth. "People who come to a Spiritualist church from different backgrounds are going to be skeptical. That's why I push my students to be the very best they can. You have to stretch yourself, Janet."

"I know."

"This class is only the beginning. I'll be offering four more over the next two or three years."

The thought of making that trans-Atlantic flight every few months made me want some of what Nigel was drinking, but I'd survived the first trip ...

"Maybe I'll come back," I said.

"I think you should, but if you expect to be coddled," Nigel warned, "you'd do better with a different tutor."

"No, I want you," I said.

He didn't seem a bit surprised.

* * *

"You're not doing what I told you," Nigel barked. "Do it again, Janet!"

It was the morning after our little chat in the bar. I could see that our little soirée had made a profound difference in our student-teacher relationship.

I took a deep breath and tried to maintain my focus. "There's a man here. He died in his sixties, I have to say, and he's trying to show me something he used to do with his partner."

"Must you always say that?" Nigel snapped.

I stopped and put my hands on my hips. "Say what?"

"*I have to say, I have to say,*" he mocked. "It's like some sort of mantra for you!"

I ran back over the words I'd just said, and I realized that once again, Nigel was right. I did say the phrase a lot, but it was nothing more than a filler. "It buys me time to sense what the spirits want."

"You must make more of an effort to watch your words," Nigel huffed. "It's a dreadful distraction."

After hearing him recite the poem, I'd developed a newfound admiration for the man. Less than twelve hours later I was back to hating him. I cursed under my breath and tried to re-establish the link with the spirit. Luckily, the spirit man was waiting patiently in the shadows.

"Okay, he's still showing me something he used to do with his partner." I strained to sense what the spirit was trying to get across, but with Nigel breathing down my neck it was hopeless. "I can't do this. I'm just not getting what it is they used to do."

"For God's sake, Janet, look at yourself!"

His tone was harsh, but I noticed that Nigel was laughing now, as were my fellow classmates.

"You're on your toes, moving about like a clumsy ballerina. The chap is obviously trying to tell you that he and his partner loved to dance!"

I looked down at my feet, and even I had to laugh. I covered my red face with both hands, which evoked even more contagious laughter. Soon I was bent over from the silliness, wondering why anybody ever thought that talking with dead people had to be so serious. I'd seen from the Brits' demonstrations that they might seem stuffy on the outside, but they had a rip-roaring time with their mediumship.

At the end of the week, I loaded my bags in the boot of the taxi and looked up at Stansted Hall. Little did I know when I first arrived that it was only the start of my relationship with the college and the SNU.

And with Nigel.

The night that we talked in the bar he'd mentioned that he was coming to the States in just over a week. He was scheduled to teach and to demonstrate at a spiritual center in New Jersey. He thought he might have time to get together if I wanted to. I'd eagerly agreed to pick him up at JFK. But that was before our parting conversation.

We had shaken hands outside the classroom and I thanked him for a wonderful experience.

"The pleasure was mine," he said graciously.

"I gotta say, you may be a Spiritualist minister, but I think you should have become a drill sergeant instead."

He laughed, then grew serious. "I've had many students from your country, Janet, but from what you've shown me this week, I can already say that you're second to none in America."

I lowered my head, humbled beyond words. Coming from Nigel, this was high praise, indeed.

Then he turned on his heel and as he walked off added, "But that's not to say there isn't room for improvement."

Chapter 18
The Journey Within

When I first got the idea to start my own church, I knew I wanted something different. Most of the Spiritualist services I'd attended called themselves Spiritualist, but they were really more *anything-goes* metaphysical churches. There's a world of difference between a metaphysical service and a Spiritualist one. I was determined to keep the focus on the principles of an afterlife.

I envisioned my church as a bridge for people who were trying to find a new religion. If you came to my service after attending mass, that would be fine with me. If you were an atheist and just came for the fellowship, that would be fine, too. All would be welcome.

I started to look around at options of where to hold the services. By then I had expanded my space in the basement of the massage school to include the large empty room across the hall. I didn't even consider having my church there. It wouldn't do to worship in a black hole that my friends called *the dungeon*. The place had roaches so big they could carry off a picnic table. I cleaned it up as best I could for my readings and workshops, but I was forever finding some crackly brown carcass with its legs up in the air.

Richard at The Wise Man bookstore was willing to rent me his back room on Sunday mornings. I was used to attending services at the Open Mind, so his offer was acceptable, if not my first choice. In my mind and heart I dreamed of a beautiful building in the style of a traditional church. I wanted a peaceful place where people could come to feel closer to God and feel safe in practicing their beliefs. Unfortunately, I didn't have the money to get out of the dungeon, let alone the riches of the Catholic Church to back me. Without the financial support and infrastructure of mainstream religion, the Wise Man would have to do.

Spiritualists did have a national organization, but I wasn't sure I wanted to be tied down to it. I'd heard about a Spiritualist minister in New Jersey from World War II days named Reverend Harrison. This was back in the heyday of Spiritualism when there were 10 churches in my area. People used to line up at Reverend Harrison's door, but now there wasn't a Spiritualist church left standing. I heard it was the infighting within the organization that killed them.

I never did like having others tell me what to do, so I decided to remain independent and start my church from scratch. Then the Spiritualists' National Union honored me with an offer I never could have dreamed of: Because of my high level of mediumship, they wanted to grant me affiliation. No church in America had ever received such a tribute.

Having seen the high standards the British adhered to, I was thrilled to accept. Their organization encompassed 350 churches throughout Great Britain. Being associated with the SNU meant I would be part of a body that was respected around the globe. I didn't take that lightly. It was truly the best of both worlds: I would be on record as one of their affiliates, but they couldn't impose any rules on me.

An added bonus of SNU affiliation was my continued contact with Nigel, with whom I enjoyed a deepening friendship. He came back to the States the week after my first class, exactly as planned. When I found out he had some free time during the trip, I offered to let him give readings in my offices. The clients he saw were thrilled with his work.

Nigel never failed to complain about the dungeon when he came to visit, but who could blame him? The ambience of my little roach motel was a far cry from Stansted's stately charm. I made up for it by getting him a room at the retreat center, and he loved staying there.

Three months after my first visit to Arthur Findlay College, I went back for Nigel's second class. Our growing friendship did nothing to mellow out the monster. He didn't let up on me in the classroom one bit. He did, however, find opportunities for me to demonstrate in churches around England, always pushing me to stretch myself and build my confidence.

After that, we bounced back and forth between our respective countries like a couple of yo-yos. I got to know my way around Heathrow like a seasoned pro, but that didn't mean I cared much for the long trip.

During a subsequent visit to the college, they held an auction to raise funds for the school. One of the prizes was a one-hour hypnosis session with Nigel. With the prospect of starting my own church looming on the horizon, I saw this as a golden opportunity to erase my long-held fear of being in front of people.

The bidding started at $75 and it quickly became clear that Nigel's services were in high demand. Within minutes the stakes rose to a hundred bucks. People started dropping out when the bidding reached $150, and there was almost no one left at $200. I ended up going head to head with one very determined British lady, but she didn't know who she was dealing with. I had almost forty years of fear to erase, and I was determined not to lose.

She bid $275, but when I bumped it up to $300, she finally gave in. I would have gone as high as $400, but I'm glad I didn't have to. That little hypnosis session cost me the same as a full month's rent for my offices, but it was money well spent. While I didn't get over my fears immediately, one session with Nigel proved faster than years of therapy.

He came to the States for a third visit the summer before I started my church. On the last day of his visit, we sat in the cafe at Barnes and Noble, sipping coffee and talking shop.

"Look at that chap over there," Nigel said, nodding at a man in blue slacks and a short-sleeved white shirt. "What do you think he does for a living?"

I studied the man for a moment. He was a customer just like us, reading a book whose cover I couldn't make out. I didn't notice anything special about the guy, so I made a wild guess. "He's probably a butcher."

"Nonsense!" Nigel set his cup down so hard that the coffee sloshed onto his napkin. "He's no butcher. Look at his hands, Janet. You must learn to be more observant. Try to notice every detail you can about both your sitters and the spirits who come through for them and see what they tell you."

"I know, I know," I said, "I have to stretch myself."

"Precisely."

"But you gotta admit, I did pretty well at that public dem last time."

Nigel's face lit up. "Yes, I must say you really nailed that one."

I thought back to what turned out to be my best demonstration ever. There was something about the energy at Stansted. I brought forth a male spirit and amazed even myself when I came up with the exact day, date, and month he died. Detail after evidential detail came out of my mouth, all with Nigel's peers in attendance. He looked like a proud father.

"But you're still wrong about the roses," I said, deliberately trying to goad him.

He took the bait, just as I knew he would. "No, I'm right. Some symbols are universal, Janet. If a spirit shows you roses, they're referring to someone named Rose."

I downed my iced coffee and shook my head. "No, the symbols mean what I think they mean, and to me, roses are a message from St. Therese." Having been a nun, the spirits often used the saints to get a particular name across. If I saw Saint Joseph, that meant somebody knew a Joseph, and Saint Michael referred to a Mike, but if I saw roses, I was supposed to talk about Theresa.

"I don't have time to argue with you," Nigel said. "We still have work to do, and I have a plane to catch."

We got in my car and drove back to Brookhaven. As I parallel parked along the main street Nigel said, "This certainly is a sleepy little town."

For once I agreed with him. Brookhaven had once been a booming place. When I was growing up over in Franklin Lakes, Brookhaven had a Woolworth's, a Singer's, and an Army-Navy store. Then the big malls opened up and the town had to struggle to stay alive. The massage school was happy to have me as their tenant.

We crossed the street and entered at the street level through the double glass doors. When we got inside, Nigel stopped at the top of the stairs. "You go first and turn on the light."

I turned to him and laughed. "You're not gonna tell me you're afraid of the dark!"

"Certainly not. I don't care to be assaulted by one of those furry creatures that inhabit your office."

I rolled my eyes, but Nigel stood his ground. I went down and did a bug-check, then called out that the coast was clear.

He joined me in my office and began sifting through the papers on my desk. "What have you done with the draft of your church by-laws?"

I reached past him and searched a couple of piles. "I don't know, but if you give me a couple of days I'm sure I'll find them."

He made a noise that sounded like a death rattle.

The phone rang, and I asked Nigel to pick it up as I continued to look for the by-laws.

"Janet Nohavec's office," he said, sounding ever so proper. He listened, then said, "One moment please."

He peered at me over his glasses and in a mocking tone said, "Is *Sister* Janet available for a reading this evening?"

I rolled my eyes. "Not if you want me to take you to the airport."

Nigel passed my regrets to the caller, then cupped his hand over the receiver. "She wants to know if we have any other nuns who can give her a reading."

We stifled our laughs and Nigel hung up just as I produced the errant by-laws. I passed them to him and he sat in the chair where my clients usually sat. After a moment he began to scowl.

"What?" I asked, instantly defensive.

"I thought America was the land of democracy, but you seem to be taking a rather imperial stance here."

"What do you mean?"

"By the wording in these by-laws, it appears that you don't intend to grant your board members an equal say with you in decisions regarding the church."

"That's right." I crossed my arms. "I'll listen to the board's advice, but my say goes."

He made a little tsk-tsk sound, then said, "I recommend you not go that route, Janet."

I understood where he was coming from, but I'd seen too much stuff happen with other Spiritualist churches. I thought of Reverend Harrison, who did it the way Nigel suggested, only to have the whole thing pulled out from under her.

"Look," I said, "if I'm gonna bust my ass, I want to have complete say on everything. This is my church, and that's the way it's gonna be."

A lesser man might have walked out on me after that little tirade, but that wasn't Nigel. He understood that this was my turf and he respected my wishes. We both knew that if we were at Stansted, he could order me around all he wanted, but down there in the dungeon, Queen Janet ruled.

* * *

I might not have planned to run my church democratically, but I still had to deal with the very democratic U.S. government. Thanks to the separation of Church and State, Congress stayed away from defining what makes a church a church. The IRS, however, would have been happy to take their share from the collection plate if I didn't prove I was legitimate. They had a list of 14 criteria I had to meet to legally be considered a church.

Yes, I was ordained. Yes, we would have a recognized creed and form of worship. Yes, we had a distinct religious history. Yes, we would have an established place of worship—even if it was the back room of a bookstore—and yes, I would hold regular religious services. I had no problem checking off most of the items on the IRS list, but there was one matter over which I had no control: To be a recognized church, we had to have a regular congregation. *That* little rule left me staring, sleepless, at my bedroom ceiling.

What if nobody came?

The number one IRS requirement for a church to be recognized by the government was that it have a distinct legal existence. All I wanted was to bring people together in fellowship, but this daunting rule meant I had to be incorporated first. Corporations need a board of directors, articles of incorporation, and by-laws. If I hadn't wanted my church so badly, I would have gladly made a bonfire with all the paperwork that entailed.

Asking Nigel to be on the board was one of my better decisions. He knew the kinds of things to include in the by-laws, even if I didn't always listen to his suggestions. For my other board members, I chose a handful of good, kind people from my psychic development classes who I knew had really strong ethics. Like me, their hearts were truly into making the church something special, and I thanked my blessings for having their help.

One of the steps in becoming incorporated was choosing an official name. This wasn't something I could just try out for a while to see if I liked it. Once that name went on the record, that was it; set in stone. I gathered my board members and we started batting around ideas.

One thing we all agreed on was to officially call it a *center* instead of a church. That way, it would appeal to people coming to us from all faiths. Our second requirement was that the letters in the name add up to a favorable number. This was a numerology thing—something I'd picked up from the folks at the Open Mind. In numerology, every letter in the alphabet has a corresponding number. You try to come up with a sum that holds special meaning.

We settled on *The Journey Within, a Center for Spiritual Evolvement*. It was kind of wordy, but it reflected exactly what we wanted the church to be. Best of all, the letters added up to what was called a *master number*. The only catch with master numbers is they sometimes came with hard lessons. If I'd had any idea of the difficulties we'd face, I might have changed the name completely.

For now, my intuition told me to keep on plugging. Finally, after months of effort, the paperwork was done. Nigel had warned me that I needed to mail it on a favorable day. Now we were talking astrology, which Nigel was really into. With everything I had riding on this church, I wasn't taking any chances. I called him in England and asked him to cast a chart.

He just happened to be in New Jersey on the date the planets lined up in my favor. The two of us had made plans to go to the festival of San Genaro in Manhattan that day, so I took the paperwork with us. We sat in a parking lot in Little Italy and I signed the final form. It was the day before Easter—Holy Saturday. I sealed the envelope and dropped it in a blue mailbox on the street.

Just like that, it was done. I smiled nervously at Nigel, then we headed for the circus. We ended up in this *Ripley's Believe it or Not* place. There were all these bizarre characters that had Nigel in hysterics, but I barely saw them. All I could think about as we wandered past the two-headed babies and the Man Who Ate Swords was something far more unbelievable: *if everything went well, I was going to have my own church.*

* * *

I don't know if it was the stars, the numbers, or the fact that I did all the paperwork right, but one year after my first trip to Stanstead—in October of '96—I got the go-ahead from the government. *The Journey Within* could officially hold services.

By law, we were required to post an announcement in a public place to make us official, so we put up a flyer at the Wise Man. Nigel couldn't make it for the first service, but I knew I could count on my other board members and a handful of students from my classes. Still, I continued to have nightmares of standing there in front of a bunch of empty chairs.

I couldn't control who came, but I could at least plan a decent program. For me, that included doing away with the old worn-out hymns I'd been singing in churches for years. Every song has an energy of its own, and I wanted songs that would lift up our spirits and fill us with joy. There were plenty more upbeat, popular pieces that moved me, yet were still respectful of God.

I collected CDs that we could play on a boom box. My board helped me put together 3-ring binders with the printed lyrics. If people showed up expecting organ music, they were going to be mighty surprised to hear Wynona Judd and Elvis, instead. Those two, like others I chose, sang some beautiful, spiritual pieces. To me, what made a song sacred wasn't who sang it, but the feeling the words and music gave you deep down in your soul.

My very favorite song was a native American tune called *Where I Sit is Holy*. It started out with a haunting flute, followed by drums, then the soulful voice of Shaina Noll. Every time I heard the first few notes of that flute, I got an instant lift. The song had this energy that sent me straight to heaven. It started off slowly, then built and built to the point where I could just step right into the spirit people's world. I chose *Where I Sit is Holy* as the song I'd play to kick off the demonstration part of every service.

As the day approached, I checked all the details. We had a couple dozen folding chairs, and I found an old podium in the attic of the guest house at the retreat center that they said I could have. I was glad nobody asked why I needed it as I loaded it in my car. I was proud beyond words to be opening my own church, but I still didn't care to discuss it at work. That part of my life was personal.

The morning of my first service finally arrived. Rather than robes, I dressed in a simple dress with pearls. I was glad that Nigel couldn't see me—not because of the way I dressed—because I'd spent 300 bucks for his hypnosis session, and there I stood at that rickety old podium, shaking in my shoes.

I was nervous as hell, but excited at the same time. I tried not to be obvious as I scanned the room and counted heads. Twenty bright faces smiled back at me, most of them familiar. *Twenty non-empty chairs.* Twenty open-minded souls who gave up their Sunday morning to worship in my church. You didn't need to be a medium to feel the loving energy in that bookstore back room.

I began with an opening prayer, followed in true Spiritualist tradition by a healing session much like the one I'd sat through in Lily Dale's healing temple. Two women from my classes were Reiki practitioners—a universal healing methodology—and they volunteered to work with me during the service.

After that, I gave my homily. For the first service, I thought it would be appropriate to focus on the history of Spiritualism in our area. I stood at the podium and spoke about the legendary Reverend Harrison who was a true inspiration to me. I had to hold onto the podium as I talked—not because I was nervous … most of the shakes had disappeared as soon as I got rolling—but because the strip of wood on the podium that held my notes in place kept falling off.

After the homily, it was time for the heart of every Spiritualist service: the demonstration of mediumship. If the group before me was like those in other Spiritualist churches, half had come because other religions didn't have the answer for them. The other half were people who had lost a loved one and came in hopes of hearing from them. I didn't want to disappoint a soul.

I pushed the *play* button on the boom box and *Where I Sit is Holy* wafted through the tinny little speakers. All remaining jitters disappeared as the flute and powerful drumming raised me to another level. As the song ended, I looked out at the expectant faces and felt immediately drawn to a lady on the left side of the room.

I pointed at her and said, "The woman in the red blouse ... may I hear your name please?"

"Good morning," she said. "I'm Gail."

I tuned in to the energy in her voice and nodded. "Thank you. I need to tell you that there's an older man who comes to you ... he's standing right behind you."

She looked over her shoulder and gave a nervous laugh. "Right now?"

"Yes. I'm aware that this gentleman is from your father's side of the family. I feel he smoked quite a bit." I put my hand to my chest and said, "He's showing me problems with his heart. Does this mean anything to you?"

"If it's who I think it is," she said, "you're right on all accounts."

I nodded. "For whatever reason, I want to go down past Tom's River ... or maybe this is somebody with the name of Tom."

"My father lived in Tom's River," she said, clearly surprised.

"And your father is on the other side?"

"Yes, he is."

"Then this is your father ... and can I ask if he collapsed before he died?"

"Yes, he did."

"Okay, because my knees just buckled."

Gail looked stunned. Those around her looked back and forth between the two of us as if watching a ping pong match.

In a regular reading, I would have stayed with the spirit and given her more details, but in a demonstration, you have to keep things moving. I finished by telling Gail that her father came to her with love and wanted her to know he was fine.

I scanned the room and stopped at an unfamiliar face near the back.

"The woman in the blue sweater," I said, pointing. All heads turned and followed my finger. The lady glanced to each side, then pointed at herself with a questioning look.

"Yes, you," I said. "May I hear your name, please?"

"My name is Connie."

"Thank you, Connie, may I ask you, is your husband on the other side?"

"Yes," she said, looking at me with big owl eyes.

"Was he sick for awhile? Because I do have to say I feel he wasn't well."

She gave a few quick nods.

"Okay, he wants me to thank you for taking care of him. He really appreciates what you did for him at the end. He also feel badly that he left a lot on your shoulders."

The room was small enough that even from my spot at the podium I could see the tears in her eyes.

"Would I be correct in bringing the name Michael around you?"

Connie's hand flew to her mouth. "My husband was Michael."

I fought the urge to make a fist and shout *Yes!* Instead, I merely smiled and said, "Can I ask you, are you a bit of a pack rat?"

She laughed, embarrassed. "Yes, I am."

"Okay, because your husband visits you, and your house is quite cluttered, I have to say."

She scrunched her face.

"Nicely cluttered," I added quickly, "And he's showing me cats and a small dog, like a shitzsu."

"That's right."

"Okay." I tuned in closer and felt a squeezing sensation. "Your husband misses you and your home, and boy, he comes around with a big bear hug. Was he kind of stocky?"

"Yes," she gave a smile that was pure affection.

"Okay, because he's stocky again, and he gives you that big bear hug." I paused and squinted as an image passed through my mind. "You kiss a picture in your bedroom."

Connie caught her breath. "I do."

I nodded, feeling my own throat tighten. "He sees you kiss it goodnight, and you talk to this picture."

She pinched her lips together so tightly they were two thin white lines.

"And you should keep doing it," I told her, "because he hears every word you say."

"Thank you so much," Connie said. Her tears spilled onto her cheeks now, and I knew I'd see her back the next Sunday.

I continued in the same manner, focusing on two others I felt drawn to by the spirit people. I sensed that everyone in the room would have loved for me to call on them, but there was only so much time set aside for the demonstration. I concluded by reminding everyone that the sole purpose of mediumship is not to amaze people, but to prove the continuity of life. I liked to wow people as much as the next medium, but that wasn't the reason I did it.

Before the final prayer, I asked everyone to join me in song. A couple of people shifted uncomfortably in their chairs, and I felt their unease.

"I don't care how you sing," I said, "Just sing however you can, and sing *loud*."

I'd been waiting a long time to tell people that. Way back in the second grade, I wanted to sing in the school talent show. My second grade teacher—a real winner of a woman who never should have been entrusted with impressionable young minds—actually told me I wasn't good enough. That comment crippled me, and I vowed that no one would ever feel bad in my church for singing a little off-key.

To put everyone at ease, I turned on the boom box and cranked up the volume. A few people laughed when they figured out it was Elvis singing *Somebody Bigger Than You and I*. I smiled and sang along at the top of my lungs. By the end of the second chorus, Elvis had plenty of company.

After the service, I hung around a while, soaking up the positive comments. Then my trustees and I loaded up our cars with all the gear, and I drove over to my office. I sat at my desk and ran through every minute of the morning like a mental videotape. The sounds of those joyous voices echoed in my ears and bounced off the walls of the dungeon.

I sifted through the papers on my desk, then pushed them aside and leaned back—drained, but exhilarated. Unable to concentrate, I did the one thing I'd come to count on to calm my nerves. I closed my eyes, surrounded myself with love and light, and gave my thanks to God.

* * *

I would have been satisfied to continue with my congregation the size of that first service, but I guess that wasn't part of The Plan. We attracted more and more people who came to us looking for alternatives. When people from my old church found out we were holding weekly service rather than once a month like they were used to, they came on over to *The Journey Within*. Soon we were up to 60 people every Sunday.

Then the Bergen Record ran a full-page story about us. It was a real positive piece, talking about the healings and our Spiritualist principles. Not only did we fill all the chairs after that, we ran out of room in the parking lot. We could squeeze in 80 if we really crammed them in, but the room was crowded with half that. I'd never dreamed we'd add a second service, but within that first year, we had no choice.

I know that Nigel had a role in helping us grow. The first time he came to a service, he brought two special gifts. The first was a large round plaque with the SNU logo. He presented it during the service, then stood beside me to give demonstrations. A story about that, complete with a photo of us holding the plaque, ended up in the papers as well.

The second present was a big round candle that came with specific instructions. "Take this candle home and let it burn for 24 hours," he said. "Then put it somewhere safe, and don't burn it again until you have your own building."

I stared at him, almost afraid to let myself dream that big. But I did as he said: I put it in my bedroom where I could keep my eye on it, lighted the wick, and snuffed it out a full day later. I stared at the last wisp of smoke, not knowing when I'd light that candle again, if ever. It didn't hurt to dream, but I had to be a realist. It had taken a year's worth of effort to open *The Journey Within*, but only a minor investment in terms of money. It would take nothing less than a miracle to find the funds for a dedicated building.

Still, I'd come a long way in a short period of time. Just a few years earlier, I didn't even know what Spiritualism was. Now I was the pastor of my own Spiritualist church—however modest as it might be. I was helping others, bringing them comfort in a way few others could. Satisfied for now, I tucked the dream away in my bedroom closet, right beside the candle.

Chapter 19

Resistance

When I began to work as a medium, I had no idea how much grief existed in the world. I mean, sure, I had my share of pain growing up—physical as well as mental. Still, I never imagined how many people were walking around out there with a big aching anvil sitting smack in the middle of their chest.

I'd never met Amy before her priest sent her to see me, but you didn't need to be a psychic to sense the woman's pain. I had no idea who was waiting for her on the other side, but right away I sensed an old woman.

"I have a lady here who gives me the feeling of a grandmother. She's telling me her name was Mary and that she lived in the Bronx."

"Wow, that's right," Amy said softly, with that touch of awe I'd grown used to by now.

"I'm sensing that your grandmother was in a coma before she passed."

She shook her head in amazement. "Yes again."

I closed my eyes, and as I did so, I became aware of a small toddler standing beside the grandmother. The spirit girl pointed toward my sitter, Amy, and with a big smile said, "That's my mom!"

My heart sank. Amy's grief was greater than you'd expect from the loss of a grandmother. Now I knew why. The little girl couldn't have been more than two or three when she died. When I told Amy that her daughter was here, she burst into tears and cried out, "Sara!"

I stressed to Amy that Sara was smiling and healthy, and that calmed her down a bit. Sara helped me by sharing some happy memories that raised a bittersweet smile from her mother. The grandmother waited patiently, but she seemed to have a more important message to get across.

She's worried about your husband," I said. "She's telling me he can't get over your daughter's passing ... that he can't forgive himself. Is that right?"

Amy merely nodded and stared at her hands, twisting them over and over in her lap.

I asked Sara to show me how she died. I immediately sensed some kind of impact. Then, in a single burst, I saw the entire scene unfold. Sara had run out of the house to follow her daddy as he got in his truck. I could tell he didn't see her, and my stomach clenched as he started backing up. I described the heart-breaking scene to Amy, stopping short of the description of the big black wheels rolling over the fragile little body. I did the best I could to soften the image of her husband standing in the driveway, cradling his broken baby in his arms as she took her final breath.

I found it hard to breathe, myself. I'd never spoken with Amy except to set up the reading, yet in a matter of minutes I was in the deepest part of her soul. We cried together as I brought through the message that her little girl was whole now, standing hand-in-hand with her grandmother. And Sara had a special message to give to her father: That she knew he never meant to hurt her ... that she knew he loved her more than life itself, and that she loved him just as much in return.

I could see the effect this message from the other side had on my client. It truly touched her to have me—a complete stranger—describe the gut-wrenching memories that she kept hidden in her heart. I prayed that the evidence from the reading would help her husband walk through the darkness as well.

Carolyn came to me like Amy—overwhelmed with grief—but Carolyn wore hers like a suit of armor. She sat across from me with her arms crossed and her eyelids riveted shut, tough as frickin' nails.

Giving readings can really drain you, and some days I get tired. This was one of those days.

"Who's Darrin?" I asked without much of a preamble.

She flinched, but she didn't open her eyes. The look on her face came across as pure arrogance.

"You know," I said, "I'm not sure this is going to work today, because if you're not going to be receptive ... "

She heaved in a big breath and opened her eyes. We held each other's gaze for a moment, then she finally moved her lips.

"I'm sorry," she said, "but when you said the name Darrin, I just couldn't talk."

I sat there and waited, still uncomfortable with her energy. Carolyn uncrossed her arms, only to put her hands over her mouth. She left just enough space between her fingers to let her words slip out: "He was my son."

I softened right up from that, but I couldn't help her if she was going to keep a shield between us. I glanced toward the door. "I'm sorry, but I don't know if I'm the right reader for you."

"No," she lowered her hands and cupped them over her heart. "You don't understand. I'm Catholic. I go to Mass every day. It took everything I have to walk through your door. If you can't bring my son to me, I'll never give anyone else the chance."

Physically, I was beat, but that lady's pain went past my tired body and straight to my soul. It was almost as if the angels were testing me: *What're you gonna do, Janet?* In that moment I knew that I was holding Carolyn's heart in my hands, and that's not something I took lightly.

I forgot my fatigue and went on with the reading. When it was over, I wouldn't let her pay me. It's never about the money, but especially not when someone's that devastated. A grieving mother found some peace that day, and that was all the payment I needed.

Cindy's reading was a little different, but only because I did it over the phone. I don't have to be in the same room with someone to tap into their energy. I attune myself to their vibrations just by hearing their voice. I couldn't see Cindy's face, but that didn't make her grief any less tangible.

I closed my eyes and right away I saw two little spirits—a boy and a girl. I took a deep breath and shivered. This was gonna be bad.

"You lost a couple of kids," I said.

Her answer came through as a grunt.

I tuned in a little more and sensed there'd been a divorce. A really nasty one. Cindy confirmed this. Then, when I saw what happened next, I had to fight the urge to hang up the phone. What could I possibly say to this woman?

"Your husband had your children for a visit, didn't he?"

I could barely make out the weak "yes" on the other end of the line.

I reminded myself that Cindy already knew the outcome of the story. It was my job to give her the facts as I saw them—to prove to her that her kids were around by giving her the intimate details, no matter how painful.

"I'm seeing that your husband killed your two children." My voice was barely a whisper. Hers would not come out.

"Then he killed himself," I said, as a band of sorrow squeezed the remaining air from my chest.

Cindy was whimpering now, but the mewing noises lessened when I stressed how I knew her tragic story. The evidence came from her children, themselves. They were standing right in front of me.

I asked the kids to give me some details to show their mother that I wasn't just reading her mind. They really came through for me, naming their favorite toys and describing the bedtime ritual they'd enjoyed each night with their mom. Best of all, they gave me a new image for Cindy to hold in her heart: that of her two young children playing happily in the Summerland, as they called it, and blowing her kisses from a field of yellow daisies.

By the end of the call, Cindy's voice had regained its strength. "I need you to know something."

"What's that?" I asked warily.

"If you hadn't told me what you did tonight, I was going to kill myself."

I realized then that no one other than a psychiatrist, or maybe a family doctor, had the kind of access to a person's soul that a medium did. My clients told me things they wouldn't share with anyone else ... things they kept inside, if only to spare themselves further pain.

I've always been a little guarded thanks to how I grew up, so getting that close to people took some getting used to. I'd leave the really heavy readings and be totally wiped out, barely able to think. I learned real quick that I had to have some balance in my life. No one could take a steady diet of that kind of grief without having some way to vent. I'd pick up the phone and give Nigel a hard time or call my girlfriends and shout, "Road trip!"

I mean, when drowning people constantly call on you to save them, how else are you gonna keep from sinking, yourself?

* * *

Some of my closest friends started out as students in the school of mediumship I put together with Nigel. I figured if I was going to have a church, I was going to need other mediums. I started the school right about the same time we had our first service. Sometimes we held classes in the big room across from my office. Other times we rented this million dollar B&B on Blueberry Point in Milford.

The place sat on a private lake in 450 acres of woods. We'd do our training during the day and build big bonfires on the beach after sunset. Because we were a church, the folks gave us the key and said, "see you when you're done." For some reason, our students liked Blueberry Point better than the dungeon.

Nigel helped me set the curriculum for the school. I have to admit that getting him involved was kind of selfish on my part. I figured I could go to England and have him as my teacher for a mere two hours a day, or I could bring him to New Jersey and hog him for a full eight hours.

After we started the school, he came to the States more often. He came three to four times a year and stayed for a month each time. He was as demanding here as he was in Stansted, and unfortunately, not everyone cared for his style.

"He doesn't pat us on the back enough," one girl complained.

"You just don't understand who you're learning from," I said. "You're being trained by one of the best in the world."

But as tough as he was, we always had a good time. It was part of that balance thing. The ones who stuck with us and became my dearest friends were the ones who knew how to laugh.

Like most of our students, Sharon Siubis heard about *The Journey Within* through an article in the local paper. I wanted to attract people from different religions, and with Sharon, I got a little of everything. She attended a Baptist church as a kid, but when her family moved they switched to Presbyterian. She ended up marrying a Catholic and went to work for a Jewish company. She told me once that she never felt right in any church until she came to mine. With us, she finally found a home.

My friend Carole Boyce was a Catholic through and through. Her kids went to Catholic school and she even served on their board. She went to Mass regularly and would go through the motions, but she always felt like something was missing. One day she got up the nerve to attend one of my services at the Wise Man. She told me later that she sat there watching me from the back of the room and thought, *Holy shit! She's talking to dead people!*

But it was my homily that got to Carole more than my demonstration that day. I don't remember the specifics, but I'm sure I talked about love. Carole said she felt as if I were speaking directly to her, and she never went back to her church. The priests and nuns got upset when they didn't see her at Mass and they cornered her at her kids' school.

"I've been going to another church," she told them.

They looked a little miffed and said, "We hope at least it's Catholic."

"No," Carole said, "It's a Spiritualist church."

They stared at her, stunned, then said, "We'll have to talk about this."

The next day she got a call from the monsignor. "I need to discuss the state of your soul," he said. Carole—bless her heart—told him that her soul had never been in better shape.

Carole became my secretary, and later one of my ministers. She put in more hours in the dungeon than at her real job with a dentist. Sharon turned out to be a darned good medium. I made her one of my ministers, too, and today she's my assistant pastor. Both of them became the girls I'd call when I needed to blow off some steam.

We never lacked for laughs when the three of us got together, but we shared one memory in particular that always got us going. It happened during one of the classes in Brookhaven. The chairs were arranged in a big circle in the larger room. Nigel had the lead, and he was going over the definitions of some basic metaphysical terms.

"An *apport*," he said, "is the sudden materialization of an object through the powers of a medium."

A few people scribbled notes as he talked.

"A *poltergeist*," he went on, "is a spirit who is often up to no good and tends to disturb the lives of others."

A woman sitting next to Sharon raised her hand. "What's the difference between a poltergeist and a ghost?"

"A very good question." Nigel removed his glasses. "A ghost is generally not a mischievous spirit—merely one who likes to visit a particular place."

The woman nodded in understanding.

Just then, a big old roach fell on her lap out of nowhere. Everyone gasped and gaped at her in horror, but none so horrified as Nigel. In the years since then, the girls and I have spent many an hour arguing over which was funnier: the look on Nigel's face or the poor woman's reaction. There she sat, staring at this big furry bug on her legs. Then she pointed down and said, "Look! It's an *apport!*"

* * *

I never cared much for the dungeon, but that incident with the roach gave me the push I needed to look for something better. I heard about a place for rent nearby. It was big enough for everything we needed: I could have my office and we could hold our classes and services all in one place, without having to lug our gear back and forth every Sunday. All that, and it even had windows.

I approached the landlord to see if we could afford it.

"What do you want it for?" he asked.

I told him we were a small church group.

"What kind of church?"

I wanted to say, *What difference does it make?* but I kept my voice even as I explained that we were Spiritualists.

He squinted at me. "What's that mean?"

I gave him the short version: that we believed in life after death, and that it was possible to communicate with those on the other side.

He put his hands on his hips and asked, "Who gives you the right to believe that?"

"Well ... God," I said.

"I don't think so, lady." He crossed his arms then, effectively erecting a barrier between us, and asked, "Don't you believe in Satan? Aren't you afraid?"

His words took me back to a demonstration I'd given just a few days earlier at a Barnes and Noble. A member of my congregation worked in the store and helped me set it up. I got a really good crowd, and things were going great, when this big guy stood and said, "You people are all going to Hell!"

I couldn't just ignore him, so I politely asked him to have a seat. That only made him more angry.

"You don't know the Bible!" he declared.

"I know the Bible better than you think," I said as politely as possible. "Jesus said we can do what he did. If you'd like to discuss it with me afterwards, I'll be happy to do so, but please don't disrupt this public demonstration."

He acted as if he didn't hear me and started quoting verses from the New Testament.

"Sir, this isn't fair to the other people here," I said. "Would you please take a seat?"

Luckily, he backed down, but not before someone called Security.

And there I was, less than a week later, dealing with another Neanderthal. I tried hard not to get discouraged. I wanted to tell him to go and talk to clients like Amy or Carolyn or Cindy—to ask them if *they* thought I was flirting with the devil. But I knew better than to try and reason with the guy, especially when it became clear that he wasn't going to let me have the property.

I shared the episode with a friend over lunch the following weekend. Julie had initially come to me for a reading and was now a faithful member of the church.

"So what are you going to do now?" she asked.

I pushed my food around my plate with my fork. "I don't know. There's a closed-up bank for sale in Brookhaven that would be really great for us, but we can't afford to buy it."

"That's your dream, isn't it? To have your own building."

I gave a little snort. "Yeah, but that's all it's gonna be at this rate: a dream."

Julie laid her napkin on the table and sat back. "I don't know, Janet. I love *The Journey Within*. I feel so comfortable there. You guys deserve better than the back room of a bookstore."

"Thanks, but we don't exactly have money just falling from the sky. Only the roaches do that around here."

Julie had heard the story and she laughed. "Well, I believe in your dream, Janet, and I'm going to give you $50,000 to make that dream come true."

"Get outta here!" I had to grip my fork to keep from dropping it.

"Would that be okay?" she asked, and flashed me a beautiful smile.

"Oh my God!" I said, picturing the candle sitting on my bedroom shelf, just waiting to be lighted again. "Oh my God!"

Julie laughed and patted me on the arm. "I take that as a *yes*."

* * *

With Julie's generous gift, we had enough for a down-payment on the bank. I discussed it with the board, and we decided to move ahead. We made an offer, and I held my breath until the answer came back from the realtor: The sellers had agreed to our price.

We signed the contract and started making plans. I could barely concentrate as I worked in the kitchen at the retreat center, all the while picturing where to put the podium and how to arrange the chairs. There would be plenty of space for classrooms and a nice big office for me. An office with a window.

Then I got a phone call from the bank—not the one we were trying to buy, but the one we'd applied to for our loan. They liked our big down payment, but not the fact that we were only two years old. Without a credit history, they were unwilling to back us.

Julie, Sharon, Carole, Nigel, my board—heck, the whole congregation—everyone commiserated with me. They wanted new facilities as much as I did. We'd just had a couple of cases of bad luck, that was all. We decided to fall back on plan A and find a place to rent. After all, we agreed, *the third time's a charm.*

Not too much later I noticed a "for rent" sign in the front window of a store-front just down Main Street from my office in Brookhaven. I knew the building well from the outside. Part of it was occupied by a school for performing arts. I peered inside, but needed a better look. The sign listed a Mr. Howard Jenkins as the realtor. I copied down his number and hurried back to my office to give him a call.

The next day I met Mr. Jenkins, who led me through the spaces. We were joined by Jerry Hancock, the leasing agent who acted as a sort of building manager, overseeing property throughout the town for various owners. I tried to keep my excitement in check as I looked around. At $1800 a month, it was pricey, but well within our budget thanks to Julie's generosity.

"So what do you want it for?" Jerry asked after I'd checked everything out.

Here we go again, I thought, then told him we were a Spiritualist church.

"A church, huh?" He stroked his chin and looked around the big room. "About how many people would be in here at any one time?"

I wasn't sure if it was safe to breathe yet, but I answered his question.

"Plenty of room in here for that many," he said.

I smiled, and decided to go out on a limb. "We were hoping to have separate rooms for a classroom and an office."

He ran his eyes across the ceiling, then tapped his knuckles in several places on the wall. "I suppose we could put a couple of walls up and put in some doors."

"What would that entail?" I asked warily.

He stuck out his lower lip and thought for a moment. "Probably take four to six months to do the work. I have a good contractor I work with, and he'd take care of all the permits."

"Yeah, but what would it cost?"

He scanned the room again. "Well, I suppose I could cover the cost of the renovations if you sign at least a three year lease."

I let out a little hum. It was now almost three years since *The Journey Within* had opened its doors. I expected the church to be around a lot longer than that, so a three-year lease would be okay. The fact that he wasn't going to charge for the changes was almost too hard to pass up.

"You got a deal," I said, and held out my hand.

* * *

With our new spaces just down the street from the dungeon, I took every chance I could to stop by and watch the progress. We started paying rent the day I signed the lease, and as I watched the workers I sent them silent prayers to move a little faster. As the 2 x 4s went up, then the dry wall, and finally some fresh white paint, I started lining up helpers to move in all our things.

Jerry Hancock was helpful every step of the way. On the day we were due to take possession, he escorted the township fire marshal for the final inspection. Everything checked out fine and the place looked great. All that remained was to get our certificate of occupancy from Brookhaven's zoning and construction officer.

I was in my office down the street when I got a call at 5:00 from Jerry. He'd waited half an hour for the zoning officer, but the guy failed to show up. I was more confused than worried.

"What's the problem?" I asked.

"I don't know," Jerry said. "But because you're a public group, you can't move in without that certificate. Why don't you come down here in the morning and we'll go to his office together?"

"In the morning?" I groaned. "We were supposed to move in tonight!"

"I'm sorry, Janet, but it's too late at this point. I doubt anyone over there works past five."

I spent the evening making phone calls to the people who were supposed to help us move in. I told everyone not to worry—that I'd clear everything up in the morning. They gave me their assurances in return, but I had a bad feeling about this zoning and construction officer. I went to sleep repeating my mantra: *The third time's a charm ... third time's a charm ...*

I met Jerry the next morning at 9:00. Brookhaven's town hall sat at the end of a short side street just around the corner from the dungeon. The zoning officer had his office in a trailer out back.

Jerry and I introduced ourselves and shook hands with Anthony Marino. He was about my height and burly, with dark, slicked-back hair. He had pock-marked cheeks that probably came from a bad case of acne a few decades earlier.

Jerry told him that we'd come for the certificate of occupancy for the space at 525 Main Street. He told Mr. Marino that they'd had a 4:30 appointment the day before, and that our church group had hoped to move in by today. I waited for some kind of excuse as to why he stood us up. Instead, Marino looked at me and asked, "What kind of church is it?"

I stiffened, wondering if I was stuck in some kind of bizarre time warp. "We're *The Journey Within*, a Spiritualist church that's associated with the Spiritualists' National Union in Great Britain."

"Spiritualist, huh?" Marino frowned. "What's that stand for? I mean, do you believe in God?"

I had to remind myself how much I had resting on the certificate of occupancy. "Yes, we do. In fact, I used to be a Catholic nun."

"No kidding? A nun?" He gave me a once-over, then asked, "So what's the makeup of this church?"

"Excuse me?" It took me a second for his question to register.

"You know ... like, what kind of people go there? They white? Black? What?"

I glanced at Jerry who made no perceptible reaction. "We're an older congregation," I said, "mostly white, with about 10 percent people of color." Then I couldn't help but add, "But what does that have to do with whether or not we can occupy the building?"

He waved his hand as if his whole line of questions was perfectly normal. "I'm dealing with the same kind of situation over in Kent with a Korean group that's giving me all kinds of problems."

I waited for him to ask me how many people we expected to put in the rented spaces ... how many square feet we had ... *anything* even remotely relevant to zoning issues and the certificate of occupancy. Instead, he shuffled some papers on the counter between us and said, "I'll get back to you, but I'm going to have to make some calls about this."

Yeah, I thought, *to the mayor and the rest of your good old boys.*

Jerry held the door and let me go first as we stepped outside the trailer. Once the door was closed, I turned to him and said, "Can you believe he was asking those questions?"

He shook his head. "Incredible, in this day and age."

We started walking back toward Main Street and I asked, "So what do we do now?"

Jerry shook his head. " Can't do much except wait."

I waited all day, unable to think about anything but the zoning and construction officer's inappropriate questions. That evening I made the same round of phone calls that I'd made the night before. Each person I told about the meeting in the trailer reacted with the same sense of outrage and distress that had been boiling inside me all day. All we wanted to do was help and comfort people and worship as we chose in our own building. Why did this have to be so hard?

The next morning I decided to stop by the rental property on my way to work. With any luck, Jerry would be there with the certificate of occupancy, and we could move in later that day. I found a parking spot on Main Street, less than half a block down. I got out of the car and started walking, but stopped when I noticed something different about the door.

As I got closer, I saw that there were big stickers pasted on the glass and across the door frame in such a way as to block anyone from opening it. My heart sped up when I stepped near enough to read what was unmistakably a warning: Anyone foolish enough to cross that virtual picket line would be in violation of state orders and slapped with a great big fine by the town of Brookhaven.

Oh my God, I thought.

I read the stickers a second time.

Oh my God.

I had no idea what to do—how to proceed. I thought about making yet another round of phone calls to my board and all my friends, but I didn't know how I'd get through it. That would make three times in as many days that I'd called them with bad news and no answers to their questions.

I'd been kidding myself to think that the third time was a charm. Brookhaven was a small town, with a typical small-town mentality. It was 1998—almost '99, and even though the rest of the world was looking forward to the new millennium, I felt as if I'd stepped backwards in time. For as much as people understood about Spiritualism, it might as well have been the 1800s.

No, I thought, as I walked slowly back to my car, our third attempt to find a new home was most definitely not a charm. We had it wrong from the beginning, I realized then. The truth, at least in Brookhaven, was that bad things came in threes.

Chapter 20

Inalienable Rights

When I saw the warning stickers slapped all over what was supposed to be my new church, I pretty much panicked. I had no idea what to do, but one thing I knew for sure: Anthony Marino's questions were way out of line. The fact that we were barred from occupying our spaces was based on one man's prejudices, not on whether or not it was safe for us to meet there.

My mind may have been muddled, but I had enough sense to seek professional advice. I went to see a lawyer whose office was right there on Main Street—a Mr. J. Wesley Fenton. Hearing myself repeat the questions that Marino asked me made my blood boil all over again. To his credit, Mr. Fenton didn't rub his hands together and get that dollar-signs-in-the-eyes look. Instead, he advised me to talk to the borough administrator and explain what had happened.

It took a few days to get an appointment. When I finally got in, I told the man I had an issue with the zoning and construction officer. I explained that Mr. Marino had asked me inappropriate questions having more to do with the make-up of our church and our beliefs than whether we could safely occupy the building. The administrator's response?

"Go talk to a lawyer."

I went back to Mr. Fenton's office. He admitted that a case like ours was out of his league and recommended an attorney who specialized in civil liberties. I wasn't comfortable with all this legal stuff and called a meeting of my board. Together we decided that we had to trust other people to help us.

Until I had the run-in with Marino, I never noticed how many lawyers disliked their first names. Either that, or you weren't allowed to practice law unless your name started with an initial. Our new lawyer, Mr. T. Jeffrey Parker, took a lot of notes as I went over the conversation with Marino that by now was indelibly stamped on my brain.

"What you want is resolution to your problem," T. Jeffrey said, in a profound assessment of the obvious. Then he added something that I never expected to hear from a lawyer: "And nobody should ever go for a lawsuit if there's another way to resolve it."

He recommended that I take the matter to the monthly meeting of the town council. At the end of their sessions the council held an open forum in which members of the public could address issues of concern. Our lawyer was right: it was an appropriate step and the proper venue in which to air our complaint, yet I felt jittery just thinking about the potential confrontation. The mayor would be there, along with all the other big wigs in town. I didn't mind standing up in front of my congregation or giving a demonstration of mediumship, but going head to head with the town leaders was a whole different ball game.

I stared at the calendar on Mr. Parker's desk. The date was March 16th. The town council had held their meeting just days before; the next one was now weeks away. We'd hoped to move into our new spaces back in February. Now we wouldn't get to meet with the council until April. All this time our spaces were sitting empty, yet we were paying the full $1800 in rent every month.

I carried the pressure of the stressful situation everywhere I went like a briefcase full of bricks: at work, at home, giving readings in the dungeon, but most especially at church on Sundays. On that day I lugged my stress along with the boom box, CDs, songbooks, and all our other gear from the dungeon to the Wise Man. There I faced my congregation from the rickety podium, knowing we should have been in our own building months ago.

The only saving grace was the faces looking back at me. There I saw understanding, sympathy, and undisguised indignation. There wasn't a single member of *the Journey Within* who didn't share my outrage. They each took as much offense as I did that we weren't allowed to claim what was rightfully ours due to one man's perceptions of who we were and what we believed.

April arrived and with it so did Nigel. He came to teach in the school of mediumship, but I took advantage of his presence and asked him to address the congregation. I knew from hearing him recite the poem in the chapel at Stansted that Nigel could hold people spellbound. This was a man who had studied great speakers like Winston Churchill and Margaret Thatcher. He proved to me on that Sunday before the council meeting that he hadn't lost his touch.

"This is the United States of America!" he bellowed. "The land of the free!"

I couldn't help but be struck by the irony. The man who stood before my congregation preaching to them about their cherished freedoms came from the very country so many early Americans had fled from in search of religious tolerance.

"You have a wonderful Constitution," Nigel said. "You must fight to uphold the rights it grants you!"

The energy in the room crackled. I half expected to hear someone shout, "Amen, brother!"

Then Nigel lowered his voice and slowed down the cadence. People leaned in, hanging on his words as he wrapped up his sermon. "Freedom means being in control, but not being controlled. Religious freedom, which operates within the confines of any country's laws, is not a threat, but an opportunity for that country to show the world a way forward which is both tolerant and flexible."

His words had the desired effect. I don't know how many people usually attended Brookhaven's town council meetings, but the Wednesday after Nigel addressed the congregation they must have set a record. The place was standing-room-only, thanks to the presence of my board and forty members of my congregation—forty faithful friends who weren't about to sit at home and let me face the lions alone.

Even with so much support, I grew more and more nervous as the open forum session approached. I wiped my wet palms on my dress as I ran through all the tricks Nigel had taught me about overcoming my fears. None of them seemed to help as I stared at Mayor Arthur Teasdale, his lawyer, and the other council members gazing back from their thrones.

The open forum began and I wondered how I was going to get from my chair to the microphone, let alone discuss what I'd gone there to say. I clung to Nigel with my eyes, wasting my wishes that he could take my place. We had discussed his position ahead of time: He had plenty to say, but being a non-citizen, he felt it best that he not speak up.

He gave me a nod of encouragement, and I dragged myself to my feet. An eternity later I stood at the front of the room with nothing between me and the council members' table but a microphone stand.

"Good evening," I said, and jerked at the sound of my own voice amplified throughout the room. "I'm Janet Nohavec from—" I had to pause to unstick my tongue from my lips. Every drop of moisture had evaporated from my mouth somewhere between my seat and where I now stood.

I took a deep breath and leaned in closer to the mike. Someone behind me cleared their throat. When I glanced over my shoulder, my arms broke out in goose bumps. Behind me in that council room my entire congregation had risen to their feet. I'd thought I was standing alone, but there they stood—forty-strong—in a show of unmistakable solidarity.

I turned back to the microphone and said proudly, "I'm Janet Nohavec, from *The Journey Within, a Center for Spiritual Evolvement.* I come before you because we feel there's been an injustice done here."

I went on to describe the meeting with Anthony Marino. I relayed his questions about our beliefs and our racial make-up and the fact that he had made a determination about the occupancy of our building based on my answers to those questions. I stressed that Mr. Marino had failed to ask any questions pertaining to actual zoning or construction issues.

"It's not our intention to cause a problem," I said, "This is the town we want to be in. We simply want to move into the space we rented months ago."

When I was finished, I stepped aside. Several members of my congregation were residents of Brookhaven, and they approached the microphone next. My heart threatened to burst as they praised me and the good things *The Journey Within* had done for them and the community.

Just when I thought everyone who wanted to speak had done so, one of our youngest members, 10-year-old Davy Martin, stepped forward.

"This really makes me sad," he said, stretching on his toes to reach the mike. "My mom taught me that in America we have freedom of religion. She said we're allowed to believe whatever we want to believe."

Someone in the gallery coughed. The members of the council shifted in their seats.

I don't know what I expected would happen that evening. If I thought the council would hear our story and tell us we could move right in, I was dreaming. Instead, we trooped out of the meeting with nothing but the assurance that they were aware of our problem and were "looking into it."

I wanted to shout, *You don't understand! We're paying rent on this place! We're stuck in the back of a bookstore and a roach-infested basement while you guys look into it!* But of course I couldn't say those things. The council and Anthony Marino held our future in their hands.

Several reporters stopped me in the hallway outside the meeting room. I answered their questions as unemotionally as I could, trying my best to stick to the facts. I followed my congregation to the parking lot and thanked them all for coming. I often wonder if they knew how much their support meant to me that night.

I walked with Nigel back to my car.

"What did you think?" I asked.

He shook his head. "Sadly, I did not witness the religious tolerance and freedom from the mayor and the council that I've always associated with your country."

I shook my head, embarrassed by my fellow citizens, until I remembered that not everyone had shamed me that evening.

"I can't believe everyone stood up with me like that."

"It was quite the show of support, wasn't it?"

"Your talk really fired them up on Sunday."

"Perhaps," he said, "but it took some pluck to get up there tonight, Janet. One could see that they respect you tremendously."

I waved off his praise and asked, "Did you hear the things they said?"

"Yes, and with such conviction!" Nigel agreed. "Your founding fathers would have been proud."

* * *

The next day the local paper ran an article about the town council meeting and the flap with our church. It felt strange to see my name in print about something other than my mediumship. I read the words, but felt no more assured than I had the night before. I felt slightly better when I learned that at least one city official was on my side: "The church's attempt to move into the mall was supported by Chamber of Commerce president Alfred Harper. Nohavec, he said, has maintained a church office at another address on Main Street where she is considered a 'very good tenant.'"

Whatever good feelings Mr. Harper engendered were wiped out by the reality of the situation when I read the statement I'd made to the reporter: "The goal down the road is to have a little white chapel somewhere, but now the congregation is stuck paying rent for space in Brookhaven it is unable to use."

If the town council was looking into our case, we didn't see any evidence of their efforts. As the days passed, I talked with my board almost daily. I relied especially heavily on one member, Joey Vallani, as we tried to figure out what to do. Joey was a big bear of a guy—a tough Italian with a slew of tattoos, but to me he was a doll: caring, supportive … the nicest guy in the world. As the president of the stage handlers union, Joey was used to handling tough issues.

"We gotta fight this, even if we lose everything." Joey said.

I went back to see my attorney, who wrote some strong letters on our behalf. In one response, a council member wrote that we'd been denied occupancy because they were worried about the place being a fire hazard—that people might not be able to get out in case of emergency. That didn't make any sense to me or to our lawyer.

"I know I advised against a lawsuit," he said, "but at this point, I'd say you have a good case. I recommend turning this over to the state Division of Civil Rights. You don't want to issue a lawsuit yourself, but if the state thinks you have a case, they'll file on your behalf."

My heart sank as I saw more months of rent going straight down the drain. "How long will that take?" I asked.

"Could take a while, and I have to be honest with you, Janet, if you go forward with this, it's going to cost you quite a lot in legal fees."

I took a deep breath. Joey Vallani's words echoed in my ears: … *even if we lose everything.*

The entire board had agreed with Joey: this was a fight for what was right, for what we believed in. But did we really want to watch all the money Julie had given us get eaten up by expenses? Lawsuits didn't always favor the one who was right. I'd watched my father go under when he sued our neighbor. We'd ended up in the street.

"What would we be suing for?" I asked Mr. Parker, swallowing past the lump in my throat.

"Again, it's not you who would be suing," he clarified, "but the State of New Jersey. I can tell you they'd probably seek compensation for the funds you spent to lease the building. The complaint would be based on two things: the ability to practice a chosen religion and discrimination against race and color."

Hearing him state our case, I would have recommended the same course of action to anyone who came to me with a similar complaint. I had discussed it with Joey and the board until there was nothing more to discuss. We were all in agreement: we would fight to the end. Still, there was one last thing I had to do before I agreed to my lawyer's advice.

I looked at T. Jeffrey and said, "I'll get back to you."

I went straight to the dungeon and closed my door. I sat in my chair, closed my eyes, and said, "*St. Therese, I need your help.*"

My favorite saint always said that if you prayed to her, she'd answer you with roses. I asked her to send me a sign if we were meant to proceed with the lawsuit. The next day I picked up the newspaper, and the headline jumped right out at me: *Lynn Rose Opens Bakery on Walnut Street.* I glanced at the clouds and smiled. I smiled again when the mail arrived that afternoon. In it was a note from an old friend—on a card decorated with roses.

I picked up the phone and called my lawyer.

Chapter 21

Taking a Stand

T. Jeffrey was right: the New Jersey Division of Civil Rights agreed that we had a "viable and cognizable cause of action for a violation of the Federal State Civil Rights Act." In other words: we had a good case. In May of '99 they filed a suit on behalf of the Journey Within against the town of Brookhaven. The complaint sounded as serious as it was: "that the respondents (the town and Marino) refused to issue to Janet Nohavec a Certificate of Occupancy for her church because of the color of her congregation (black) and because of her creed (Spiritualist) in violation of the New Jersey Law Against Discrimination."

I felt no urge to celebrate as I read the paperwork. In fact, I felt sick to my stomach. The only thing that made me feel better was the bottom line—the part about seeking "compensatory damages for economic loss." Our bills were only growing bigger.

The law suit was big news in Brookhaven. Once again the papers told our story, but this time they included a quote by Anthony Marino: "I take great exception to the accusations made about me by Rev. Nohavec," he said.

I continued reading, aware of my pounding heart. "During the meeting with the pastor and the renting agent in February, Marino said he attempted to ascertain the makeup of the congregation solely to determine how many individuals would be meeting at the site on Main Street, how often, and whether they might require special access accommodations depending on their age and whether or not they might be handicapped."

I picked up the phone and called Joey. "Did you read what he said?"

"Yeah, I read it."

"He didn't ask anything remotely related to those questions!"

"I believe you Janet. So what about the leasing agent that went with you? You said he heard it all, right?"

Suddenly, I relaxed. Joey was right. Jerry Hancock had been standing right beside me. We specifically talked about Marino's inappropriate questions after we left the trailer. Unfortunately, the reporter hadn't interviewed my sole witness, but I promised Joey that I'd make sure the Department of Civil Rights talked to Jerry.

Whoever it was that said "The wheels of justice turn slowly" knew what they were talking about. Two months passed before the state assigned a docket number and an investigator to our case. I wanted to cry when the guy called me to let me know he was "looking into it."

At that point it became clear that the whole fiasco could drag on for months. We had signed the lease based on our "ability to occupy." Thanks to the lack of a certificate of occupancy, we never got that ability. In the summer of '99, we were released from the lease. We'd gone through all those months of renovations and all that rent money, only to end up right where we started: in the back room of the Wise Man bookstore.

A few weeks after we got out of the lease, my friend Sharon called me.

"Did you hear who they rented the spaces to?"

"Who?" I asked, instantly on guard.

"A group of handicapped kids."

"You gotta be kidding me."

"I'm serious."

"But the town said they wouldn't rent to us because we couldn't get out in an emergency!"

"What does that tell you?" Sharon said.

It told me what I'd known from the start: The whole situation was one big mess.

Without new spaces to move into, we were fighting our case now strictly on principle. I turned two more pages in the calendar before I heard anything from the Division of Civil Rights. The letter, dated September 12th, requested that I meet with them for a fact-finding conference in Paterson. They hoped to "define and clarify the issues ... to obtain evidence, and to ascertain whether there was a basis for resolution of the complaint." They set the date of the meeting for November 12th. November ... two more months away.

I closed my eyes and called on St. Therese.

* * *

Picture your favorite law show on TV ... the ones where the lawyers in their fancy suits sit at a big, long table and talk in somber tones. That pretty much describes the setting for the fact-finding conference with the state's investigator. I gave my testimony, glad for the pitcher of water in front of me. It's hard to talk when your mouth is full of cotton.

Afterwards, I talked to the investigator off the record. "What about Jerry Hancock—the leasing agent who was with me when I met with Marino? Have you talked to him yet?"

The investigator shook his head. "I'm afraid he's not going to be any help to our case."

"What do you mean?" I asked. Jerry—my only witness—was my one big hope.

"He claims he didn't hear anything."

"What?" I reeled as if I'd been slapped. "He was right there! We talked about it afterwards. I remember my exact words: *'Can you believe he was asking those questions?'* And Jerry said it was incredible in this day and age!"

The investigator shrugged. "I'm sorry, but he's not talking now."

I walked back to my car, crushed. On the drive home I figured out what happened. The property on Main Street was only one of several buildings Jerry Hancock managed. He probably thought he'd lose business if he stood up for me and told the truth.

Without Jerry Hancock's testimony, it was my word against Marino's. To people who didn't know me, I was the pastor of some wacky New Age church. Anthony Marino was a respected city official. Until Jerry backed down, I thought we had a chance to win the case. Without him, all bets were off.

* * *

It's just as well we got out of the lease on Main Street when we did. After the fact-finding conference in November, we heard nothing conclusive in December, January, February, or March. Spring turned into summer and we still had no decision. I didn't know what they were doing over there in Paterson, but the case dragged on into the Fall and past November—a full year from the time I sat down with the investigators.

Finally, in December of 2000, T. Jeffrey Parker called me to his office.

He held up a piece of paper embossed with an official-looking seal. "We finally heard from the Division of Civil Rights."

My heart sped up. "A decision?"

"Yes."

"And?" I asked, wondering how long he was going to drag this out.

"Well," T. Jeffrey said, "It seems the respondents argued that the Division didn't have the jurisdiction to adjudicate that a municipal zoning ordinance is discriminatory."

I squinted at him. "Could you put that in English, please?"

He cleared his throat and looked down, then back up at me. "The complaint was dismissed for lack of jurisdiction."

I was still confused, but one word jumped right out at me. "Dismissed?"

"I'm afraid so."

He handed me the letter and I scanned it, but nothing made sense. It was as if my brain refused to interpret the words on the page. "But why? I don't understand."

For the first time since I hired him, T. Jeffrey looked embarrassed. "Well, as you and I have discussed, it's unlawful for any municipality or officer of a municipality to regulate land use or housing based on race, creed, color, or otherwise …"

"I'm with you," I said and prompted him with my hand to go on.

"But Brookhaven's lawyers showed that any person claiming to be aggrieved by unlawful discrimination shall enforce the law by private right of action in Superior Court."

I must have looked as confused as I felt, because T. Parker spelled it out for me.

"The Division of Civil Rights didn't have the right to sue. Only New Jersey's Superior Court could have done that on your behalf."

"You gotta be kidding me."

"I wish I were."

"You mean that after all this time, we lost on a technicality?"

"Technically? Yes."

"Not because of the questions Marino asked me, but because somebody didn't do their homework about who should file our case?"

"I'm afraid so."

"Oh my God." I covered my face with my hands.

I thought about the months of worry and all the money we'd wasted. We'd racked up $18,000 in legal costs and lost rent. Eighteen *thousand* dollars that was supposed to buy us the little white chapel of my dreams.

I lowered my hands and said, "So what are our options?"

"At this point you need to decide if you want to take it to Superior Court."

I shook my head without even thinking. I would talk about it with Joey and the board, but after our two-year nightmare, I held no more illusions of winning. All along I'd had the sneaking suspicion that the town was trying to bankrupt us. If we took them to Superior Court, bankruptcy was a distinct possibility.

The board agreed with me, as I knew they would. We were all tired. It was time to leave the nastiness behind us and focus our full attention on each other and our Spiritualist principles. I was willing to forgo further action, but there was one thing I'd never forget: Not once through all that turmoil did anyone in my church say, *Did he really ask you those questions?*

So we continued on at the Wise Man on Sundays, and I gave my readings in the dungeon. We rented the B&B at Blueberry Point for our classes when Nigel couldn't stand the roaches any longer. Then, one day, when I thought I'd put the lawsuit to rest, I picked up the mail for the church. There, at the bottom of the stack, was a large manila envelope with a return address from the Division of Civil Rights.

I dropped the rest of the mail on my desk and tore into the flap, half afraid of what I'd find. The cover letter was written by a clerk. It explained that she was tying up loose ends and had found some correspondence from my case. She was sending me copies as a courtesy.

I leafed through the papers, giving a quick scan to each of the pages. I was familiar with most of the documents until I came to the last piece of paper. When I saw the signature at the bottom, I did a double take. The letter, addressed to Mayor Teasdale, was signed by Anthony Marino. I raced through the letter, then went back and read it more slowly, digesting every word to make sure I wasn't mistaken.

"Yes, I asked her what the makeup of the congregation was," he wrote. "*As the Construction Official, I think I had the right to ask that question. How do I know if these people were drug addicts being cured, people on parole, wife beaters, ax murderers, etc.?*"

I stared at the letter. After Jerry Hancock clammed up, I had nothing to go on but my word. Now, in my hand I held Anthony Marino's admission that his line of questioning had gone exactly where I said it had. I sank into my chair and gazed into space, reliving every painful moment of a two-year battle that was doomed from the start. In hindsight, I knew the letter hadn't changed the outcome of the lawsuit. The jurisdictional problem was still the central issue, but that letter vindicated me. It proved my case. I could wave it at my fellow wife beaters and ax murderers and say, "Thank you for trusting me. Thank you for standing with me."

I leaned forward and picked up the phone, smiling—however bittersweetly—for the first time in ages. The lawsuit had cost us $18,000, but you couldn't put a price on the taste of absolution.

Chapter 22

Pressure

The lawsuit became old news in Brookhaven, but my mediumship drew increasingly more press. When the Arthur Findlay College granted me Overseas Tutor status—a pretty big deal—I made the papers both here and abroad. I began doing guest spots on local radio shows, which led to a couple of appearances on News Channel 12.

The local TV station broadcast throughout northern New Jersey. It was your typical interview scene: I sat across the table from the host of the show, who introduced me and asked a few questions. Then people called in and I brought through the spirits of their loved ones—live—on the air.

The first time I appeared on channel 12, the host was as skeptical as they came. He waited until the cameras got rolling, then asked, "You really don't believe you see spirits, do you?"

I smiled at him and said, "You mean, like your father, who's standing right beside you?" The guy shot a glance to his left and gave a nervous little laugh. I rattled off a few personal details that his dad asked me to pass along, then watched as the guy's skin turned red from his collar to his cheeks.

He flashed a smile at the camera, and said, "Why don't we take the first caller?"

I began to build up a waiting list for readings. New faces showed up at church every week. One Sunday as the final notes of *Where I Sit is Holy* drifted away, I felt drawn to a man I hadn't seen before at the service. He had a high forehead and blonde hair combed straight back. I turned to address him, and as I did so I bumped the podium. The lip of wood on the front had always been precarious, and that little nudge was all it needed to fall off, followed by my notes, which fluttered to the floor.

Sharon, who by now was a deacon in the church, rushed to help me pick up the papers. When everything was back in order, I took a breath and returned my attention to the demonstration.

"The man in the brown sweater with the blonde hair … May I come to you?"

He looked amused, but pleased, and said, "Sure, why not?"

"May I hear your name, please?"

"I'm Jimmy. Jimmy Kropkowski."

I thanked him, then said, "There's a gentleman that comes before me. I sense that this is your father."

One side of Jimmy's mouth turned up, as if to say, "Oh, really?"

I squinted and listened to the spirit man, then asked Jimmy, "Are you working on a red truck?"

His amusement turned to surprise. "Yeah, I'm rebuilding one in my garage."

"Well, your dad wants you to know he watches you as you work. He also tells me that you used to use Cooper Tires."

Jimmy turned to the dark-haired woman beside him and gave her a *do-you-believe-this* look.

"I sense that your father died suddenly," I said. " … from a heart attack. And he didn't get to say goodbye."

Jimmy's smile disappeared. "That's right."

"But he's here with you now, and he wants you to know that he's fine."

The father seemed to want to hang around, so I cocked my head and tuned in closer to his personality. "Your dad was a quiet guy, but he definitely ran the ship. He would joke around, I have to say, but if he looked at you *just so*, you knew not to mess with him."

Jimmy turned to his companion as if no one else was in the room and said, "She's really talking to my father!"

I became aware of a second spirit standing beside the man. "I have someone else here now. I believe this is your mother, and that she died not too long after your dad."

Jimmy's eyes grew bigger and he confirmed what I'd said.

Then I saw an image that stirred up memories of the Polish bakery my father used to take us to over in Passaic. "I'm seeing your mother making *babka*, and she's putting them in front of the heat vents around the house so they'll rise."

Jimmy threw back his head and laughed. The rest of the congregation smiled, not so much at the homey image of the *babka*, but at Jimmy's obvious delight.

I moved on to address others in the congregation, but Jimmy came up to me as soon as the service was over. He introduced the pretty, dark-haired woman at his side as his wife, Rita, then said, "I know you're busy, but I gotta tell you: that thing with the *babka* ... that's exactly what my mother used to do. At Christmastime, every heat vent in our house had *babka* in front of it with a towel over the top."

I laughed. "I know *babka* when I see it."

"Well, I just want to thank you," he said. "That was incredible."

"Jimmy heard about you from a friend who saw you at Barnes and Noble," Rita said. "He wanted to come and check you out, but he was a little skeptical."

He thrust out his chin. "I don't believe anything right off the bat."

"That's good," I said. "You gotta be careful."

He slipped his arm around Rita's waist. "Ever since my parents died, I've been reading a lot of books about life after death. I wanted to know they were some place other than in the ground."

"Well, I hope my demonstration today proved that to you."

"Oh, yeah." Jimmy shared a look with Rita. "After the things you told me this morning, I know they're okay."

I could see the healing effect that my reading had on Jimmy and Rita. That kind of result was the whole reason Spiritualists gave a demonstration at every service. It was what we were all about.

As they walked away hand-in-hand, a woman who'd been hovering behind them quickly took their place. "I saw you on TV, Janet, and I had to come and meet you." She stepped in so close that I could smell her shampoo. "I was really hoping you'd call on me during your demonstration," she said.

"I'm sorry," I apologized, "but there's just not time to come to everyone."

"Yes, but I really need to have a reading with you. I drove two hours to get here this morning, and I was hoping you could see me while I'm here."

I wanted to help the woman, but I was running on empty. The high of leading the service always led to an equivalent low as the adrenaline wore off. Giving readings took a lot of focus, and I only had so much energy. The problem was, there were always people who wanted a reading *now* rather than later.

That problem, combined with my inability to say no, had recently led me back into therapy. I'd grown up in a family that didn't know what boundaries were. None of us had ever learned how to stand up for ourselves. My father had been gone for years, but I continued to struggle with the legacy he left me. Part of me was still that scared little kid, and the whole ordeal with the lawsuit hadn't helped. All those men in powerful positions telling me what to do took me right back to the days when one man held all the power in my life.

Maybe none of my issues would have come to light if I'd stayed in the shadows, but I chose a path that put me more and more in the spotlight. People were calling me from all over the country looking for healing, both physical and mental. The more requests I got, the more I realized that I shouldn't be healing others until I fully healed myself.

Someone recommended I talk to a Franciscan priest named Father Michael. They said he was a really good counselor. The fact that he was a priest made no difference to me. I didn't care if he wore a brown robe and sandals or blue jeans and boots, as long as he could help me.

We spent a lot of time talking about anger, which had been out of control growing up. I had no examples of normal behavior to learn from; no rational adults to model. In my house, everyone reacted the same way whether you broke the rules or broke a fingernail. Like I said: no boundaries.

Father Michael was a godsend. He helped me see what was appropriate. His counseling made me a better boss of the kitchen and housekeeping staff at the retreat center, and a better pastor of my church, where people were always saying *help me, help me, help me.* He showed me how to stand up for myself instead of living in fear. He taught me that it was okay to say no—that I could help others better when I took care of myself first.

I looked at the lady standing in front of me and smiled sympathetically. "I'd like to give you a reading, but now is not a good time."

"But I drove two hours," she complained.

I pointed across the room before she could say more. "Do you see that woman in the blue dress?"

She turned to look at Carole, who was stacking chairs along the wall.

"That's my secretary," I said. "She'll set you up for a reading at a time that's best for both of us."

And with a silent *thank you* to Father Michael, I turned and walked away.

* * *

The two places in my life with the greatest healing energy were the grounds at the retreat center and the town of Lily Dale. I enjoyed Holy Spirit's chapel and wooded trails five days a week. I made the trip to Lily Dale as often as I could get away.

I'd loved Lily Dale from the first time I drove through the gate. Years had passed and it still had the same calming effect on me. I didn't need to sit in the Healing Temple to feel renewed; the whole place was one big sauna for the soul.

I'd been going to Lily Dale a couple of times a year when it finally occurred to me that I wanted to spend more than just a few days at a time there. The Maplewood Hotel was nice, but I decided to buy a house and become an active member of the community. There were always a couple of cottages for sale, but I didn't want to be cramped up on one of the side streets. I was a Pisces, and people with the sign of the fish needed to be near the water.

I picked out two houses with unobstructed views of Cassadaga Lake. Either one would have been perfect, except that they weren't for sale. I figured it was worth waiting to get what I wanted, so I wrote two letters: one to Joe Merrill and one to Pat Bartlett, the owner of each house. I gave them my number and asked them to call me if they ever decided to sell.

I could have used a place to slip away to during the lawsuit, but I didn't hear anything from Joe or Pat. Then, a few months after the case was dismissed, I got a call from Larry Clark, a friend of Joe Merrill's. Larry called to tell me that Joe had died. I expressed my sympathy, of course, but I couldn't help but think about Joe's house—a big two-story, three-bedroom cottage with an enclosed porch that looked out on the lake.

I held my breath. "Did you find my letter? Is that why you're calling?"

"Yes," Larry said, "But what you don't know is that Joe had been keeping his eye on you."

"What do you mean?" I asked, confused.

Larry explained that he'd been going through Joe's things and found some copies of the *Psychic News*, a Spiritualist newspaper published in England by the SNU. Several issues featured articles about me, and there, scribbled at the bottom in Joe Merrill's handwriting, was the statement: "She would be a good asset for Lily Dale."

"Joe left the house to me," Larry said, "but you were meant to have it."

I drove up that day and made a deal for the house with Larry before anyone knew it was available. While there, Larry showed me the articles that Joe had saved. With all the attention during the lawsuit, I hadn't always appreciated the press, but this was one case where a little exposure hadn't hurt.

* * *

I wiped a smudge of flour from my black skirt and straightened my blouse. Father Benedict, Holy Spirit's latest director, had asked to see me. I had no idea what he wanted to talk about. It could be anything from a change in the menu to a problem with one of my staff. Hoping it was the former and not the latter, I grabbed a note pad and headed for his office.

"Good morning, Janet."

I looked up to see Father Marcus, one of the staff priests, standing at the landing by the staircase. "Good morning, Father."

"How are things going?" he asked.

"Pretty good, I have to say." I was just back from two days in Lily Dale, where my new house was shaping up nicely.

Father Marcus smiled. He was one of the few people at the retreat center who knew about my other life. I'd been working there for 16 years now. I'd been a medium and a Spiritualist minister for more than half that time, but the retreat center was one place where I never had an issue with boundaries. From Day One I always kept my personal life separate from my work. After I appeared on the news shows, retreat guests would occasionally stop me and say, "I saw you on TV." I acknowledged their remarks, but if they wanted to talk about my mediumship, I politely let them know that I didn't discuss that subject at work.

The only exception was Father Marcus. He'd expressed an interest in Spiritualism and had no qualms chatting with me in private. He would come to the kitchen and we'd talk about the spirit world, but we always stopped if any of the guests came within earshot.

"Let's talk again some time when you're not in a hurry," he said.

"Any time you want," I called over my shoulder.

I arrived at Father Benedict's office and knocked on the open door.

"Come in, Janet." He motioned for me to have a seat.

"You asked to see me, Father?"

"I did."

I propped the note pad on my lap and held a pen at the ready.

Father Benedict tugged at his white collar as if it were too tight. I waited and watched as he cracked his neck to the left, then the right. I could tell from his energy that this wasn't about the menu, and I wondered which staff member had done something wrong.

Then he leaned forward and pulled a piece of paper from under the blotter on his desk. When he held it up between us, I saw that it was a clipping from the *Bergen Record*. I recognized the story right away: a positive piece about me and *The Journey Within*. I suddenly realized that the meeting wasn't about one of my employees; it was about me. My pulse quickened, but not fast enough to shield myself from a blow that I never saw coming.

"If there's any more press about you," the director said as he pushed the article toward me, "you will be out of a job."

Chapter 23

Severed

It had taken me years to get to the point where I could openly tell people, *Yes, I'm a Spiritualist.* Now, because of my beliefs, I was in danger of losing my job. Had I not been back in counseling when Father Benedict issued his ultimatum, I might have crawled inside myself and crumbled. As it was, he caught me so off guard that I left his office without saying much at all.

More than anything, I felt betrayed. It was true that I was making a name for myself as a medium and a minister, but I worked equally hard at the retreat center. I broke my back for that place for 16 years. I put my love into the food. There was one winter when I risked my life to go to work in the middle of the blizzard. It was a crazy thing to do—leaving my car at the bottom of the hill and trudging through waist deep snow to make sure people got fed. It never occurred to me to stay at home. My work there was part of my ministry.

After I had a chance to gather my wits, I saw the situation for what it was. I'd been going to therapy to learn to stand up for myself, and like the lawsuit, this was yet another test. My counselor echoed what I already knew: that I couldn't let Father Benedict get away with his threats. I had to be strong and face him.

I couldn't help but wonder what kind of religion could hold a gun to a person's head based on what they believed. In my mind, that was ruling by fear—which was exactly how my father had always ruled my family.

I knew that I would remain a Spiritualist and that there would probably be more press. Faced with that dilemma, I went back to that place inside myself where I'd been shining all the flashlights and asked, *what am I going to do here?* The last thing I wanted was to get involved in another legal battle, but I had the sense to see that once again, I needed professional advice.

I saw a new lawyer this time—one who specialized in workplace issues. He focused right in on the fact that the director at the retreat center was treating me differently than other employees. He suggested that I go back and talk to Father Benedict—to tell him that threatening my job was inappropriate. Most critical of all, the lawyer advised me to record the meeting.

Having already done the *he said/she said* thing with Anthony Marino, I didn't hesitate to buy a small cassette recorder and slip it into my purse. That little bit of insurance helped me feel less nervous when I knocked on Father Benedict's door for round number two.

I'd asked to speak with the director, so he knew I was coming. This time he didn't tug at his collar or crack his neck. Instead, he sat behind his big desk and waited for me to speak. I gave one last glance at the talking points I'd written out in advance, then began.

"I was very surprised by your statement that if there was any more press I'd be out of a job," I said. "I find that highly inappropriate. No one here has ever complained about my work performance, and to threaten my job because of my beliefs is unfair."

He didn't deny that he'd threatened me. He didn't talk about my performance. Instead, he leaned back in his chair and crossed his hands high on his chest. "What you believe conflicts with what people here believe."

"There is nothing in my file that says I'm not doing my job," I said, sticking to my script. "My work here is not about what I believe or don't believe. My job is to run your food service and housekeeping departments. My beliefs are part of my personal life. I do not bring them to the job."

He swept his hand in front of me and said, "But look at you—you always wear black."

I almost choked. Who did he think I was? Satan's sister? "I'm a chunky girl," I said. "Black makes me look thinner!"

"Whatever the reason, I'm sure you can understand that we can't have you imposing your personal beliefs on our guests."

I wondered if the tape would pick up the arrogance in his voice. "My concern has always been for our guests," I said. "I consider feeding them and having a friendly chat with them to be part of my ministry."

"Your ministry?" He gave a cocky snort. "You weren't really a nun. You didn't take your vows."

I had to remind myself that we were both adults. I refrained from mentioning that he shouldn't be slinging hash with all the trouble his fellow priests were having at the time.

"You're right," I said. "I left before final vows, but in the hospital where I worked they called me sister."

He laughed as if my words amused him.

The conversation was going nowhere, but I'd gotten what I needed on tape. I walked out of his office on trembling legs and went back to work.

It would have been easy to become discouraged with the Catholic Church as a whole, but I could only hope that Father Benedict was acting alone. He was just one priest who found my beliefs unacceptable. I had other priests who sent me clients for readings. My counselor, a Franciscan, was highly supportive of my mediumship. Father Marcus, a Carmelite like my boss, was fascinated by Spiritualism.

The big question was: which way would the director's bosses lean? Following my lawyer's advice, I sent Father Benedict's superiors a formal letter. I let them know that my job was being threatened and that such threats were unacceptable. I didn't mention the tape, but I kept it close at hand in case it was needed.

The U.S. Postal Service was efficient. I could tell within days that my letter had arrived. Just like turning the calendar from August to September, the whole atmosphere at the retreat center grew noticeably cooler. In the space of a week I went from someone my colleagues respected to someone they went out of their way to avoid. Even Father Marcus let me know that our days of chatting in the kitchen were over.

I made the mistake of telling Father Benedict that he was creating a hostile work environment. Once I used those words, he knew I'd been talking with a lawyer. The mood in Holy Spirit's hallways went from uncomfortable to unacceptable. My lawyer advised me that the next step was to offer them a deal: I'd leave quietly if we could agree upon an acceptable severance package.

I didn't know if I was ready for such a major step, but maybe it was time. I had no doubt that I could support myself as a full-time medium, but it hurt to even think about leaving. Faced with such a tough decision, I did what I always did now: I turned to God. If and when the time was right, I felt sure I'd be given a sign.

* * *

To many people, church is a refuge. I wanted my church to feel that way to my congregation, but it became my safe harbor as well. In the days following the unpleasantness with Father Benedict, I spent my hours at work enveloped in hostility. I found my sanctuary at *The Journey Within*.

One Sunday after a particularly rough week, I arrived at the Wise Man with my trunk full of gear. Carole, Sharon, and Hope, a faithful member of my board, helped me carry the CD player and songbooks inside. We stepped into the back room and the four of us stopped cold. The crappy little podium I'd picked out of the garbage at the retreat center was gone. In its place stood the most beautiful podium I'd ever seen. The President of the United States had never addressed his fellow Americans from such a magnificent podium.

"Do you see what I see?" I asked the girls.

The varnished blonde wood appeared to be hand-carved. The base was strong and sturdy, the top wide and welcoming, with a shelf underneath to store my papers. A lip of well-affixed wood along the back edge meant I'd no longer have to hold things in place as I spoke. The top edge curved in from both sides like a fancy headboard. At the center, sheltered by the sculpted wood, stood a tiny golden angel. Beneath her, framed by swirling wood overlays, a regal plaque read, "*The Journey Within.*"

I felt my throat clamping shut. I looked at Sharon, Carole, and Hope and saw that they, too were holding back the tears.

"Where did this come from?" I asked as I ran my hand over the smooth wood.

The girls knew nothing about it.

"Whoever made it must have spent months working on it," I said.

Then I noticed a little envelope stuck to the top. I tore into it as my friends peered over my shoulder.

"*You did something for me that nobody else could ever do.*"

I turned the card over and frowned. It was unsigned. I knew that Jesus said we should give gifts of kindness anonymously, but anonymity wasn't gonna cut it. I looked at my girls and said, "Find out who did this."

I tucked the note under the shelf and turned my focus to the service as people started to gather. I wanted to mention the podium—to thank whoever had done such a wonderful thing—but I knew that once I brought it up, I'd lose my composure completely. I needed to keep my energy high—at least through the demonstration.

As I delivered my homily, I looked out at my congregation. There sat Carolyn and Amy, Jimmy and his wife Rita, and countless others for whom I'd given readings. I'd sat with many of them through some of their darkest hours. I wondered if that was the thing to which the gift card referred—the thing I'd done that nobody else could ever do. If people felt so touched by my work that they would do this for me, did I really need to go back to a job where people actually thought I was sinful?

When it was time for the demonstration of mediumship, Carole popped *Where I Sit is Holy* into the boom box. Distracted until now by my thoughts, I was grateful to have my old stand-by to center me. The flute and the drums worked their magic, as did the lyrics that always spoke to my heart. By the end of the song my energy was right up where it needed to be—vibrating in sync with the spirit world.

"The woman in the back" I said, pointing to a lady with short brown hair and a round face that I'd never seen at the service. "May I hear your name?"

She pointed at herself. "Me?"

"Yes, you, please."

"Oh," she looked embarrassed to be singled out. "Good morning. I'm Patty Moran."

"Thank you. I have a woman here, and I feel like this is your mother. Is your mother on the other side?"

Patty glanced nervously at the man beside her, then said, "Yes, she died six months ago."

"Uh huh. This feels like a recent passing, and for whatever reason, she's showing me keys in her hand."

Patty went rigid and stared back at me wide-eyed.

"They aren't driving keys, but she tells me they're important—especially the way she's holding them. She's showing me the keys on some kind of red clip."

Patty leaned over to her partner and they whispered back and forth.

I put my hands on my skull. "She had a bad head injury. I feel like she was hit by a car."

Both of them nodded now.

"I see her lying on the ground, and you're taking her hand."

"I did," Patty said, the grief now evident on her face.

I felt bad about dredging up such an agonizing moment, but I knew that my next words would help ease her pain. "Your mother's telling me that she wasn't happy her last years here after your father died, but she wants you to know that they're dancing again."

I moved on then and brought through the loved ones of several others in the room. Each person I addressed reacted with smiles, tears, and undisguised appreciation. I couldn't help but think about the lyrics to my demonstration song. They epitomized what everyone in my church believed: that where we sit is holy, what we do is holy, and who we are is holy—in spite of what others thought about us.

The service was coming to an end and I could no longer keep my mouth shut about the podium. "Those of you who've been with us for a while may have noticed we have a new addition to our service." I stepped back and held my hand out. "This is unbelievable."

A surge of emotion welled up in my throat, making it nearly impossible to talk. I pulled out the gift card and choked my way through it as I read it aloud.

"I'm pretty sure someone here is responsible for this," I said as I wiped at my eyes, "and I'd like to know who it is."

There was an awkward moment of expectant silence until one of my regulars called out from the back, "You just got through talking to the spirit people, Janet. How come you don't know who built the thing?"

The ensuing laughter helped me get myself together.

"It doesn't work like that!" I shot back. We all laughed together, then, and even though we'd already sung the musical selections from the day's program, I suggested that we join together in one final song. I asked Carole to pull out the CDs and pop in *Share a Little Bit of Your Love*.

Carole cranked up the volume and we sang as loud as we could. In light of the new podium, it just seemed to fit.

After the service, the first woman I'd called on during the demonstration came up to me and said, "I have to tell you, you are amazing."

"You're Patty, right?"

"Yeah, and this is my husband, Thomas."

I shook the hand of the large man who'd been sitting next to her.

"That thing about my mother holding the keys—" Patty said with a thick Bronx accent, "You don't know how significant that was."

She explained that her mother had been out walking when she was struck by a car just a block from her house. Thomas heard the commotion and went to the scene. He saw a woman lying in the street, but the police wouldn't let anyone get close. Then he noticed a set of keys on a little red clip in the woman's hand and knew immediately that the victim was his mother-in-law.

"The fact that you saw those keys ... and that red clip ..." Patti shook her head in amazement.

"That's what evidential mediumship is all about," I said.

"You have no idea what that meant to me ... to hear you say that my mom and dad are dancing again took away the ache I've had since she died."

I clasped Patty's hands and thanked her and her husband for coming. She turned to go, then stopped. "You used to be a nun, didn't you?"

Not according to Father Benedict, I thought, but I nodded and said, "That's right."

"I've been a Catholic all my life, and this was a whole new experience for me. We don't talk about these things in church."

"Well, the saints spoke to dead people," I said. "We just take it a step further."

"I like that," Patty said. "And I really liked the music." She laughed, then added, "I never thought I'd hear Bette Midler and Simon and Garfunkel at a church service."

I laughed and shrugged my shoulders. "We're a little non-traditional."

"Yeah, well, I have a feeling I'll see you again."

She and Thomas walked off, leaving me with a warm, fuzzy feeling in my heart. The feeling grew even warmer as I stared once more at the podium.

The contrast between my life as a medium and my work at the retreat center couldn't have been greater. For three months I'd suffered in an environment where I no longer felt welcome. The place where I'd once found such peace had become a living Hell. Yet here at the Wise Man and back in my office, people brought me unexpected gifts of love. They respected me and didn't scoff at my beliefs.

Those thoughts followed me as I collected the songbooks. I worked my way down the rows of chairs, stacking one on top of the other. In the last row, one of the notebooks lay open to the Simon and Garfunkel hit we'd sung earlier that morning. I stared at the lyrics to *I Can See Clearly Now*, and felt a thud between the eyes as if I'd been hit by a giant rubber mallet.

Here—in my church—*was the rainbow I'd been praying for*. I realized that when I immersed myself in the work I was meant to do, *all of the bad feelings just disappeared*. In a single instant, *gone were the dark clouds that had me blind*.

I'd asked God for a sign and received it in the words to a song. I knew then that I'd been at the retreat center long enough. I could see clearly now that it was time to move on.

* * *

Once I told the director that I was willing to accept a severance package, he and his superiors wasted no time drawing up the papers. Not only was I The Evil

Spiritualist in Black, but I was a whistle-blowing troublemaker who they couldn't kick out the door fast enough. On my last day at the retreat center they watched me so intently that it broke my heart. I felt as if my dress bore a giant scarlet S— not for Spiritualist ... for *Scourge.*

I wanted to take one last tour of the grounds—to sit under the tree where I'd learned to meditate—but I was too uncomfortable. With the director hovering nearby, I bypassed the chapel where I'd spent so many hours in peaceful prayer. I recalled sitting in that sanctuary twenty years earlier as a member of ACOA. Had the rules not forbidden me from taking Holy Communion, I might never have gone back to the Church. I didn't want to feel left out at the time, and had embarked on a path that changed the course of my life.

I skipped a visit to the guesthouse as well. The day I'd sat there to write my first vows was ancient history now. In more recent times, Nigel had enjoyed staying in its rooms. I felt sure that he would no longer be welcome because of his association with me. The fact that he was a Spiritualist wouldn't enter the equation. The retreat center welcomed people of all faiths; Spiritualists just couldn't *work* there.

I took one last walk through the kitchen. There I hugged and shook hands with my staff, who were as devastated at my leaving as I was. I didn't learn to stand up for myself until my final days of working at Holy Spirit, but I had always stood up for my employees. They'd seen me go to bat for them on every level, fighting for fair salaries and fair treatment. I might not miss the paperwork that went with being a supervisor, but I would definitely miss the people whom I'd come to love like family.

I picked up my purse and walked down the hallway of the main house. I paused as I passed Father Paul's old office. There he had shown me—his little bird—how it felt to be loved. Years later, I'd sat in the big leather chairs with Father Leonard, who helped me come to terms with leaving the convent. Both priests had made Holy Spirit a haven for me. I knew that the center still offered that feeling to many of its guests, but in my final months there I was treated unjustly.

I continued down the hallway and was about to walk out the front door for the final time, when I stopped. My thoughts had reminded me of a man who not only shared my feelings of injustice—he died for them. I turned back and climbed the wide staircase, well aware of watchful eyes following my footsteps.

At the top landing I approached the tribute to Titus Brandsma, the Carmelite priest. It was he who had sung songs and hummed through the darkness of his days at Dachau, imprisoned for standing up to the Nazis' treatment of the Jews. Like him, I had always believed that people should be able to go through life humming. I'd left the convent when I realized I wasn't doing so, and had come home to the retreat center.

I used to hum here, Father, I said to his portrait. *But I'm not welcome any more.*

I reached out and touched the cool glass inside the frame. I stared at the warm eyes in the photo, but failed to sense his spirit. My energy was so low in that moment that I couldn't have tuned in to a radio. But I knew that if Father Titus was there with me, he was proud. I'd stood up for myself, just as he had.

You should come to my church some time, I told his picture. *We really know how to sing.*

And for the first time that morning, I smiled. My history with Holy Spirit had been happy until the ugliness at the end. My only option now was to look ahead and welcome this next stage of my life. I was nervous, but excited about the prospect of fully dedicating my life to my mediumship and my church. And to my dream of that little white chapel.

I may not be humming now, I told Father Titus as I turned to leave, *but you just wait.*

Chapter 24

Angel in Disguise

It took a couple of months, but we finally found out who made the podium. It was Jimmy Kropkowski. His own wife, Rita, ratted him out. She told us that Jimmy was so blown away when I brought through his parents that he wanted to do something nice for us. According to Rita, he spent four months working on it in the basement. Just as I suspected, he'd hand carved all the wood. When I was finally able to thank my secret Santa, he gave me this cute little smile and asked if he was gonna get brownie points in Heaven. I assured him that he was.

My favorite part of the podium was the little angel on top. I don't know how Jimmy knew I liked angels, but by then I'd come to believe that there are times in your life—particularly in desperate times—when the universe sends you helpers. Angels don't necessarily have wings like the one on the podium. Sometimes they manifest through people. God puts just the right person in your path when you need them the most, and in that moment they're an angel. I guess for Jimmy, I was his angel—helping him to know that his mom and dad were okay. And Jimmy was an angel for me, bringing me that special gift.

I liked angels so much that I decided to open a little angel gift shop. We'd been turned down for a loan because we didn't have a credit history. I figured a little business on the side would show the bank we had a steady source of income.

I found a place to rent in the next town over from Brookhaven. It wasn't big enough to hold services in, but it had just enough room for a shop out front and an office in the back where I could give readings. I hung onto my original office just in case I needed extra space.

When people at the church found out about the shop, any worries I had about staffing it went out the window. I had a list of volunteers ready to keep it open six days a week. As for making the space usable, we had our own contractor in the form of Jimmy. He painted the walls, hung new doors, and re-did the bathroom. I lost count of how many trips he made to Home Depot, but he surprised everyone the day he came back with an angel border for the top of the walls. Pretty good for a man, I have to say.

As busy as I was, I had to wonder how I ever had the time to work at the retreat center. I rose every morning now at 5:00 and was in my office by 6:30. I'd do a few readings in the morning, then spend a good part of the day on church business. My sister and I had bought a large house together some years back and shared it with my mother. I'd check on my mom at lunch and take care of personal stuff, then go back to the office. I'd give a few more readings in the evening, and head home some time after nine.

I didn't mind the long hours because I loved my work. Now and then I took a break to go to Lily Dale or have fun with the girls, but for the most part, my mediumship and the church were my life. I was happy to throw myself into my work—to fulfill my life's legacy by building a church to God. With hard work and faith, our little angel shop would help us to get there. It was a worthy undertaking, I thought. My father had left behind a legacy of pain; I would leave a legacy of love.

* * *

My appointment book listed the couple across from me as Bob and Karen, with no last name, as usual. I remembered them the second they walked through the door from one of my services a few weeks back. They were both tall and fit, with an air of quiet dignity. Karen had neatly groomed brown hair. Bob's was that distinguished gray-white color that looks really good on men.

Their confident bearing made them stand out, but what I remembered most about them was the sparkly energy I'd felt from the moment I shook Bob's hand. It was an unusual service because the music took me so high that day. I was really *on* when I started the demonstration. *Supercharged*, I have to say.

I'd never seen Bob or his wife, but I went straight to him and brought through a man in uniform. Bob confirmed that Karen's brother had been in the Navy and was no longer with them. I then brought through Bob's father, giving him details about his father's personality and the work he did. Next came Bob's mother, along with information on her home and life as well. It seemed as if the whole family was waiting to talk, for his grandfather came through next, telling me he'd owned a bar.

As I passed along each evidential detail, Bob's stunned expression showed his amazement that I knew so much about his family. It was as if he couldn't believe what was happening.

Then, suddenly, I felt a burst of sadness and knew why the couple was there. "You've lost a child," I said. "A young woman."

They both stiffened.

"Who's Anne?" I asked Bob.

"Anne is my wife's mother," he replied, glancing to his side.

I nodded my head. It made sense.

"Your daughter is with your mom," I said to Karen. "Anne was waiting for her when she crossed over."

The sparkly energy continued, but for some reason the spirit people told me I wasn't supposed to talk any more about the young woman that day. I didn't know why they said that, but Bob looked genuinely upset. Looking back on it, I realized their wound was too raw, and it would have been too painful to bring through any more details in such a public setting.

Karen returned to the church the following Sunday with a young man. She introduced him to me as her daughter's husband, David. We stood together at the side of the room and I tuned in to his wife right there.

"Lori sees your key chain and she smiles," I said to David.

His eyes grew wide and Karen gripped his arm. He reached into his pants pocket, pulled out his keys, and showed me a wedding band hanging from the ring.

Now Bob and Karen sat with me in my office for a private reading. People often showed up and asked to connect with a certain family member. I always advised them not to pin their hopes on any one person in particular. The spirit people decided who came through and when. But I remembered the sparkly feeling that day in the church. I had a feeling Lori's wouldn't let her parents down.

I began the reading and right away I brought through Karen's mother and father. For most people, a thing like that would be pretty special. I wasn't surprised when she gave me one of those *That's-nice-but-I-want-to-hear-from-my-daughter* smiles.

And then, thank God, a beautiful young woman with long, curly hair stepped before me.

"Lori's here," I said and described her as I saw her.

Bob crossed his arms and took a deep breath. Karen's fingers curled in her lap. I'd seen these anxious reactions a hundred times, and it was always worse with parents. They want so badly to know that their child is still with them.

My next question broke the tension. "She's feisty, isn't she?"

Bob and Karen shared a look of wonder.

"Yes, she *is*," Karen said, and they laughed with restrained delight.

"I sense a kind of fierceness with her ... as if she tries to fit everything into a day."

They nodded and laughed some more.

"And she likes to learn ... and try new things."

Suddenly, neither Karen nor Bob seemed capable of speaking as the enormity of my revelations sank in. I passed them the box of Kleenex I kept handy.

"She's telling me how happy she was with David," I continued " ... and how much she loves both of you."

Bob and Karen hung on my last sentence like the lifeline it was. I knew it was comforting for them to hear their daughter's expression of love, but I wasn't satisfied. Anyone could say the words I'd just spoken. There was no proof in that kind of message.

I asked Lori to give me something more evidential. Right away she told me that she'd died in her mid-thirties. Her parents confirmed this.

Lori went on to talk about her siblings and other details I had no way of knowing.

"And now she's bringing up a little boy," I said. "I'm not getting a name, but she's telling me how unfortunate it was that she had to leave him so soon."

I could tell I really hit a nerve with that one. Karen broke down, but Bob held it together enough to fill in the blanks for me. My insides threatened to tear apart as he explained that the little boy was their grandson—Lori's little baby, William.

Seven years earlier, when Lori was 28, a doctor had removed some polyps from her colon. He never advised her to have regular colonoscopies to follow up, and everyone thought she was fine. At age 35, Lori found out that she and David were going to have a baby. She felt worse and worse as the months went on, and they chalked it up to the pregnancy. She couldn't eat. She was nauseous all the time. It turned out it wasn't the baby; it was Lori.

Two months after William was born, Lori died of colon cancer.

"Oh my God," I said, and reached for a tissue, myself. I'd wanted evidence to give to her parents, and I'd gotten it, however heartbreaking. Lori's mention of her baby was about as evidential as I could ask for. Nothing would ever erase Bob and Karen's pain, but I knew this proof from their daughter would make their grief more bearable.

Having established her presence with evidence, I passed along a final message from Lori to her parents: "She wants you to know that she visits this child every day."

By the end of the reading, Bob and Karen looked dazed. I asked if they were okay to drive. They assured me they'd be fine, then thanked me, and turned to go. They were halfway down the hallway when Bob stopped and said, "We forgot to pay you."

Karen looked stricken and started rummaging through her purse.

"It's not about the money," I said with a wave. "I don't need it. I just need you to believe in what I'm doing."

They must have believed, because two weeks later they came back for another reading. Karen told me that hearing from Lori had been like a phone call from Heaven.

I liked that.

"You saved us from despair," she said. "Now I know I'm just a long-distance call from my daughter."

* * *

The angel shop was up and running in time for the Christmas season. Every time the cash register rang up another sale we rejoiced. I figured that in a couple of years—three at the most—we'd be able to show the bank that we could make good on a monthly mortgage payment.

I was in my new office now. The phone rang, and I picked it up.

"Janet? This is Bob Benedetti."

The name didn't register.

"You gave a couple of readings for my wife, Karen, and me. You brought through our daughter, Lori."

It had been a couple of months and I hadn't known their last name, but I remembered the three of them right away.

We shared the usual *how are you doing* stuff, then Bob said, "Karen and I are really fascinated by this Spiritualism. We'd like to take you to dinner and learn more about your gift."

I rarely turn down a meal—or a chance to talk about my work. We met at a little Italian restaurant just down Main Street from the dungeon. The place was packed, but we found a table off to the side where we could hear ourselves talk.

Karen was dressed impeccably, just like the previous times I'd seen her. On her wrist she wore a beautiful silver bracelet. It was almost an inch wide with a shiny dragonfly resting on the top.

"That's a beautiful bracelet," I commented. "Is the dragonfly significant?"

Karen looked at Bob and they smiled at each other.

"Dragonflies are our sign that Lori is around," she said.

Karen explained that Lori and Dave had bought a house together. Karen found two dragonfly prints and gave them to the kids as a housewarming gift. Lori loved them, and they still hung over Dave's fireplace.

"After we lost Lori," Karen said, "I was at Dave's house watching the baby, when a beautiful dragonfly landed on the window screen. It was all sparkly, and it stayed there the whole time I sat with Billy. I asked Dave if he'd ever seen dragonflies around the house, and he said he never had."

"The spirit people often send us signs that they're around in the form of animals or birds," I confirmed.

"Oh, but there's more," Karen said. "The first time I took little William shopping with me in his stroller, I pulled up outside of Nordstrom's and a dragonfly came and landed on the hood. It sat there the longest time, and I said, 'Is that you, Lori? Are you watching me take your son to a mall for the first time?'"

She went on to tell me that later, she and Bob were walking at a nature center, when a dragonfly flew up and landed on his hand.

"That's wonderful," I said, "No wonder you wear the bracelet."

Karen brushed her finger over the dragonfly as if petting it. "It's just a little reminder that Lori's still around us."

"You helped us to know that," Bob said. "I was never into any of the things you talk about in your church, but I'm fascinated by your gift."

"Because of you," Karen said, "I no longer say that Lori *passed away*, but that she *crossed over*, instead. You showed me that she's in her other life now. We're only here temporarily. We're here to practice for that other life."

Bob took a sip of water. "I used to look at Lori's grave and think that was the end for my daughter, but thanks to you, I know now that I was wrong."

"How did you hear about my church?"

Karen explained that Lori had been gone for five months, when they started attending a bereavement group for parents who had lost a child.

"A couple walked in during the sixth meeting with the group," she said, "and I noticed right away that they were smiling. I turned to Bob and said, 'My God, I've never seen anyone here smile.'"

They paused as if I knew the punch line, but when I stared back at them blankly, Bob cleared up the mystery.

"The couple that was smiling had just been to a private session with *you*."

"Wow," I said, feeling humbled. "I guess we were meant to meet."

A waitress came up to our table. We stopped talking long enough to look over the menus.

"There was something really special about that first time you came to my church," I said as the waitress walked off with our orders.

"I remember feeling a surge of energy when I shook your hand," I said to Bob, "and then everything got all sparkly when I came to you in the demonstration."

Bob shook his head. "This is all really new to us. We were both raised Catholic, and we honestly don't know very much about Spiritualism."

"Lori was trying to find the right religion for her because she wasn't happy in our church," Karen said. "If she'd gone to your service, I know she would have joined."

"That's how we felt that first time at your service," Bob said. "—that Lori could be there."

"I've never heard anyone speak so warmly or so lovingly as you did," Karen said.

I shifted in my chair, pleased with their praise, but a bit relieved to see the waitress bringing our food.

We continued our chat about Spiritualism as we enjoyed our meal. Bob asked me to recommend some books he could read to learn more. I promised to make up a list.

Then Bob picked up his napkin and wiped his mouth. "What's your goal with all of this, Janet? What's your dream?"

I smiled and pictured the candle sitting in my bedroom closet. "One day I'm going to have a church of my own—a nice little white chapel where everyone is welcome."

I told him how we'd tried to buy the boarded up bank, and about the angel shop we recently opened to improve our chances of getting a loan. I didn't want to spoil the evening, so I skipped the whole fiasco with the lawsuit.

"How much money do you need for a church?" Bob asked.

"For our own building?" I said, "Probably $300,000 dollars."

Bob sat back and laid his napkin on the table. "Okay," he said, "I'm going to give it to you."

Just like that: "I'm going to give it to you."

I knew that I must have misheard him.

"What?" I said, afraid to breathe.

Bob glanced at Carol. She gave him a look that said, *fine with me.*

He nodded his head as if the whole idea had just occurred to him. "I'm going to give you the $300,000 dollars to buy your church."

I put both hands on my cheeks. "This can't be real."

Bob and Karen simply smiled at me with that beautiful, quiet dignity.

I held out my arm and said, "Pinch me. I must be dreaming."

But I wasn't dreaming at all. Like I said, God sends you angels when you need them the most. I had no idea that they had money—that Bob was the CEO of his own company. You just never know who you're talking to.

But I think Lori had the whole thing figured out all along.

Chapter 25

Déjà Vu

I know beyond a doubt that Bob Benedetti would never have offered me the money for my church if I hadn't been an evidential medium. He just never would have done it—not without the kind of proof I gave him about his daughter. But when you give people those little details from the spirit people that nobody else could possibly know, it changes the way they look at life and death.

It changes *them*.

I remember a couple very much like Bob and Karen who came to one of my group sessions. Like the Benedetti's, this man and woman were also staunch Catholics and Italian. Unlike Bob and Karen, they had very thick accents that told me they hadn't grown up in America.

I began the session with a prayer, as I always did, and immediately sensed yet another link the Italian couple shared with my benefactors: They, too, had lost a child. I spent the next ten minutes passing them messages from the young spirit man standing beside them—their only son, as it turned out.

I moved on to the others in the circle, but after the group session finished, I asked the Italian couple to stay a few minutes afterwards. I'd sensed their hunger, and wanted to give them more details about their son. I described his personality and the family members he was with on the other side. His parents hung on every word—and onto each other—especially after I identified their boy by name—their Anthony.

"How did you hear about me?" I asked as they pulled on their coats.

"We was visiting our Anthony's grave," his father said, "and we met a woman at the cemetery."

"She went there to visit her husband's grave, God rest his soul," the woman said and crossed herself. "She told us about you and gave us your phone number."

"It was meant to be," said the man.

As they left, they invited me to their home for coffee, and I agreed. On the morning of my visit, I arrived to find the dining room table set as if for royalty. The intricate lace table cloth was covered with an assortment of fancy cakes and five porcelain cups. The woman introduced her sister and brother-in-law, who greeted me with kisses as if I were family.

In between sips of strong, black coffee, we talked of little else but Anthony. I brought through a few more family members who confirmed that the young man was being well looked after.

Anthony's aunt put her hand on my arm. "You don't know how you have helped my sister. None of us has been able to get through to her since Antonio died. But now, she is like a different person."

When the time came for me to leave, Anthony's father tried to press some bills into my hand. I thanked him, but refused to take them. He looked truly upset, but I stood my ground. When someone is hurting that badly, I can't talk about money. I had my coat on by then and was ready to leave, but he held up both hands and insisted I wait.

He walked off to the kitchen and returned a moment later with his wife. In their hands they held two jars of homemade tomato sauce and a big *panetone*—the Italian equivalent of *babka*. As I accepted their gift, I was struck by yet another way in which the couple before me was just like Bob and Karen. Their hearts had been broken by their tragic loss, yet both couples gave me truly heartfelt gifts. To be sure, the small token of food wasn't going to buy me a church, but it touched my soul just the same.

* * *

Bob got involved in the search for a new church from the very beginning. I would scope out places with a realtor, then bring him in when I found something with potential. Around this time the Wise Man bookstore moved. The new place was too small for us to hold services, so we rented a room in a nearby banquet hall on Sundays. The change didn't make that much of a difference. We still had to lug the same gear in and out every week, but it made me that much more anxious to have our own place.

We hung onto the angel shop, which turned out to be more necessary than we'd thought. Bob's gift was beyond generous, but as we looked around at property, we realized that even $300,000 wasn't going to cover a mortgage in our high-cost area. We also knew that whatever place we found would probably need some pricey renovations. Every sale from The Angel Within would help, but even more helpful was Bob's offer to co-sign the loan.

For two years we searched, dreamed, and saved our pennies. Then we found a building for sale in the next town over from Brookhaven. It belonged to a doctor who was giving up his practice. I took Jimmy to see it, since he'd agreed to help with renovations. I thought the place had great potential, but Jimmy was one big downer.

"There's not enough parking," he said, "and the rooms are way too small."

Bob felt the same way, but all I could see was a permanent home. In my mind, the fact that the office was on a busy commercial street made it the perfect setting to put our angel shop out front.

We made an offer, and it was accepted. I let my hopes climb nice and high as the closing date drew closer. Then the doctor decided to be a jerk. Even though we'd agreed upon a price, he went and raised it by 50 thousand bucks. The negotiations back and forth grew downright painful.

"This place is a root canal from beginning to end," Bob said, putting it all in perspective. I had nothing to counter with when he finally announced that, "This is not going to happen."

The debacle with the doctor left me feeling depressed and defeated, but I picked myself up and went to see the realtor. I told her to kick up the search to the next higher price range. The next day she called me about a building in Brookhaven that belonged to the American Legion. The town had been trying to buy the hall to use as a senior center. Then the town council decided to spend the money on a new ball field in another location, and the property fell out of contract.

The place was less than a mile from the dungeon. I hopped in my car and drove right over. The building sat at the end of a short residential street just off the main drag. I pulled up to the curb and just stared, not sure what to think. It wasn't exactly love at first sight.

The building looked like a fortress: a big, long, cinder block box with boarded up windows. I didn't want to dismiss it outright, so I brought Jimmy and Bob back to get their opinions. It wasn't much better on the inside than outside. The walls were covered with dark paneling and the whole downstairs smelled of beer, which is exactly what you'd expect from an American Legion hall. You could have walked away from it without a second thought.

"This place is great!" Jimmy said, walking around like a kid on Christmas morning.

Even Bob saw the potential. I couldn't argue that it was big enough for services and our classes, with plenty of room left for several offices, and there was no shortage of parking. The residential neighborhood made our angel shop impractical, but we could rent out the banquet hall in the basement to help make the payments.

Bob and Jimmy were ready to go for it. I told them I needed some time. Jimmy assured me that he could turn the building into the church of my dreams. I wanted to believe him, but this was a major investment. I needed more than his word to make that kind of decision.

I called Sharon, Carole, and Patty Moran. Patty had been coming to the church ever since I brought through her mother holding the keys. Being part of the church ended up helping her in ways we never could have imagined when her husband, Thomas, went into the hospital for elective surgery. He developed an infection and died, tragically, one week later. I know that Patty's new under-standing of life after death helped her handle the dark days that followed. I tried to be there for her as much as possible. I called her every day to let her know I was thinking about her and I showed up at her house unexpected from time to time. She started volunteering in my offices when Carole couldn't make it—answering phones and scheduling readings. In time, as she adjusted to her new life, she just naturally became one of the girls.

Faced with the big decision about the American Legion hall, I knew it was time for a road trip. The four of us took three days and headed up to Lily Dale. It's impossible to get in a car with those three without laughing my head off, and I felt my tension easing the farther we got from Brookhaven.

"I don't know what to do about this building," I moaned as we zipped west along the highway.

"Surely you've prayed about it," Sharon said.

"Of course I have." I told them. "I asked God to send me a sign."

"Any sign?" Patty asked.

"Nah," Carole said. "With Janet, it's gotta be roses."

"You're wrong this time," I said. "If I'm supposed to buy that building, I asked God to send me an animal that I've never seen in my life. Ever."

The girls seemed to find this incredibly amusing, but I was dead serious. They ignored my protests and spent the rest of the drive joking and teasing me about the different kinds of animals that were likely to pop up. With all their wise ass comments, you'd think I'd asked for the Loch Ness monster to crawl out of Cassadaga Lake.

We had a great little get-away, but I failed to see any animals around Lily Dale other than the usual birds and squirrels. I take my signs very seriously, and I knew that unless God answered my prayers, I wasn't meant to buy the building. On the final day of our trip, feeling a bit discouraged, I agreed to ride along on a day trip to Lake Findley. We were driving down a two lane country road, when Sharon slammed on the brakes.

"What's that?" she cried out, and pointed in front of the car.

We all stared as a long, slinky little animal ran in front of us from right to left.

"I don't care what the Hell it is!" I shouted in jubilation. "I've never seen it before!"

The four of us screamed as if we'd just seen Big Foot. The little critter turned out to be a weasel, which I didn't learn until I found a picture of one later. All I knew was that I had my sign. We continued on to Lake Findley, but I might as well have not been there. My mind was back in Brookhaven, picturing that cinder block building transformed into my little white chapel.

I don't know what the chances were of seeing an animal I'd never seen before, but God made sure I saw that weasel. On our way back to Lily Dale, He sent the little guy running back across our path a second time. As Sharon, Carole, and Patty were my witnesses, that weasel cut right across the road in the very same spot where we saw him before, running this time from left to right. I guess he was heading home, just like we were.

I didn't need anything else to make up my mind. On March 17, 2004, Bob Benedetti and I signed the papers. The American Legion hall was mine—dark paneling, beer smell, and all.

* * *

To buy a commercial building in my area, I had to have a lawyer. I was pretty tired of attorneys by that point, but having been burned in the past, I figured it might be handy to have one around. I'd hired a Mr. T. Carter Thompson back when we tried to buy the doctor's office. When that deal fell through, I hung onto his card and called him when we bought the American Legion hall.

Mr. Thompson advised me that to use the building as a church, we had to obtain a conditional use approval from Brookhaven's planning board. To anyone other than me, that might have sounded like a reasonable request. After all, it was a pretty big switch to change a building's use from a beer hall to a church. But for obvious reasons, once Mr. Thompson mentioned the planning board, I got a little nervous. Believe me, I didn't deliberately plan to have my church in Brookhaven. That's just where the building happened to be. In my innocence, I thought we'd buy the building, get the change of use request approved within a month, and start moving in.

I don't know what I was thinking.

It took three months to get on the docket. In the meantime, without that piece of paper, we weren't allowed to do any construction or occupy the building. *Our* building, that is. We made our monthly mortgage payments and had no choice but to hold our services in the banquet hall as usual.

It didn't make sense to pay the lease on the gift shop along with a big mortgage payment, so we gave up The Angel Within. We were allowed to store our stuff on the first floor of the new building, but that left me without an office. I reluctantly moved the phones and fax machine back to the dungeon. That's when Carole put her foot down.

"I am not going back there," she said.

"Come on, Carole," I begged. "It's just for a few weeks—just until we get the conditional use approval."

She crossed her arms. "Okay, but one sign of a roach and your secretary is leaving!"

Faced with such a serious threat, I did what I always do: I prayed. But this time I did it in writing. I wrote out the prayer on a piece of note paper and hung it on the dungeon wall:

> *Dear Angels and Earth Creatures,*
> *Please surround this room with your light and let no crawling/ falling creatures pass this way, as our friend has an aversion to them. Please send them in the other direction so we can have our Carole feel comfortable here.*
> *Amen.*

We never saw another bug.

* * *

I don't know why it took so long to get on the docket, but this time I wasn't taking chances with the town fathers. Not only did I have my lawyer ready, I lined up an architect, an engineer, and Mr. Bernie Campbell, the town planner, to go with me to the meeting. Mr. Campbell advised me that by state law, a church had the right to go anywhere except under two conditions: if it was a hindrance to the town, and if it brought in a bigger capacity crowd than the building previously held.

The American Legion hall used to hold up to 400 people. Without offering beer, I knew we'd never come close to that number. As for being a hindrance, we'd certainly be a lot more quiet than a bunch of legionnaires, but that was up to the town to decide.

And that's what worried me.

It was a mid-summer's evening when Sharon and Patty and I trooped into town hall—into the very room where I'd voiced my complaints about Anthony Marino five years earlier. The situation was quite different this time. Rather than bringing the entire congregation, we decided to low-key it. We didn't want to overwhelm the board, but to wait and see what happened.

Our request for a conditional use approval was on the agenda. I was nervous when my turn came, but not because I expected trouble—the formal setting would have intimidated anyone. I sat at a table with my lawyer, Mr. Thompson, and faced the board of 7 men seated on a platform before us. Mr. Thompson began by stating our purpose for being there, which in his language sounded a lot more complicated than it was. Then I had to raise my right hand and swear to tell the truth. That, for me, had never been a problem.

Arthur Teasdale was still Brookhaven's mayor. I noticed him when we first arrived, but he quietly slipped out a side door as our session began. He was not a member of the planning board. We learned that the board chairman was absent that evening. Gary Berger, another member of the board, led the meeting in the chairman's place.

"You understand that for the use variance requested, you need a majority of the board's votes," Mr. Berger began.

"We understand that," Mr. Thompson said.

"The board's attorney is not here this evening," Mr. Berger continued, "so we're going to hear testimony, but I don't think that you're going to get any kind of action tonight."

Mr. Thompson and Mr. Berger then discussed the difference between a "use approval" and a "use variance." The only part I understood was the part where Mr. Berger had said we weren't going to get any action. To me that translated into only one thing: another delay.

Mr. Berger then turned to me. "Miss Nohavec, *The Journey Within* has acquired the property on Bridge Street. Correct?"

"That's correct," I said and sat up straighter.

"What is the purpose of *The Journey Within* Center, please?"

I leaned in to the mike. "It's a recognized church by the State of New Jersey and a recognized church by the IRS. We are a 501c organization."

"What is the church's intention with regard to that property?" Berger asked.

"We purchased the property to put a church there," I said. "We're a small church. We would have services primarily on Sunday, classes during the week, and an office with two employees at any given time."

"Do you have a registered congregation for the church?"

"We have 60 members," I said, giving him the latest average tally.

"What would church functions consist of?"

"We'll conduct weddings, funerals, and fundraisers like every other church," I said.

"How about exterior improvements?"

This was a reasonable question, as were his others, and I began to relax. "The exterior is currently peeling and chipping," I said, "so we'll improve that."

"Do you have any intent to alter the current footprint of the structure?"

"There will be no exterior changes except the addition of a handicapped ramp." I said, having already discussed the plan with our engineer and architect.

Mr. Berger asked a few more questions about renovations, then invited the board to ask their own.

A round-faced man sitting to Mr. Berger's right asked, "Where are you currently holding your services?"

"We rent from a banquet hall about five miles away."

"Are you looking to leave that location?" he asked.

I wanted to say, *Why do you think I'm here?* but I held my tongue. I explained that we'd always wanted our own building and had come to a place financially where we could pursue that goal. "That's always been our dream," I said, "to have our own home—to not lug the song books and everything we use for our services back and forth every week."

The board member thanked me, then satisfied that no other board members had any questions, Mr. Berger took the floor once more.

"Miss Nohavec," he began with a disarming smile, "this might be a stupid question to ask, and I've asked many in my life, so this is just one more, but what's the difference between a church and a cult?"

In that time-stopping moment, I remembered how I'd felt when I slammed my car into a pole. The room swirled, closing in around me as if I were being sucked into a long, dark tunnel. Completely blindsided, I sat there and wondered what the chances were of our civil rights case happening twice. Maybe they were the same as seeing an unfamiliar animal two times in the same spot. One thing I knew for sure as I stared back at Mr. Berger: Lake Findley wasn't the only place I'd run across a weasel.

"How do I differentiate?" Mr. Berger continued as I tried to gather my thoughts. "Because the IRS and the state of New Jersey say you're tax exempt, does that make you a church? Is that it, or, I don't know … I'm just curious."

He smiled at me like a wolf smiles at a trapped rabbit.

Luckily, I knew the answer to his question. Once I caught my breath, I spoke into the microphone with as much dignity as I could muster. "The difference between a church and a cult, from my understanding as a religious person, is that churches do things that are in the best interest of the public. They collect food and do other charitable acts. Cults don't take care of people. Cults hurt people. We are a church."

My voice wobbled, and I stopped. I glanced at my lawyer, who nodded for me to continue.

"We collect food for groups," I said. "We gather clothes. We raise money for organizations. We have a belief system that is recognized by 350 other churches. We are a recognized church by the government of the United States."

The wolf-weasel flashed his teeth. "Good answer," he said.

"Now we know," said the guy beside him.

"Now we know," said Mr. Weasel.

He looked then at the rows of chairs behind me and said, "Does anyone from the public want to address Miss Nohavec?"

He pointed beyond me and said, "The lady in the back?"

What he didn't say was that the lady in the back was his wife.

"I have one question," she said. "Are you a pastor?"

I turned to see the woman, but I deliberately avoided making eye contact with Sharon or Patty. I knew if I looked at either one of them I'd lose it.

"Yes, I am a pastor," I replied.

"Where were you ordained?" she then asked.

In spite of the fact that she had now asked two questions instead of one, I told her that I was ordained at a church in Oakland, New Jersey.

"I should also say that I am a former Catholic nun as well. I was a Sister of Charity in Convent Station before I left."

"The church name is *The Journey Within*?" she asked, bringing her *one question* up to three.

"It's called *The Journey Within—a Center for Spiritual Enlightenment*. We wanted to use the word "center" because it's not solely Christian, and some people who are not Christian find the word "church" limiting. That's all."

Finished with her interrogation at last, the woman sat down. When no one else from the gallery had any further questions, Mr. Berger gave the floor back to the panel.

A board member asked me about our plans for the driveway. I breathed for the first time in minutes as he followed with several more of the same line of relevant questions. When I'd answered to his satisfaction, the man thanked me and sat back.

Mr. Berger then produced some papers from a folder in front of him.

"I did a little research," he announced with that same sly smile. "And I see that you conduct a school?"

"We do classes," I said, on alert once again.

"It's a school for mediumship," Berger stated.

"Yes, sir."

"Can you tell us a little about that school and some of the modules that are offered as well as the subject matter?"

The smug look on his face told me that he already knew the answer, and as soon as he said the word *modules*, I knew I was in for more trouble.

"As a Spiritualist church, we believe that life is continuous. Our courses aim to offer proof of that fact. We also believe in spiritual healing, and we follow state laws regarding that as well, if that answers your question."

"To a degree," he said. "But again, I did some research, and I see that in module four—which probably doesn't mean anything to anyone but you and me because I looked it up on your website—but module 4 is on the subject of 'haunting, ghosts, and poltergeists.'"

"Correct," I said. It was one of Nigel's lessons. "It deals with physical phenomena and mediumship."

"Could you tell us about that in a little more detail, please?" Mr. Berger asked.

I looked at my lawyer in exasperation. I wondered how long he was going to just sit there. "Are they allowed to ask me these questions?" I asked.

Mr. Thompson held his hand over the mike and said, "We don't want to get their backs up. Just answer whatever he asks."

I took a deep breath. "For most people who believe in the continuity of life, we have to answer other people who say, 'Oh, you're talking to ghosts,' or 'You're talking to evil spirits.' That's not the basis of Spiritualism. So module four is to steer people away from those false beliefs."

"So you teach a course about poltergeists?"

"If those kind of words frighten you," I said, with *my* back getting up now, "talk to the Catholic Church. They offer classes in exorcism."

"Thank you for that," said Mr. Berger, who paused to look over his papers.

"Does all this have anything to do with anything?" I asked, unable to keep quiet any longer.

He looked up and shrugged. "Without legal advice on our side, it's difficult to say how relevant this is, but to me it's a use variance, and I guess we're trying to find out for what purpose the building is going to be used."

Then, like a broken record, he went back to the cult thing.

"The last time I looked," I said, "the United States government saw us as a religion, and it's my right in America to believe what I want to believe."

Then, much to my relief, Mr. Campbell, the town planner I'd brought with me, stood and said, "This whole line of questioning is getting a really bad taste about it. There are only two reasons you can keep these people from establishing their church, and neither one of them fits in this case."

Other people in the back of the room began to speak out, but I barely heard them through the roar in my ears. I don't know if Mr. Berger realized then that he'd overstepped his bounds, or that he'd simply finished making his point. For whatever reason, he stated once again that without their lawyer, they couldn't take a vote.

And without your lawyer, you felt free to crucify me, I thought.

He thanked us for coming and told us they would reschedule us for the next month's meeting.

I didn't know if I could get up and walk out of the room. I felt as if all the blood had drained from my feet. Somehow I did manage to get out of there, but the rest of the evening passed in a daze. The girls tried to console me, but I spent the whole next day sobbing. I couldn't talk to anyone. Like a turtle, I just pulled my head inside my shell and didn't care if I never came out.

As I wallowed in the darkness of my thoughts, a tiny voice inside me worked its way to the surface.

You've gotta fight this.

I moaned and pulled my neck in even further. All the fight had gone out of me. I felt utterly defeated. My dream was not meant to be.

Listen to me, Janet, the voice said, and I shook my head. Then, a memory from the previous winter intruded, unbidden, on my thoughts. I'd been in my angel shop, rushing around because Nigel was in town and I had to take him to the airport later that day. As always, I was trying to fit too much in at once. I'd looked at my to-do list and decided I could get to the recycling place before I had to pick up Nigel at his hotel.

I went about gathering up all the cardboard from the back of the shop when I heard a voice say very clearly, *Don't do this today.* I acknowledged the voice by saying, *I have time.*

There'd been a huge blizzard the night before, and when I stepped outside the shop I went flying. I hit the ground and immediately knew it was bad. I felt the bones moving in my shoulder. I had a lot of money in my pocketbook and I was afraid I'd pass out, so I dragged myself back inside the shop.

I had a reading scheduled, and the woman knocked on the door. I must have been in shock, because I stupidly called out, "I can't talk to you right now." She went away and I sat there saying, *ow, ow, ow, ow, ow.*

Lucky for me, Karen Parker, a psychic artist, passed by the shop and saw my car. She came up to the door and called, "Janet, are you in there?"

I said, "Karen, you've gotta call the police. I can't get back to the door to unlock it."

Instead of calling the police, she called Sharon, who had a key. They ended up getting an ambulance. Turns out I had completely shattered my shoulder. The one I have now is all synthetic and metal.

You've gotta fight this, the voice repeated, bringing me back to the present.

I didn't know if I could get back up a second time, but something deep inside me told me this was yet another test. If there was one thing I'd learned from years of giving readings, it was that everyone faces challenges. I'd met people who lost a child and were so totally crushed by their loss that they never went out of the house. Others turned their loss into a cause. How we handle our challenges is part of why we're here.

My life's challenge seemed to be facing up to strong men—starting with my father, then the zoning and construction officer, followed by the town council, Father Benedict at the retreat center, and now Brookhaven's planning board. I honestly thought I'd learned my lesson by this time, but this latest test could only mean that part of me still needed to stretch and grow.

I rubbed my shoulder and frowned. I hadn't listened to the voice the day I slipped on the ice, and I'd shattered my bones. Now the planning board's meeting had shattered my will, but the same voice was telling me to get back up and fight.

I might not have listened the first time, but I wasn't going to make the same mistake twice.

* * *

We decided not to go to the press. It was a calculated decision. We figured if we went into an aggressive fight mode, the planning board would ratchet up their resistance to the next level simply to protect their position. We had chosen to be a part of this community, and we wanted to keep things as amicable as possible between us and the town.

I can't say that the board reacted with the same consideration. They sent a police officer to the angel shop to check us out. I don't have any proof that they're the ones who sent him, but the shop had been there for years and no police ever stopped by. The policeman wanted to know what we were all about and what our intentions were. If you ask me, the timing seemed just a little too coincidental.

Then, shortly after Officer Friendly came to visit, Patty saw a woman peering in the window of the shop. She opened the door and said, "Come in! We're open." That's when she recognized the lady who'd asked me all the questions at the planning board meeting—Mr. Berger's wife. The woman looked at Patty and said, "You were at the meeting," and Patty said, "Yeah, you were, too. May I show you around?" The lady didn't even bother browsing; she just took off.

Once we realized what we were up against, we knew we had to be prepared. I sent Sharon out with a camera and she took pictures of all the churches in town. She photographed every sign that announced Sunday school classes in case they brought up our school again. I was ready to tell them that they were treating me differently than other churches in the town. If they weren't going to allow me in, they were going to have to shut down every other Sunday school in Brookhaven.

I returned to the town hall the following month with my lawyer and a handful of church members. This time the board decided to focus on parking. "There's more than enough room for the congregation's cars," I said, and stuck to my script. "If you're going to keep us out based on our parking lot, then you have to show me that St. Mary's across town is being held to the same standard."

They told us to come back the next month with a detailed parking plan. We went back the next month—it was August by then—and showed them our parking plan. They no longer cared about our parking lot. They wanted to know how we were going to deal with handicapped access. We'd already gone over this with an architect and had a plan for a ramp, but the board wasn't prepared to discuss it that evening; they only wanted to raise the question. They put the discussion on the agenda for September.

We were ready to discuss it in September, but the planning board cancelled the meeting. For the whole month. But we still had to pay our lawyer, of course. And pay our mortgage.

Those were some really dark days. My frustration level pegged out as the meetings dragged on with a different agenda every month. What the board didn't know was that the banquet hall where we'd been holding our services was getting ready to close. They were going to tear it down and put in a car dealership in just a few months.

Mr. Thompson and I met with the board in October to discuss the handicapped ramp. A lady stood up in the back and asked, "What's going to keep kids from skateboarding down the ramp? I think you should have some kind of gate on it."

"If kids are going to be on the ramp," I replied, "then they're trespassing."

That's how ridiculous things got.

The meetings would go from 8 P.M. to 10:30. Mr. Thompson and I had to sit there for hours awaiting our turn. When they got to us, the questions were always the same trivial nonsense: "How many people will be at your services?" "How are you going to arrange your chairs?" It got to the point where they asked how we intended to plant trees in the yard. We had to go back a month later with a shrubbery plan.

We ended up with a whole list of conditions imposed by the board: We could only have 80 people in the building at a time, even though the American Legion fit 400 in the same space. We had to be out of the building by 10:30 at night. We had to provide lighting in the parking lot and have an attendant on

Janet Nohavec

duty. We had to have the handicapped ramp. On and on it went, but we agreed to everything. What choice did we have?

By November they had no choice, either, but to make a decision: Would they issue us the conditional use approval or not?

* * *

Sharon and Patty sat behind me in the large boardroom. I sat shaking in my chair facing the board members. By that point, it was a wonder they hadn't put an engraved plaque with my name on it at the seat.

Once again we'd decided not to bring any others with us, even though this meeting was crucial. I could feel my friends' eyes boring into my back as the board chairman introduced the vote. There were seven members present: the chairman, Mr. Berger who'd stood in for the chairman at the initial meeting, and five other men. We needed four *yeses* to win.

The chairman voted first and gave us a *yes*. I took a deep breath. It was a good start, but there were six men to go. He turned to his right and called on the man at the far end. The man voted *no*, and my heart sank. Then the second man voted *no*, and my brain began to shut down. They gave no reasons for their decision. By then I had decided that if the vote failed, I was taking them to court. There was no doubt in my mind. They had no legal basis to vote us down. They might not have to explain themselves at a planning board meeting, but they'd have to justify themselves in a court of law.

The next man voted *yes*, and I grabbed a quick breath. We were now two and two. The chairman turned to his left and nodded at the man beside him. The man hesitated, then voted *yes*. That gave me three *yeses* and two *no's*. I didn't know if I could stand the tension. By that point, I just wanted to get it over with. The second to last board member was Gary Berger, the man who had initiated the whole mess with his questions about cults. Big surprise: he voted *no*.

There was one man left to vote, and the score was three to three. I didn't dare turn around. I didn't need to. I could feel Sharon and Patty's tension as if it were my own. I knew that they, like me, felt sick. I stared at the man, willing him to vote in our favor. We locked eyes. He glanced at Gary Berger, then looked back at me.

And voted *yes*.

A cheer rang out from behind me. I turned around and looked at Sharon and Patty. *Oh my God*, I mouthed.

Oh my God.

We had won. But at what cost?

In all we paid over $50,000 in legal fees and nearly a year's worth of mortgage payments for a building we couldn't occupy. But now it was ours. With one slight exception. We couldn't move in or make any modifications for 60 days from the date of the vote. I would have fought to oppose that ruling as well, but the local regulation applied to everyone.

There was no shortage of hugs and tears as we walked out of the town hall. I thanked Mr. Thompson and told him we'd settle up later. The night air was cold, and I shivered as he walked away, but inside I felt a spreading warmth that I hadn't experienced in a long, long time.

I looked at Sharon and Patty. "I can't believe the nightmare is over."

Sharon shook her head. "Let's hear it for freedom of speech and religion."

The three of us glanced down Main Street, where a tiny replica of the Liberty Bell sat on a plot of public land maintained by the town.

"Do you hear it?" I said, and both girls smiled.

"I hear it," said Sharon.

"I do, too," said Patty.

And maybe nobody else heard it that night, but the sound of that little bell ringing was music to our ears.

Chapter 26

Deliverance

When we were finally able to occupy our building, I asked Jimmy to be the foreman in charge of renovations. A short time later he brought me a DVD of this old movie with Sidney Poitier called *Lilies of the Field*. He handed me the box and said, "You gotta watch this! This is you and me!"

Sidney Poitier played a construction worker named Homer who was driving through the desert out west in search of work. He stopped to get some water for his car at a farm being run by some Catholic nuns from eastern Europe. The mother superior thought that God had sent her Homer to build them a church.

Jimmy told Rita the first time he watched *Lilies of the Field* that he wanted to build a church some day. Now he swears that God sent him to build mine. But I'm not sure he knew what he was getting into. First of all, the entire place had to be flipped. It was nothing but a cement box with iron windows. The downstairs was a wreck—a large open hall with a long bar at one end. There was a big, ugly exhaust fan in the roof and the walls were nothing more than cinder blocks covered with cheap wood paneling.

That was Jimmy's first challenge. His second was putting up with me. I had appointed myself the general contractor. When our 60-day waiting period expired at the end of January, I set the date for our dedication ceremony for the last weekend in March. I'd originally wanted to have the work done in one month, but Jimmy insisted there was too much to do to be ready that fast. He said that even two months was pushing it, but after all the delays we'd been through, I was tired of waiting.

The first job was to put in the handicapped ramp. We were lucky to have a warm February. The ground was soft enough that they were able to lay the pilings. Everything was going fine until I handed Jimmy the drawings.

He turned up his nose and said, "The guy who did these isn't a very good architect."

"What are you talking about? He's the best in town!"

He pointed at the plans. "If you just cleat this to the wall and don't put separate railings on, you could do it for half the price and in half the time."

I snatched the drawings from his hands. "We're doing it the way it says."

"But it's stupid!" Jimmy said.

"I don't care. This is how I want it."

Jimmy grumbled and did it my way.

There was too much work for one man, so I brought in specialists as we needed them. I have to admit, I didn't always do the best job in picking the workers. I hired an electrician based on someone's recommendation. The man was so old that he should have been rocking on a porch somewhere instead of running wires.

"Why are you still working?" I asked him one day.

"Because when you retire, you just sit around all day and rot."

The man could barely climb a ladder, and working on the roof was out of the question. I was starting to sweat it—sure that we wouldn't be done on time, but I couldn't find it in my heart to fire the guy. So I hired more electricians to come in and work beside him. Luckily, they all knew each other, so nobody's feathers got ruffled.

Even with the specialists, I knew I was putting a lot on Jimmy's shoulders. Then I thought of Jay, a handyman who helped me when I bought my house in Lily Dale, and I gave him a call. He couldn't resist the offer of some work in the wintertime, especially when I agreed to put him up in a motel.

Jay was known as *Hippy Man*. He was tall and bony with long, stringy blonde hair and a classic '60s attitude. I'll never forget the look on Jimmy's face the day his new helper arrived. Hippy Man and his girlfriend pulled up in a broken down old station wagon. He climbed out of the car with a small bag of clothes and a tool belt.

Jimmy leaned close to me as Jay kissed the girl goodbye and said, "Those are all the tools he brought to help me put a whole building together?"

I shrugged.

"It's like showing up to do a roofing job with a screwdriver!" he hissed.

I thrust my chin out. "He does good work."

"He'd better," Jimmy whispered as Hippy Man ambled our way.

I introduced the two men and studied them as they got acquainted. Seeing Jimmy with his neat work clothes and stocky Polish build standing next to Jay, it was like *The Odd Couple Comes to New Jersey.*

"Is that all the tools you brought?" Jimmy asked, nodding at Jay's belt.

"Janet told me you already had everything."

Jimmy turned to me, flashed a big fake smile, and said, "Well, good for Janet!"

We took Jay inside and showed him around the building. When we got downstairs, Jimmy told Jay that the first thing he wanted him to do was to start tearing down all the old paneling.

I went on instant alert. I had asked Nigel to dedicate the church, and he already booked his flight for the end of March. Everything had to be ready by the date we'd set.

"Can't you just paint over the paneling?" I asked.

Jimmy gawked at me. "You gotta be kidding!"

"No, I'm serious. It would be faster than fixing all the walls."

He turned to Hippy Man. "You're gonna love working with Mother Superior here. She wanted me to put drop ceilings in upstairs. Drop ceilings! The room is 25 x 30. It's got 12-foot ceilings. It's perfect for a church, but she wanted to drop the ceiling down and put fluorescent lights in. It would have looked like a dentist's office!"

"But you could have done it in half the time!" I said.

"I can't see not taking an extra day or two to make it look nicer when you're gonna be looking at it the rest of your life, right?" he prompted his new accomplice for support.

Jay stared back like a deer in the headlights.

Jimmy turned to me and put his hands on his hips. "Did they tell Michelangelo to go into the Sistine Chapel with a roller and paint it blue just so it looked nice? No! He had to make it something that was gonna last through the ages!"

I snorted, crossed my arms, and looked at all the paneling. "Go ahead and tear it down," I huffed as I headed for the stairs. Then I glanced back and added, "as long as it's done on time."

Jimmy and Hippy Man worked well together, but it wasn't enough. We needed more help, so I brought in the Longo Brothers, a family-owned construction business of a father and his two sons. They were all nice people who didn't mind putting in the same long hours as the rest of us. They often started at six in the morning and worked until late at night. Jimmy worked seven days a week like that. Rita started calling herself a church widow and would bring him his lunch just to see him in the daylight.

One morning I arrived at the building and Jimmy came up to me all excited. One of the Longo Brothers had seen a set of oak doors propped against a nearby restaurant with a *for sale* sign on them.

"They'd be perfect at the end of the hallway at the entrance to the chapel," he said.

"Yeah? But how much do they want?" I asked.

"The sign said '*Make an offer.*'"

I figured it was worth looking at them, so we got in my car and zipped across town. We hadn't even arrived at the restaurant, when Jimmy started salivating. "Look at that!" he said, pointing. "There's a transom window and everything!"

I'd barely stopped the car before he hopped out. The three-piece set looked pretty expensive, so I stayed behind the wheel and simply rolled down the window.

"This is real leaded glass," Jimmy said, running his fingers across the panes. "And these doors are solid oak. To buy these new would cost you between six and eight thousand dollars."

"I'm not paying that," I said.

"I know, but these doors are the real deal. They'd look really great once I stripped them."

Just then the owner walked up. I stayed in the car and let Jimmy do the talking.

"I don't know what you want for these," he said, "but we're putting a building together, and these doors would go great."

"Make me an offer," the man said.

I leaned out the window and barked, "Three hundred bucks."

Jimmy stiffened and turned his back as if he didn't know me.

The owner smiled at me as if I were a child, then said to Jimmy, "Do you realize the transom window alone is worth over $300 dollars?"

"I know that," Jimmy said, "and I'm embarrassed she even said that, but the thing is, we're building a church, and our funds are extremely limited. We just wanted to see what the doors looked like."

The man looked at me, then at Jimmy, then back at me again. "What kind of church?" he asked.

"Spiritualist," I said.

When the man wrinkled his nose, Jimmy said, "It's kind of like Christianity, but without all the guilt."

The guy cocked his head as if he were trying to figure out if we were pulling his leg, then Jimmy added, "We're just a bunch of nice people trying to get a church together, but I know we can't afford the doors now that we've seen them."

I started the engine and Jimmy started walking around to the passenger side, when the man held up a finger. "Wait a minute."

Jimmy stopped and turned around.

"The last time I did something nice for somebody who was building a church, my business boomed. So I'm gonna do you a favor. I'm gonna sell you everything for 300 bucks."

I gripped the steering wheel.

"Really?" Jimmy said, glancing at me with wide eyes.

"Yeah. And I'm even gonna have my guys drop 'em off."

The man shouted across the property to a couple of workers. "Yo! Grab these doors and put 'em in the truck. Follow these people wherever they're going."

Luckily, I had the cash in my purse. I paid the man and we headed in a happy little parade back to the building. The Longo Brothers couldn't believe it when we showed up with the doors. I felt bad because they'd already set up the hallway for standard double doors, and now they had to deal with the transom window. You'd have thought it was no big deal. They started cutting into the wall and bracing everything up without even a grumble. And that's the way the whole thing went—as if the place was blessed from the minute we walked in the door.

* * *

Jimmy liked the look of the transom window so much that he wanted to buy the same type of set-up for the main entrance. I didn't see anything wrong with the doors that came with the building.

"When people walk up the steps, you want it to look like a church, not a VFW hall," he said.

"New doors cost two thousand bucks!"

"What's a couple thousand more?" he argued. "They're gonna be your welcome mat to everyone who comes here."

So I went ahead and ordered the darned doors, even though the existing ones were perfectly good.

The doors arrived a week later and Jimmy propped them up in the hallway. The next day, when the Longo Brothers showed up at 6 A.M., I asked them to start putting the doors in. What I didn't realize was how seriously Jimmy took his role as Sidney Poitier's stand-in. Just like Homer in *Lilies of the Field*, Jimmy would have been happy doing everything himself. He was okay letting the carpenters do the grunt work, but unbeknownst to me, he felt the special touches were his personal mission from God. To him, those weren't just doors, they were *his* doors.

I was sitting in my newly finished office at 7:00 when I heard one of the Longo brothers out in the hallway say, "About time you showed up."

Then I heard Jimmy's voice. "I didn't leave here until 11:30 last night," he said, followed immediately by, "Who told you to put the doors in?"

The other brother answered, "Janet did."

"But those are my doors," Jimmy said.

"We're just doing what we were told," said the first brother.

I walked out to the hallway and said, "I need you to finish grouting the bathroom tiles, Jimmy."

"I can do the grouting any time," he argued.

"No," I insisted. "I want you to do it now. The plumbing inspector is coming and it has to be done today."

He grumbled some more, but stomped off to do the work.

I thought that was the end of it, but when he finished with the grouting job, he stepped into the doorway of my office and said, "That's it. I've had it with this place. I'm outta here today."

I didn't know if I believed him, but I didn't even allow myself to think of getting by without him. Everyone in the congregation was doing what they could—chipping, painting, and pounding nails, but Jimmy was indispensable. I left the building that night and said goodbye to everyone as usual, but the next morning when I went back, all of Jimmy's tools were gone. My heart went through the basement. We were all working like dogs and everyone was tired, but I knew then that I'd pushed him too hard.

I picked up the phone and called Jimmy's house, but I got the answering machine. I kept calling throughout the day and left the same message every time: "We gotta talk about this. I'm sorry. This can't end this way."

After every unanswered call my heart twisted more and more into a knot. By the end of the day, I didn't care if I had to hire a hundred workers to finish the job. No one could replace the dear friend that Jimmy had come to be.

When he didn't call back, I had no choice but to look for help right away. The deadline for the dedication ceremony was getting closer every day, and I couldn't afford to go even one hour without checking things off the endless to-do list. I looked in the Yellow Pages and called a handyman who listed himself as *Mr. Fix-it*. He showed up with some helpers, but I didn't like their energy from the minute they walked in the door.

I thought about Jimmy constantly throughout the day. The building was alive with workers, but the cement walls echoed without him. The next day I headed for the property, dreading the thought of dealing with *Mr. Fix-it* and his misfits. Even my daily stop at Starbucks didn't help to perk me up. By the time I arrived at the church I had decided to keep calling Jimmy's phone number until somebody answered. I was climbing out of my car when I heard a crunch on the gravel. Few workers arrived as early as I did, and I held my breath as I turned to see who was pulling in behind me.

It was Jimmy.

I rushed him as he got out of his car. "I don't care if you won't do the job," I said without preamble. "I won't let it come between our friendship."

He nodded gravely. "Yeah, I know."

"Are you back here just to talk or … ?" I was afraid to ask the question.

"I guess I'm here to work," he said, allowing himself half a smile. "Rita convinced me to swallow my pride give my ego a rest."

"I'm so sorry, Jimmy." My voice shook and my eyes welled up. "I didn't mean to hurt you."

"Those were *my* doors," he said softly.

I wrapped my arms around him and spoke into his shoulder. "I know, and I'm really sorry I let the other guys put them in."

He squeezed me back, then pushed me away and jerked his thumb over his shoulder. "What the heck did you do with the parking signs while I was gone?"

His abrupt change of focus threw me off balance. "What are you talkin' about?"

He marched over to the arrows I'd mounted the day before at the entrance to the parking lot. He threw out his hands and asked, "What is this? A runway? You got both signs facing in!" He grabbed one sign and gave it a shake. "They're all wrong. You shoulda put both signs on one pole. Where's my screwdriver?"

He stomped over to his trunk and pulled out a tool box. I swallowed past the lump in my throat and left him to undo my work. When he came into the building, we picked up where we'd left off as if nothing ever happened. I still kept the pressure on about the deadline—I had no choice with Nigel coming—but maybe we didn't butt heads quite so much as before.

Then I made the mistake of asking Jimmy to paint an archway at the front of the chapel. I'd found a picture in a magazine and I held it up for him and Jay.

"I want something just like this," I said.

Jimmy studied the photo, then shook his head. "You don't want to do it that way. We can get some 2 x 6's, and Jay and I can frame in a 3-D archway that'll look a thousand times better."

"No, no, no," I waved my hand. "I don't want any of that stuff. Just paint it on and paint in a window on both sides while you're at it."

Jimmy rolled his eyes at Jay then said to me, "Maybe you can get *Mr. Fix-it* to paint it." He was still pointing out the mistakes they'd made in his absence.

I thrust the photograph at him and went off to check on the electricians.

The next day I had some readings scheduled in my office on Main Street so I didn't get to the building until mid-morning. I walked in, and there was Hippy Man hammering a nail into one of several 2 x 6's already framed in at the front of the chapel. I knew that Jay wouldn't have gone against my wishes on his own, so I stalked off in search of Jimmy. I found him downstairs in the storage room with his head in his tool cabinet.

"What are you doing to the chapel?" I demanded.

"We're framing in the arch," he said just as casual as can be.

"But I told you just to paint it on!"

He pulled his head from the cabinet. "Yeah, well, we already bought the lumber. And thanks for the use of your credit card, by the way."

He banged shut the metal doors and gave me a smug smile. As he walked off with his hammer and a handful of nails, my eyes fell on what looked like graffiti scrawled on an inner city wall. On closer inspection, I knew immediately that Jimmy was the artist. *"No girls allowed at any time under any circumstances"* was scrawled across both doors of the cabinet in thick black Magic Marker.

I shook my head and laughed, but I didn't rush to get a sponge and some cleaner. I knew better than to mess with Jimmy's doors.

* * *

"I think we should do something that really wows people when they walk in," Jimmy announced in Mid-March.

I couldn't believe my ears. We were getting down to the wire, and I had enough to think about without him changing the plans at the last minute. "Whatever you do," I warned, "it better be done in two weeks."

"I'm thinking of vaulting the ceiling in the entry hallway," he said, looking up. I could give it a real nice curve and paint clouds on it like you're looking at the sky."

"You gotta be kidding me," I said as I stared at the large air conditioning ducts criss-crossed above my head. "What are you gonna do with all those pipes?"

"We'll move 'em."

I started to protest, then clamped my lips together. I'd promised myself I wouldn't push him too hard. I opened my mouth just long enough to repeat my warning. "Two weeks, Jimmy. You got two weeks."

The amount of work those guys put into that domed ceiling floored me. Not only did they re-route the ducts, but they wired in recessed lighting to shine up on their beautiful blue sky. Then they papered the bottom half of the hallway in a pretty floral pattern, put in a chair rail, and decorated the top half with butterflies. I couldn't believe a bunch of men would push for little details like that, but Jimmy was right: When they were finished, you couldn't walk in the door and not say "*Wow.*"

While the finishing touches were going on inside, a truckload of brick masons swarmed across the outside walls. A plastic surgeon couldn't have given the place a better facelift. What had been an eyesore for the residents of Bridge Street became the jewel of the neighborhood, thanks to their excellent work. The final step involved stenciling our name on the upper right corner facing the street. I chose to go with the stenciling for a very simple reason: A sign would have required approval by the town. When I looked up and saw *The Journey Within* in foot-high letters on the side of my church, I felt a surge of pride and love.

My dream was almost a reality.

By the final week, I was running on pure adrenaline mixed with frequent shots of caffeine. Everyone hated me, but for some reason they kept coming back. The girls wore ruts in the road, running back and forth to Home Depot after working a full day at their own jobs. Jimmy and Jay were practically crawling from exhaustion.

On Wednesday morning I dragged myself up the stairs and into my new office. I walked through the door and stopped dead in my tracks. There, staring back at me from my big leather chair, was a two-foot tall witch, complete with hooked nose and high, black hat. I recognized her from a Halloween party we'd held some years back. I'd last seen the witch downstairs in the storage closet, but somehow she'd found her way to my chair. Someone had put a Starbucks cup in her hand and hung a hand-lettered sign around her neck that read, *"I want it done now!"*

I heard snickers behind me and turned to find Jimmy and Hippy Man peering in the doorway. They could barely keep a straight face.

"Very funny," I said, trying not to laugh as well. "You guys are a real riot."

Then the dam let loose and we all burst out laughing. After all the coffee I'd drunk on the way in, I had to cross my legs to control myself. I thought I'd be okay, then Jimmy leaned out in the hallway and yelled. "Hey, Bernie! Come in here a minute!"

Bernie was a young Mexican who Jimmy hired to help him. He was a good kid and he worked as hard as everybody, but he never said more than a couple of words at one time.

"Bernie, look!" Jimmy said as he steered him toward my chair. "Who's that?"

Bernie looked at the witch, then with great seriousness turned to Jimmy and said, *"Esa?* That is Miss Janet."

Jimmy and Hippy Man roared, and I ran for the bathroom.

* * *

They could tease me all they wanted about cracking the whip, but by Friday of the last weekend in March, we'd met our goal. The downstairs wasn't complete, but it was functional. The upstairs was enough to take your breath away. I'm the first to admit it wouldn't have been nearly as beautiful if Jimmy hadn't insisted on so many nice touches. More than anything, though, you couldn't help but feel the devotion of all the people who'd worked so hard. The walls were infused with love from everyone who had their hands in that masterpiece, from the hired workers to every member of my congregation.

Everything was set for the dedication ceremony on Sunday. Nigel was flying in the next day, and I was scheduled to meet him at the airport. All of the inspectors had come through and signed the required forms. There was only one thing left to do before the weekend: To occupy the building, we needed one final signature from the town's zoning and construction officer. I gathered the completed inspection reports and headed over to the town offices.

It felt strange to be back in the very same trailer where I'd been questioned by Anthony Marino years earlier, but the situation this time was vastly different. Then, I'd merely been trying to rent part of a building. Now, I was about to realize my long-held dream. Luckily, Anthony Marino had long since moved on. The new zoning and construction officer was a woman.

Dorothy Durban wasn't in at the moment, but her secretary, Martha Carter, greeted me with a cheerful smile, then glanced through my paperwork. "Looks like you have everything in order," she said. "I'll give you a call when it's signed."

"Do you know how long that'll be?" I said. "I have to have this approved by the end of the day."

"That shouldn't be a problem," Mrs. Carter said. "Ms. Durban usually leaves by noon on Fridays, so I'm sure she'll be back any time now."

I returned to my office to tie up some loose ends. At 11:00, when I hadn't yet received a phone call, I drove back to the trailer to check on the papers in person. When I walked in the door, Mrs. Carter saw me and she flushed.

"Is something wrong?" I asked, instantly on alert.

"Well," she said, standing up. "Ms. Durban was here, but I'm afraid she left for the day without signing your papers."

My knees went weak. "What do you mean?" I asked, my mind racing with the implications of her words. "Why didn't she sign them?"

"I don't know. I told her that you were working against a deadline, but she left anyway."

I felt a tingling in my tear ducts. "But how could she do that?"

"I'm sorry," Mrs. Carter said. "Why don't you speak with the borough clerk and explain your problem."

Her words impaled themselves in my chest. Suddenly, after everything had fallen into place, I had a "problem." I could barely think as I walked across the street to the town's administrative offices and found Ruth Sampson, the borough clerk. I tried to stay calm, but I broke down as I explained the importance of the zoning officer's signature.

"We have someone flying in from England to dedicate our church," I said through my sniffling. "Everyone has worked really hard to be ready for the ceremony on Sunday, and now this woman is holding the whole thing up."

I saw nothing but sympathy in her eyes. "I'm afraid we've had some issues with Ms. Durban," she admitted. "Unfortunately, she works for the state, not the town. Give me some time, though, and I'll see what I can do."

I had no choice but to trust her. I went back to the dungeon, where poor Carole didn't know what hit her.

"That bitch!" I cried as I burst into the office. "She left without signing our approval and turned off her cell phone so nobody can reach her!"

I went through the whole story while I dialed Nigel's phone number. I needed to let him know that he might not want to get on his plane.

He tried to give me encouragement, but I was beyond consolation. My batting average with Brookhaven was not going to get me into the World Series—nor into my church.

I left the dungeon and drove over to the church, where I was greeted by Jimmy's long face. Carole must have called him in the five minutes it took me to get there.

"It ain't looking good," I said.

"I heard."

"We're running out of time."

Jimmy knew the stakes as well as I did, but there was nothing either of us could say. With such a short deadline, the only thing we could do to fight Brookhaven's bureaucracy was pray. And that we did. I didn't stick around to hear Jimmy's prayers, but I kept up a constant conversation with God and St. Therese as I drove back and forth between Dorothy Durban's trailer and the dungeon. I knew that prayers are always answered, but not necessarily in the way we want. By 4:00, when the town hall started emptying out for the weekend, I was a wreck.

"I've never seen you like this," Carole said, trying to console me through my jagged sobs. "It'll be okay," she said. "We'll deal with it like everything else. We'll get through this."

"No," I said, gasping and choking from the crying. "I give up. I just give up."

Now Carole started crying. I couldn't stand to just sit around, so I told her I was going out. I didn't know where I was going, and it didn't matter. I just got in my car and drove, my mind far from the road in front of me. Luckily for me and the other cars around me, I didn't get too far when my cell phone rang. It was Carole and she was screaming.

"The mayor wants to talk to you! He has the police out looking for you! The mayor, Janet! He overrode her! He called that woman's boss in Trenton and got permission to sign in her place!"

"Tell me this isn't a joke," I said, too numb to react appropriately.

"It's no joke, I promise. You're supposed to go over to the town hall and pick up the papers from the borough clerk."

She didn't have to tell me twice. I rushed over to Ruth Sampson's office before anyone could change their mind. I wiped the tears from my ravaged face, but I refused to get excited until I saw the mayor's signature for myself.

Mrs. Sampson stood up when I walked in the door and waved a sheath of papers. "You can thank Mayor Teasdale for this," she said. "He spent the whole afternoon on it—four hours going back and forth with the state. First he got permission to order Ms. Durban back to work, but she refused. Then he got permission to sign in her place."

"I still don't understand," I said. "Did she have something against us?" It certainly wouldn't be the first time.

"No," she shook her head. "Not that we know of. Like I said before, we've had problems with her."

She handed me the paperwork and I stared at Arthur Teasdale's signature, awash in gratitude and relief. Under normal circumstances I would have danced around and celebrated right there in Ruth Sampson's office, but I was drained—both physically and mentally. Then, ever so slowly, like the sun peeking above the horizon on a clear morning, it gradually dawned on me that nothing stood between us now from dedicating our church.

I drove straight to the dungeon and showed the signed papers to Carole. I was beginning to recover, and we squealed and cried and laughed together. Then I called Nigel for the second time that day.

"We got it!" I shouted loud enough to be heard in England without the phone between us. "The mayor signed the paperwork!"

"Thank God!" he said. "I've been praying for you, Janet—asking God to give this to you after all you've been through."

"Well, all of our prayers must have worked." I said. I thanked him and told him I'd be there the next day when he got off the plane.

I called Sharon next, then Patty, then headed over to the church to tell Jimmy. He ran out to greet me as I pulled into the parking lot.

"The mayor was here looking for you! You just missed him!"

His announcement floored me. "The mayor came here?"

"Yeah. He was a really nice guy. He said he had some good news for you—that you're gonna open this weekend!"

"I know," I grinned and waved the papers like a victory flag.

"I told him he was the man of the hour," Jimmy said as he took the papers from my hand and studied the mayor's signature. "He wanted to make sure we knew that this wasn't the town's fault."

"Yeah, it was that woman. And it had nothing to do with who we are. Can you believe that?"

We walked up the stairs to the main entrance and stopped at the landing.

"I asked the mayor what kind of church people thought this was," Jimmy said. "I told him I wouldn't go to a church that didn't stand for something good."

I put my hand on his arm, overcome by the emotional day. "When this weekend is over," I said, "I'm going to track down the mayor and thank him in person."

"But first," I said, as we stepped through Jimmy's doors into my little white chapel, "we have a church to dedicate."

Chapter 27

Dream Come True

I like to do things my way, but I felt no need to take center stage at the dedication ceremony. I asked Nigel to preside for a number of reasons: He trained me. He helped write our by-laws. He was with us through every fight. But most of all, Nigel has an unbelievable connection with the spirit world. Having him bless our church would set us up to have that kind of connection in the future.

I picked him up at JFK airport and took him straight to the church. He'd last seen the building when it was an American Legion hall in total disarray. At the time, he was concerned that it wouldn't all come together. Anybody would have felt the same way. I'd kept him updated with regular phone calls as the renovations progressed, but my detailed descriptions couldn't prepare someone who'd seen the place before for the total transformation we managed to pull off.

Walking from the parking lot toward the entry doors, I felt like a proud parent presenting my new baby to its uncle for the first time. We stepped into the domed hallway and stopped. He kept his comments to himself for the moment, but his face spoke volumes as he took it all in. I led him ahead through the chapel and he swept his eyes over all the changes.

For the crowning touch, I'd ordered a framed stained glass picture that now hung under Jimmy's 3-D archway. It was lighted from behind and showed a luminous winged angel in a beautiful pastoral setting. A square of glass embedded beneath the angel read, *"In celebration of Lori's life."* I knew beyond a doubt that Bob and Karen's daughter was our angel, and as long as the church stood, that special picture would hang as a reminder that Lori was watching over us.

"Bob and Karen can't be here for the dedication," I told Nigel. "But Lori's husband, David, will join us."

His eyes moved from the glass angel's to mine, and he finally spoke.

"What more can I give you?" he asked solemnly, and I knew instinctively what he meant. Nigel had been my mentor, and I his protégée. With the realization of my dream—this brick and mortar church that had finally become reality—his role in my life would no longer be the same.

Now it was me who couldn't find the words, but Nigel filled in the silence.

"It's truly miraculous what you've done here, Janet. And I don't just mean the work on this building. It's a miracle that you took your church from the back room of a bookstore to a rented banquet hall, and now to this beautiful edifice that stands as a symbol of God's love."

"Yeah," I smiled, "I think I'll finally be able to hum here."

He gave me a puzzled look until I reminded him of Titus Brandsma.

"Ah, yes," he tapped a finger to his lips as he remembered the famous priest's story. "You'll be happy here, indeed. You were sent to do this work," he said, looking around. "Of that I have no doubt."

I took him to see my office, and he nodded in approval. "It's a great improvement from the dungeon, I must say."

"I think you'll miss the old place," I teased.

"I should think not! The energy here is far more suited for spirit communication."

I reached across my desk and picked up two of the pamphlets we'd had printed. I handed one to Nigel and read my own copy for the hundredth time:

Come visit us in our beautiful new home. A church of our own. A spiritual oasis. A dream come true. A place to grow and be. Blessed by God and the angels. A place to search for the truth within your own heart.

"Good show," he said as he handed back his copy.

I thanked him, then led him back through the hallway to the chapel as we walked through the next day's program. We planned to combine the dedication ceremony with a regular service, complete with a demonstration of mediumship.

He clasped his hands across his chest and said, "Please tell me that you're not going to play that song again."

"What song? You mean, Where I Sit is Holy?"

"Yes. Precisely. You've played the same tune at every service for how many years now?"

"I don't know … ten? Since I started The Journey Within."

He waved his hands at me. "You seem to think you need that song to raise your energy, but you're a brilliant medium whether or not you play music beforehand."

"Thank you very much, but I happen to love that song. Those drums and that flute give me a lift like nothing else."

He rolled his eyes. "I can see I have no choice but to listen to it once again."

"Yeah, but this time it's gonna sound better than you've ever heard it. We spent 1800 bucks on a primo sound system. Denise is gonna operate it during the service."

Denise was a member of our advisory board. She had agreed to be in charge of music for the ceremony.

"Perhaps you can instruct Denise to choose a different song this time."

"That ain't gonna happen, Nigel."

He gave a dramatic sigh and said, "It's your church, Janet."

I heard his words, and a burst of adrenaline flooded my chest. "Yeah," I said as I gazed around the chapel. "It is, isn't it?"

* * *

I stood at the door in my purple dress and pearls and greeted guests as they arrived for the ceremony. The whole congregation came, of course, but so did all the workers who had helped with the renovations. I didn't recognize some of the plumbers, electricians, and carpenters at first. They looked out of place in their coats and ties, but everyone smiled proudly and stood as tall as if it were graduation day.

When everyone had taken their seats, Denise put some choral music on to set the mood. Meanwhile, a select group of us gathered on the landing with Nigel. The program called for him to bless the building outside, then do the same on the inside. My three ministers: Sharon, Carole, and Hope, joined Nigel and me, along with Jimmy and Rita, and Lori's husband David.

The eight of us approached the right rear corner of the building with Nigel in the lead. He wore a plain blue suit and swung a thurible—a metal ball with holes in it suspended from a chain— as he walked. Inside burned a hunk of charcoal topped with a piece of incense. As he swung the thurible, smoke swirled around us, symbolizing his invitation for Spirit to surround us and our new church.

"All glory and praise to You, our Father," he said at the first corner.

"May this land be consecrated to the glory of Your name," he prayed at the next.

"From a dream came a reality," he said at the third corner as the fragrant smoke drifted upwards.

When we arrived at the fourth corner, we all stopped and looked up at the name stenciled in the bricks. Nigel swung the thurible, then shouted, "This is The Journey Within!"

I'd been holding myself together up to that point, but my emotions had been right at the edge. When I heard him announce the name of my church to the heavens, my tears just spilled right over. This was without question the greatest accomplishment of my life—my gift to God and anyone who chose to worship with us. There were more than a few times over the years that I never thought this moment would arrive.

We completed the circuit and climbed the steps to the landing. There we gathered in a semi-circle behind Nigel. He raised his right fist, then pounded three times on the door.

"Open this door in the name of God and the spirit world," he called out. "May this be a sacred place, where the two worlds may meet and the truth in Your love be found. Bestow upon us, Your people who worship here, the light of Your love."

We entered the church and stopped in the hallway, where each of us picked up a candle. For Spiritualists, candles are an expression of the power of God. Their flame symbolizes the essence of all creation.

"Sanctify this candle to the glory of Your name," Nigel intoned as he lit my special candle. It was the one he'd given me ten years earlier to celebrate my first service at the Wise Man. I'd burned it then for 24 hours as instructed, and it had remained in my closet untouched until this day.

With all candles now burning, the eight of us proceeded to the chapel and moved to the right rear corner.

"May the light of God be present!" Nigel said.

The congregation now joined us, calling out "Hear us!" in response to his words.

"In the land of the free, may the light of God be present here!" Nigel said at the second corner.

"Hear us!" the crowd repeated.

We continued on to the remaining two corners in the same manner. Having completed the full blessing, everyone took their seats while Nigel and I moved to the front.

He faced the congregation and spoke as eloquently as I'd ever heard him.

"Throughout the ages," he began, "almighty God has moved his people to build houses of prayer and praise and to set apart a place for the ministry of spirit. With gratitude for this building—for *The Journey Within*—we are now gathered to dedicate this space and to consecrate it in God's name. The doors are open, friends, let us be glad! Let us rejoice, for the day of our dreams has come!"

He then turned to me, smiled triumphantly, and said, "After so many years of trying to get it, you finally got it!"

The abrupt change in his style caused an equally abrupt change in the atmosphere of the room. The hushed and sedate crowd suddenly burst into cheers. Everyone there knew what we'd been through. They whistled, clapped, and hollered like a bunch of baseball fans after a grand slam by the home team. The happy hubbub went on and on and on.

I stepped to the podium and stood there—wondering if they were ever going to stop. *They're cheering for my church,* I thought as I grinned back at everyone. *Hooray for us!*

When the room finally grew quiet, I thanked everyone for coming and thanked Nigel for honoring us by presiding over the ceremony. I turned the floor back over to him, expecting more of his moving oration. Instead, he shocked me by shouting, "Let's hear it for Janet!"

The smoldering embers of the cheers erupted once again into a blazing bonfire of noise. I smiled, but shook my head, uncomfortable with the personal attention.

As the applause subsided, Nigel reached under the podium and pulled out a rose. Flowers are the gems of God. For me, roses were my special sign from St. Therese that everything would turn out okay. He extended the rose toward me in both of his hands and said, "I want you to keep this in a special place and remember this day."

As if I'd ever forget it, I thought as I accepted the gift.

Nigel then turned to the congregation and invited anyone who wished to come forward for a personal blessing to do so. I didn't know how many people would take him up on his offer, but every person who came to the church that day rose and walked to the front of the chapel.

"May God bless you and all that you do," he said to the first person who stopped before him. Then, one after another they stood facing him as he took their hand in both of his. Many of them he knew, and some were strangers, but he gave a blessing to each of them until the only person left was me.

I crossed the carpet and turned to face him as the others had done. I was keenly aware of all of the eyes fixed on my back as I held out my hand. Nigel and

I locked our gaze, then he did something totally unexpected: he bent his legs and got down on his knees before me.

I froze, and my heart stopped beating. I'd never dreamed he'd do such a thing—to kneel like that in front of everyone. I wanted him to get up. I *begged* him to get up with my eyes. Instead, he took my hands and placed them on the top of his head. I realized then that he wasn't going to bless me. He wanted me to bless him.

I heard a murmur rustle through the chapel, but my eyes stayed fixed on Nigel's. All of my life God had put strong men in my face to test me, and now—on the day my dream came true—one of the strongest, most spiritual men I knew had humbled himself before me, in full view of my flock.

I melted. Right there on the carpet I simply dissolved. Through my tears, I found the words to bless my teacher, then helped him to his feet with trembling hands. I returned to my seat and faced the rows of smiling faces. The dedication ceremony had been filled to that point with special symbols. Many of the guests might not have understood the meaning behind the smoke, the candles, and the rose, but I could clearly see that everyone present that day had understood the significance of Nigel's singular act of respect.

I didn't know how I was supposed to function for the rest of the service, but God had carried me through far tougher challenges in my life. The demonstration of mediumship came next and my nerves began to settle down. I would have to speak, but there wouldn't be any more surprises. I could count on the spirit people to carry me through.

We gave a demonstration every Sunday, but this day was more special than most. It would be the first time that the workers who had helped us would see what we were about. I knew that Nigel and I—working together—would convey the main message of Spiritualism in a way that they would never forget.

I looked across the room to where Denise stood ready to start the music. I gave her a nod, and she pressed the *play* button on our spanking new sound system. Seconds later, the deep thrum of the Indian drums reverberated off the walls. The haunting tones of the flute followed shortly, floating from speakers mounted high in every corner. The church members who'd been with me through the years tapped their toes in time to the oh-so-familiar rhythm.

I glanced over at Nigel as the music filled the air, and I swear I saw him grimace.

But me?

I just closed my eyes ... and I hummed.

Epilogue

Bob and Karen Benedetti missed the dedication ceremony, but they made it to the service the following week. They didn't know anything about the stained glass angel or about the "Lori's Chapel" sign we hung above the big oak doors, but I could see that they were touched. They hadn't asked me to do anything special in their daughter's honor, but how could I not do something after what they gave me?

A little while later I brought a psychic artist from Britain to the church. She drew beautiful pieces of artwork about people's lives that were full of symbolism. She didn't know anything about our story when I asked her to do a picture for the church. When she handed me her drawing, I knew right away that I had to give it to Bob and Karen. The picture showed a church with a little girl on a swing who I'm sure was Lori, and this huge dragonfly hovering over everything. I told the artist, "You don't know what you just did with this dragonfly."

Things have settled down some since those chaotic days when we were trying to get our church together. But not by much. My life gets a little hectic sometimes. I bring over a lot of mediums from England to demonstrate, and I usually end up running them out to Lily Dale while they're here. I still give classes, and my waiting list for readings is longer than ever. If things get a little too crazy, I just call up the girls and tell them it's time for a road trip. Some things never change, but it's all good.

We're very happy in Brookhaven, and our neighbors love us. Hawks circle the church all the time. Buddhists believe that hawks bring people to you, and people walk in now and say, "My God! This place is so peaceful!"

It takes their breath away.

We're trying to do new things at the church. Since the dedication, we put up an "All Faiths Wall" with symbols from every religion and a prayer for world peace. We're raising funds to build a room on a school in Africa. Jimmy says that if we can get enough money to send him over, he'll build it himself.

Spiritualism is still not as well known as it should be, but we're changing that one soul at a time. When people push past their fears and see what we're all about, their whole perspective changes. Knowing that life is continuous takes away the darkness and makes death something they can talk about. When my father died, we didn't want to discuss it. Now we talk about death in my family.

My mother had to have open heart surgery not too long ago. Before she went in, I told her that we needed to have a chat. I said, "I think you're gonna face a choice in there, Mom. At some point in that operating room, the spirit people may say, 'You can go with us, or you can go back,' and it's gonna be your choice. Don't be afraid."

What I didn't realize was that my mother honestly believed that when she crossed over, my father was going to be waiting for her. All those years she'd worried that he was going to have the chance to go at her again. You just never know what people are thinking unless you have these conversations.

I said, "Even if you choose to go to the other side, Mom, Pop has no more power over you."

Luckily, she made it through the surgery. A couple of weeks later she said, "I had a dream. Your father came for me in a station wagon, and I told him I wasn't going with him."

I'm not sure if it was only a dream or if she had an actual vision, but it was definitely symbolic. Somehow she got a little power from our conversation. For her to tell my father, "I'm not going with you," was huge. I believe this lifetime is about finding out how strong and powerful you really are. I have no doubt about that, with the obstacles I've overcome.

As for me, I've finally found my peace. I love what I do. It's a privilege and an honor. What more could you want from this life than to touch people's lives with love? My belief in taking responsibility for my choices and being in charge of my life has brought me the most peace of all. Coming from a place where everything was imposed upon me growing up, I've come into my own power. It's true that my path has taken many turns, but there's one thing I now know for certain:

No matter what happens in this lifetime, no one can touch your spirit.

CPSIA information can be obtained
at www.ICGtesting.com
Printed in the USA
FFHW010332010519
52159798-57530FF